MATE AND STALEMATE

The Practice of Social Work

General editors: Bill Jordan and Jean Packman

1   MATE AND STALEMATE
Janet Mattinson and Ian Sinclair

2   GROWING UP IN CARE: TEN PEOPLE TALKING
Barbara Kahan

3   CREATIVE SOCIAL WORK
David Brandon and Bill Jordan (editors)

4   CHILDREN, GRIEF AND SOCIAL WORK
Gill Lonsdale, Peter Elfer and Rod Ballard

Mate and Stalemate

Working with Marital Problems in a Social Services Department

JANET MATTINSON
and
IAN SINCLAIR

In collaboration with
Patricia Coussell
and
Robert Morley

Basil Blackwell · Oxford

First published 1979 by
Basil Blackwell (Publisher) Ltd.
5 Alfred Street, Oxford OX1 4HB

British Library Cataloguing in Publication Data

Mattinson, Janet
  Mate and stalemate.
    1. Family social work - England - London
    I. Title II. Sinclair, Ian
    362.8′2   HV700.G7

ISBN 0 631 11821 7

Printed in Great Britain by Billing and Sons Ltd ,
London, Guildford and Worcester

iv

Contents

Foreword by Dr Jean Packman   ix

Acknowledgements   xiii

Part One	*The Project*	1
1	Introduction	3
2	The Framework of the Project	12
3	The Scope of the Problem	25
4	Four Theoretical Themes	45

Part Two	*The Clients*	65
5	'The Corpses in the Graveyard'	67
6	Dilemma and Demand	83
7	Meeting Demands	101
8	Patterns of Attachment	119

Part Three	*The Clients and the Workers*	133
9	Suckers or Bastards	135
10	The Problem of Limits	141
11	The Problem of Control	157

Part Four	*The Clients, the Workers and the Work*	177
12	Getting Engaged	179
13	Wading Upstream	197
14	Mr and Mrs Ingledow and Mr and Mrs Cabassi	223

Part Five	*The Clients, the Workers and the Organization*	241
15	Therapeutic Response and Institutional Temptation	243
16	The Problem of Institutional Limits	253
17	The Problem of Institutional Splitting	274
18	In Conclusion	290

Appendices

1	Survey of Referrals	300
2	Survey of Long-term Cases	308

Index of Clients

General Index

vi

THE SANDGATE GIRL'S LAMENTATION

I was a young maid truly,
And lived in Sandgate Street.
I thought to marry a good man
To keep me warm at neet.

He's an ugly body, a bubbly body,
An ill-fared, hideous loon;
And I have married a keelman,
And my good days are done.

I thought to marry a parson
To hear me say my prayers;
But I have married a keelman
And he kicks me down the stairs.

I thought to marry a dyer
To dye my apron blue;
But I have married a keelman
And he's a perfect fool.

I thought to marry a sailor
To bring me sugar and tea;
But I have married a keelman
And that he lets me see.

He's an ugly body, a bubbly body,
An ill-fared hideous loon;
And I have married a keelman,
And my good days are done.

Traditional ballad

Foreword

There are books about the theories which underlie, or perhaps
ought to underlie, social work practice; there are a few works which
describe and analyse in detail what social workers do with their
clients and, occasionally, what clients do to their social workers;
and there are texts which examine the structure and functions of
social work organizations. Sometimes two of these approaches are
combined, but it is rare to find a book which grapples with all three
perspectives. This is what the authors and their colleagues have
done. In the process, they show not only an acute understanding of
some clients, their workers and their social service organizations,
but also offer us fresh insights into the complicated interaction
between them.

As experienced caseworkers with the Institute of Marital Studies,
they worked alongside basic-grade social workers in an inner
London social services department for three years. In response to
growing concern about marital violence and breakdown, they
offered to work with marital problems as presented to local
authority social workers, aiming to contribute something from
their specialist knowledge and skill, but hoping also to learn from
and adapt to the new and unfamiliar setting.

The first revelation was that only a minority of referrals to the
social services department involved 'couples', the vast majority
being concerned with individuals, or with one-parent families.
Further, only a tiny minority were specifically referred for marital
problems. At first sight it seemed that they were offering an
irrelevant service. Yet closer examination showed that a sizeable
proportion of couples were, indeed, in extreme conflict with one
another, though it was their related and pressing needs for
accommodation, or finance, or psychiatric help or care for their
children for which they were referred and to which the department

tried to respond. It also became clear that this group of clients made demands on the time and expertise of social workers out of all proportion to their numbers. There were therefore strong arguments for tackling the conflicts that seemed to be at the heart of so many other problems.

The clients they thus tried to help are described in unforgettable detail; so too are their own struggles and those of their local authority colleagues to understand and assist them. These, in turn, are seen within the dynamic and often hectic context of a social services department that endeavours to meet a vast range of needs and to satisfy apparently limitless and often conflicting demands.

The result is, I believe, a unique and compelling contribution to social work literature. It is depressing, because the problems of the couples concerned are so painful, chronic and overwhelming. It is daunting, because the families who are described represent only a small proportion (albeit a time-consuming one) of the total caseload of any social services department. It is perplexing, because the problems seem so intractable and solutions so elusive. It is exasperating, because clients, workers and department often seem fixed in what is, indeed, an unproductive stalemate. Yet the book is also hopeful, humane, humorous and illuminating.

We see how practice led gradually towards theories which made some sense of the chaos of these families' lives, and helped explain the reactions to them of workers and agency and, ultimately, gave shape and direction to their endeavours to help. There were moments when, most movingly, the clients were enabled to find the words to describe their dilemma and even to suggest ways in which it might be eased. Some couples, after a sustained period of help, were clearly a little more comfortable, more optimistic and more self-reliant than they were before.

Our understanding of some of the most difficult interpersonal problems which face social workers is unquestionably enlarged by this study, but so too is our grasp of how the best of helpful endeavours may founder and how complex is the task we have willed upon social services departments. We are enabled to see that, in order to help some of the most deprived and damaged people who come to the departments, partial or practical solutions are not enough, and a style of consistent, highly-tuned, long-term social work of a most resilient and imaginative kind may be the most hopeful response. Yet, to sustain staff in such gruelling work, departmental supports and responses must be similarly consistent and strong. This is not easy, given the number and variety of all the other demands that are made upon it. The study cannot answer the question of whether social services departments should attempt such work, given the implications for organization and practice or, indeed, whether they can afford not to. Rather, it highlights the choices that have to be made, and by addressing itself to the difficulties of all three parties to the social work endeavour — clients, workers and employing organizations — the book, in the words of one client, truly 'grasps the nettle'.

It is most fitting that it should launch a series which aims to inform and improve social work practice.

Jean Packman

Acknowledgements

Our major debts are to our clients, and to our colleagues and their managers in the social services departments who worked with us on the project. Both the project and this book benefited greatly from the guidance of the project's management committee and the generous contribution of its members. We are particularly grateful to them and also to the members of the teams who invited two of us to join them and extended to us the support they gave each other. We have chosen not to identify the borough in order to give additional anonymity to the clients. The inevitable loss is that we cannot name those from whom we learnt so much.

The project would not have been possible without the generous financial support of the J. Arthur Rank Group Charity; the Tavistock Institute of Medical Psychology; the I.J. Lyons Charitable Trust; the A.F. Wallace Charity Trust; The Baring Foundation; and a trust which wishes to remain anonymous. The borough contributed to the cost, as did the Institute of Marital Studies, which receives its major grant from the Home Office.

Our colleagues in the Institute of Marital Studies not only commented on the manuscript, but bore with the moods and feelings engendered in us by the project, and carried additional work in our absence. We thank them and Claire Sieradski and Maureen Rooney, who carried the burden of the secretarial work.

Of the staff of the Tavistock Institute of Human Relations, we thank Dr Eric Miller, who helped us in the planning stage; the Secretary, Mr Sidney Gray, who as always put his wisdom and experience at our service; and Mrs Margaret Walker and her staff in the library who, in their usual way, so fully involved themselves in the work they did for us.

We owe much of the theory used in this book to Dr John Bowlby and Mrs Isobel Menzies Lyth. We thank them both for permission to quote their work and for the discussions we had with them. Mrs Menzies Lyth also worked with us as consultant to the project and helped us to understand some of the institutional problems and what, at times, was happening between us and our local authority colleagues.

Members of the Marital Studies Advisory Panel of the Tavistock Institute of Human Relations also discussed the text and we thank them all. We are particularly grateful to the Chairman, Professor Gordon Dustan, for his concerned and astringent criticism.

We thank the Society of Authors as the literary representatives of the estate of A.E. Housman; and Jonathan Cape Ltd, publishers of A.E. Housman's *Collected Poems*; Faber & Faber Ltd, publishers of *The English Auden: Poems, Essays and Dramatic Writings 1927 - 39,* edited by Edward Mendelson; Routledge and Kegan Paul Ltd, publisher of C.G. Jung's *The Practice of Psychotherapy*, Vol. 16 of the Collected Works; and Anthony Shiel Associates Ltd, in respect of an extract from *The French Lieutenant's Woman* by John Fowles, published by Jonathan Cape.

PART ONE

The Project

On the death of a child in suspicious circumstances:

> *In came the doctor,*
> *In came the nurse,*
> *In came the lady*
> *With the alligator purse.*
>
> *'Dead', said the doctor,*
> *'Dead', said the nurse,*
> *'Dead', said the lady*
> *With the alligator purse.*
>
> *Out went the doctor,*
> *Out went the nurse,*
> *Out went the lady*
> *With the alligator purse.*

Children's song; source unknown

1 Introduction

See how yon justice rails upon yon simple thief. Hark, in thine ear; change places and, handy-dandy, which is the justice, which is the thief?

William Shakespeare

This book is about work with marital problems presented to a social services department. It reports an action research project undertaken jointly by four caseworkers of the Institute of Marital Studies (IMS) and the social workers and their managers of an inner London borough.

It is a book about interaction; the interaction within client families, between these and their workers, and among the workers themselves. Inevitably these interactions are affected by the organizational setting within which they take place. The constellation of clients, workers and setting provides the framework for this book, as it did for the project.

In many ways our analytical framework is similar to that of the official reports concerned with individual cases in which children have died as the result of their parents' behaviour.[1] As we have

---

[1]   For example:
  (i) Health and Social Security, Department of (1975), *Report of the Committee of Enquiry into the Care and Supervision Provided in Relation to Maria Colwell* (HMSO).
  (ii) Lascelles, R., *et al.* (1975), *Report of the Joint Committee of Enquiry into Non-Accidental Injury to Children with Particular Reference to the Case of Lisa Godfrey* (London, London Borough of Lambeth).
  (iii) Norfolk County Council and Norfolk Area Health Authority (1975), *Report of the Review Body Appointed to Enquire into the Case of Steven Meurs* (Norwich, Norfolk County Council).

done, these reports made it their business to consider the complex interactions among the families and extended families of the children, the performance of the professional workers and the institutional framework within which they operated. We do not dissent from most of the conclusions of these reports, yet there remains an uneasy feeling that something has been missed. It is clear that the workers missed cues, failed to communicate or failed to communicate what was important. Quite rightly the reports say this should not have happened. To draw such obvious conclusions, however, does not advance our understanding of why such mistakes continue to be made by intelligent, concerned and frequently well-trained and experienced people.

We believed that to get nearer to the heart of the matter we needed to begin by immersing ourselves in the kind of experience so neatly processed in the government reports. Following a similar logic, this book also starts with an experience. The example which follows is taken from the diary compiled by one of us while we were working as basic grade social workers in the department. Because it was written without hindsight and soon after the events, it reflects the anxiety aroused at the time. We present it in its confused and untidy state.

Cases like the one we describe, although not typical of much of the day-to-day work of the department, have an impact out of all proportion to their frequency. In this chapter we consider some of the questions raised by this example and in the following one we describe the methods we used to try to answer them and the framework of the project. All names in this book are pseudonyms. Quotations taken from the research diaries, surveys or reports in case files are inset.

EXAMPLE

The family consisted of Mr and Mrs Jafferji, their one-year-old daughter, Angela, and their four-week-old son, Christopher. Mr Jafferji was of Middle-Eastern origin, Mrs Jafferji was English.

Thursday

I visited Mr and Mrs Jafferji by appointment. Both of them were at home and expecting me. Close on my heels, however, a lady who said she was Dr Huggins arrived. She said she had been asked to call by the social services department. I denied that I had asked her to call, but she insisted someone had done so. I presumed Mrs Jafferji had asked her in connection with Mr Jafferji's behaviour the previous week when he had slapped Angela and smashed the windows.

To my astonishment, which I had great difficulty in containing, Dr Huggins examined Mr Jafferji's pills and gave him an injection which, she said, would cure him. I was amazed that Dr Huggins did not discuss with Mr Jafferji what was the matter with him, nor ask any questions, nor tell him why she had come, despite Mr Jafferji's request to be told who had sent her. Mr Jafferji submitted very docilely, kneeling at her feet while she administered the injection. I resisted all Mrs Jafferji's attempts to draw me into the conspiracy and I joined with Mr Jafferji when he said how confused he was: I added that I felt the same.

A variety of questions are immediately raised by these two paragraphs. We do not know if Mrs Jafferji did summon the doctor, but, if she did, what must her feelings have been in order to ask for such aid without discussion with her husband? Moreover, what must the world be like for Mr Jafferji when, without consultation, doctors can descend, treat him apparently as being incapable of rational discussion, and administer an injection?

Other questions relate to the workers. It is apparent that, although dealing with the same problem, they did not know each other. Like Mr Jafferji, the male worker was confused. Like Mrs Jafferji, the doctor presumably considered Mr Jafferji a dangerously irrational person and gave him an injection of what she at first told the social worker was a powerful psychotropic drug. Already this situation seemed likely to result in a row between two highly trained professional workers. More confusion followed.

I became even more confused when the health visitor also turned up. I was particularly startled as I had an appointment with her later in the day to discuss the Jafferjis' problem.

When the doctor had left, I endeavoured to have the interview with Mr and Mrs Jafferji and I wanted to know what had happened since my visit the previous week. The row had started when Mrs Jafferji had ticked him off for slapping Angela when she had been scrabbling in a drawer and taken no notice of his admonition. The slap had left finger marks on the child's face and this was confirmed by the health visitor. Mr Jafferji had felt ashamed by his wife reprimanding him in front of the child and he had then twisted Mrs Jafferji's nose and thrown a chair through the window.

Then, on Mrs Jafferji's instigation, Christopher had been admitted to hospital because, as she said, he had tonsillitis or gastro-enteritis. (I later learnt from the health visitor that the hospital had not known what had been wrong with him except that they suspected Mrs Jafferji had difficulty in relating to him.) He was still in hospital but could have been collected the previous day. Mrs Jafferji was now wondering whether to go and get him later in the afternoon.

Mrs Jafferji did not seem bothered by the injury to Angela, but complained of being neglected by Mr Jafferji who had been working long hours with his friends and had not visited the baby in hospital. (I later learnt that she had not visited either.) They continued to argue about Mrs Jafferji's mother who had arrived during the week and had been turned away by him; Mrs Jafferji firmly took the side of her mother. I made several attempts to help them understand their deep feelings of neglect by the other, a strong wish always to be put first and their reaction when this did not happen.

Mrs Jafferji tried to put Mr Jafferji in a bad light at every opportunity and tried to involve me in this. I refused to be put in this position and again made it clear that I had nothing to do with the doctor's visit. I asked Mrs Jafferji why she had asked her to come. She lost her temper, shouted that she hated all foreigners and that she did not want her husband. After her outburst we were able to discuss their having the baby home and I, anxious about the way she provoked Mr Jafferji in a way that made him irrational and left her the ill-treated victim, arranged to call the following day.

'Battering' arouses anxiety and often anger in most people. Why was it that, despite Mr Jafferji's apparently being the one responsible for the attacks, the worker continued to put more weight on Mrs Jafferji's provocative behaviour, and was less concerned about any further attack on the child? Again, why did he apparently accept the feasibility of Mr Jafferji's view that he lost face in front of a one-year-old child?

Faced with the worker's response, Mrs Jafferji redoubled her efforts to get him on her side. Failing to do this, she lost her temper, not with him, but with her husband. Why?

Friday

I registered the 'battering' of Angela and telephoned Dr Huggins. She was not Mrs Jafferji's doctor and had not until yesterday seen Mr Jafferji for some time. She had administered the injection only on Mrs Jafferji's request. She did not think she had done anything irregular, but agreed not to treat Mr Jafferji unless he himself asked for this.

I visited Mr and Mrs Jafferji. They were both depressed. Mrs Jafferji had collected the baby and clearly was having considerable difficulty in feeding him. She was holding him in a most uncomfortable position for them both and Christopher was not sucking and taking the milk. I could see why the health visitor was anxious. After watching for some time, I suggested how Mrs Jafferji might alter the way she held him and how she could put the teat more firmly into his mouth. When she did this, he was able to suck much better. I suggested she should discuss this problem with the health visitor who I knew was calling the same day. I did not feel at this point that I could open up this problem between her and the baby. Mrs Jafferji made several comments about Mr Jafferji's being out so much working with his friends and leaving her alone, and I wondered if she found it very difficult his going out to work at all. Again I commented on their feelings of being so neglected by the other.

After the weekend

On Monday I learnt that Mrs Jafferji had been seen by the department's night-duty officer over the weekend and, showing her bruises, had complained of being beaten and raped by her husband. She had been taken to a voluntary agency who had arranged accommodation for her and the children at a women's aid hostel.

The worker from the voluntary agency telephoned to say Mrs Jafferji was seeking an injunction.

On Wednesday the health visitor telephoned to ask if I was going to do anything about the injunction. She seemed rather surprised when I said, 'No'.

On Thursday I visited and saw Mr Jafferji who was in a depressed state and not really understanding what had happened. He denied there had been any violence over the weekend, but said he had asked Mrs Jafferji for intercourse which she had refused. Subsequently he found her crying in the kitchen. He did not know why she was crying and, when he asked her, she told him to go away. He said he did not know why she had left and he could not understand anything about it.

On the Monday she and another woman had come into the flat while he was asleep. He had woken up and she said she had come to collect her things. He had gone to sleep again. I asked him why he had not asked her why she was leaving and he said very simply that if she wanted to leave she could do so and he was not stopping her. I told him that she was applying to the court to have him leave the flat so that she could come back into it with the children. He did not know why she had to go to court for that as, if she asked, he would leave anyhow. But he did not show any signs of doing so and just seemed very depressed and unsure of what he wanted to do and what the marriage and its breakdown were about. So far he had not received any notice of his having to appear at court and he seemed to be just biding his time. I arranged to call next Thursday.

These paragraphs have continued the themes of the first recorded interview but raise the question of whether the situation has been improved by the social agencies. In what follows it will be seen that more and more people become involved. The basic conflict between the couple is mirrored in the relationship between the workers and highlights ethical questions on the proper role of the social workers. In the background are professional jealousies and differences in the way such cases are understood. It will be noticed that most of the people involved do not seem to have had previous contact with each other, and that as they find it harder and harder to cooperate they tend to involve bureaucratic structures either to ensure 'cooperation' (through a case conference) or to get a person's superior officer to force him to do what is required.

The following week

On Tuesday the health visitor or the worker from the voluntary agency (I cannot remember which) telephoned to say Mrs Jafferji had obtained an injunction against Mr Jafferji, who had to leave the flat by 6.00 p.m. on Wednesday evening. She asked me whether I was going to do anything about it and my 'No' again caused her some consternation.

On Thursday Mr Jafferji telephoned to make sure I was coming. I found him in possession of the injunction which, he said, had been served on him only the previous evening but ordering him to be out that day. I talked to him about what was happening and he felt the whole procedure had been unfair as he had not been given a chance to say what he had to say nor been given time to find anywhere else. He had felt unable to leave and I learnt that he had resisted the health visitor and three policemen who had called. We had a long discussion about it and I advised him that he really ought to go and that he would be in some trouble if he refused to do so. I think he felt sufficiently trusting to be able to leave with me, so I helped him pack his bag and took him to an address of one of his friends. I left a message for the health visitor to say Mr Jafferji had left the flat and Mrs Jafferji was free to return.

On Friday I was telephoned by various people all of whom were demanding to know where Mr Jafferji was because of a warrant issued for his arrest. I refused to give the address, but told all of them that I would give it to the officer of the court when he asked for it.

It began with a senior health visitor who telephoned to complain about me and refused to discuss the case with me personally. I telephoned her back and eventually we agreed that I would meet with her and the health visitor to discuss the problem, but I would not agree to there being a full case conference.

Then the worker from the voluntary agency telephoned, complaining that I had given Mrs Jafferji's address and her own home telephone number to Mr Jafferji. I denied I had done this. She threatened me that the tipstaff would want to speak to me if I did not give her Mr Jafferji's address. I said very firmly that I would not give her this just as I would not give Mr Jafferji hers, and I again repeated that I would give his address only to an officer of the court.

Next it was Mrs Jafferji's solicitor who accused me of being obstructive. I denied this and yet again said I would give Mr Jafferji's address to the tipstaff when he asked for it.

Subsequently the assistant director telephoned having received a complaint about my behaviour. I explained what had been happening and my refusal to give Mr Jafferji's address to anyone other than the officer of the court.

Finally the tipstaff, in no apparent urgency to arrest Mr Jafferji, telephoned. I told him the address at which I had left Mr Jafferji, but could give him no assurance that Mr Jafferji was still there. I also told him that I had advised Mr Jafferji to take legal advice and, as far as I knew, he was doing this.

The rest of the day was comparatively uneventful.

In the subsequent work with Mrs Jafferji and the two children, Mrs Jafferji was very angry that the worker had not conspired to get her husband punished and imprisoned. A few weeks later she was wanting a reconciliation. By this time, however, Mr Jafferji had had enough and wanted no marriage. He had been very uncertain whether he had ever wanted it in the first place.

An interesting thing about this example is that there was only one reference to anyone being anxious or worried although they behaved as if they were. Certainly there was reason enough for anxiety. There was a child of one year with slap marks on her face caused by her father. There was a baby of a few weeks old whose mother was having enough difficulty in relating to him to seek sanctuary for him in hospital. There was a wife and mother with her nose twisted, who, the more she craved for herself the attention the baby needed, screamed the more that not she, but her husband, was the patient. There was a husband and father who, feeling as inadequate and angry as his wife, expressed his fury with his fists.

Violence, screaming and distressed adults, babies failing to thrive and maltreated toddlers arouse anxiety in most people and it is extremely difficult to contain and handle this type of anxiety usefully. The problem for all social workers is how to make what is a natural and appropriate anxiety work for them and for their clients and not against them all. But the more anxiety-provoking the situation, the more difficult it is for the workers to hold on to their basic professional skills and ethical standards of work.

In the example there were three social workers — two from the statutory department (one for the days, one for the nights) and one from a voluntary agency — one doctor, one health visitor, one solicitor, one tipstaff, three policemen, one assistant director and one senior health visitor. The pressure the workers put on each other and the way they behaved towards each other was a modified and more sophisticated version of what the clients did to each other. The workers used words rather than fists, but the accusations, denials, demands, threats and complaints were all there. The marital war was imported into the workers, who, in their turn, exported it further up the organizational hierarchy. The workers, no less human than the clients, functioned less well when anxious and when under pressure from the disturbed Mr and Mrs Jafferji.

The social worker managed to 'get talking' again to the health department, but had to fight to do this by insisting on speaking to a senior worker who had previously refused to speak to him. The separation of the health visitor and the social worker was fortunately not as total as that of husband and wife. They had to continue to work with Mrs Jafferji over her difficulties of relating to and handling the two children when she became a one-parent family.

The effect of all the earlier interactions of the workers, however, was probably not helpful to the clients. Mr Jafferji was seen by his wife as violent and irrational and his handling by the doctor and policemen can hardly have diminished this impression. Mrs Jafferji was almost certainly worried and guilty about her inability to care for her baby, and desperate for attention and concern. Attention she certainly got, but it took the form of alleged rape and battering from her husband, which, in turn, were the grounds on which she appealed for sympathy and more attention. Whether her methods of getting attention ensured that it was focused on her real needs remains doubtful.

There is a drama about this type of case. No one got what satisfied them and yet the hectic activity of the participants covered, if only superficially, the sadness of Mr and Mrs Jafferji. It was very hard to think about what was happening.

If we are to grow wiser as a result of this kind of experience we need, as we argued at the beginning, not only to immerse ourselves in it, but also to pull back and reflect on what has been happening. Our first chapter has been concerned with experience. Our second describes the background against which we undertook the project and the research methods we used.

2 The Framework of the Project

*It seems often to be the case, that the more
sophisticated the counting, the less sophisticated
the understanding of the phenomenon being counted.
... It is probably less damaging to miscalculate a
well understood phenomenon than most elegantly to
quantify a heap of nonsense.*

N. Christie

HOW WE STARTED

The project was first proposed in a climate of public concern and
professional conflict.

In Parliament and the press there was increasing anxiety about
marital violence. This concern, however, was not matched by an
equal enthusiasm on the part of professional workers for marital
casework with the spouses involved. There were calls for more
shelters for female victims, changes in the law, and more active
police intervention. The help offered by caseworkers in such
situations seemed to many as relevant as the admonitions of a
maiden lady at a bar brawl.

Uncertainty, in fact, surrounded the whole practice of casework
whether with individuals or with families. (In certain circles, for
example the Civil Service, casework means simply work with cases
and can involve no more than decision-making in relation to
information acquired from a file. In social work the word has come
to denote a set of practices and values employed in face-to-face
contact with individuals. We use the word in this more specialized
sense.) By some casework was upheld, taught or practised as the
major method of social work. Others had grave doubts about its

12

effectiveness. Some studies had found that randomly selected clients receiving intensive casework did not do better in terms of objective criteria than similar clients who had been left alone.[1] Psychoanalysis, the traditional underpinning of casework, had long been subject to similar attacks,[2] and more recently social scientists had suggested that the consumers of casework usually wanted something more practical and less verbal than they got.[3]

The doubts about casework were given added force in some people's view by the amalgamation of the children's, mental health and welfare departments, and by the expectations placed by the Seebohm Committee[4] on the new social services departments. The change almost certainly made the practice of casework, whether desirable or not, more difficult. The training of social workers and the first years of their working lives now encompassed a wider variety of clients, with the result that specialist skills took longer to acquire. Many of the tasks imposed on social workers seemed to call for little by way of casework expertise, and they themselves seemed to feel more than ever overworked and to stay an even shorter time in contact with clients before leaving for promotion or other reasons. It would not have been surprising if the practice of casework had come to be regarded not as the stuff of a social worker's professional life, but simply as a brief preparation for higher and better things.

Now, as then, the IMS occupies a particular place in this climate of professional conflict. In the total network of welfare provision it is one small specialized unit which offers both a casework service to people who are experiencing marital difficulties and educational programmes for social workers on marital and related family

---

[1] Adams, S. (1967), 'Some Findings from Correctional Caseloads Research', *Fed. Prob.* 31.
  Powers, E., and Witmer, H. (1962), 'Does Counselling Prevent Delinquent Behaviour?', in Johnson, N., Savitz, L., and Wolfgang, M.E., *The Sociology of Punishment and Correction* (New York, Wiley).
  Fisher, J. (1973), 'Is Casework Effective?', *Social Work* 18, 1.
[2] Eysenck, H.J. (1952), 'The Effect of Psychotherapy. An Evaluation', *J. Cons. Psychol.* 16.
[3] Mayers, J.E., and Timms, N. (1970), *The Client Speaks* (Routledge & Kegan Paul).
[4] Seebohm, F. (1968), *Report of the Committee on Local Authority and Allied Personal Social Services* (Cmnd 3703, HMSO).

problems. Its full-time workers have between them had working experience in probation, children's, welfare, health and mental health departments. It believes in the value of the family and its structure supports the practice of casework.

As members of the IMS, we also believe that our specialized experience with marital problems is relevant to agencies with more diverse tasks than our own and that an interchange between agencies is fruitful. Members of courses which we run have kept us continually in touch with the change and development in these services, and we have been able to relate this knowledge to our own previous statutory experience. In support of our teaching programmes, however, at this point in our history, we wished to extend our practical experience with a clientele different from the one which finds its way to the IMS and in a department which did not exist in the days when we were first out 'on the beat'. We were curious.

Although we thought it likely that the amalgamation of the previously specialized services made the practice of casework more difficult, much of the casework which is done in Great Britain is carried out by workers in social services departments and the majority of them spend most of their time working with individuals, some of whom are living in two-parent families. More important, perhaps, many of the more difficult problems brought to them, such as delinquency, child neglect, mental illness and homelessness, are known to be associated with marital difficulties.[5] Among local authority clients, no less than elsewhere, the marital

[5] Davies, M., and Sinclair, I.A.C. (1971), 'Families, Hostels and Delinquents', *Brit. J. of Criminology,* July.
Fisher, S., Boyd, I., Walker, D., and Sheer, D. (1959), 'Parents of Schizophrenics, Neurotics and Normals', *Archives of General Psychiatry,* 1.
Laing, R.D., and Esterson, A. (1964), 'Families of Schizophrenics', Vol. 1 of *Sanity, Madness and the Family* (Tavistock).
Nye, F.I. (1958), *Family Relationships and Delinquent Behaviour* (New York, Wiley).
Philip, A.F. (1963), *Family Failure* (Faber).
Vogel, W., and Lauterbach, C.G. (1963), 'Relationships between Normal and Disturbed Sons' Percepts of the Parents' Behaviour and Personality Attributes of the Parents and Sons', *J. Clin. Psych.,* 19.
Wilson, H. (1962), *Delinquency and Child Neglect* (Allen & Unwin).

relationship in a two-parent family is the primary relationship — the basic dyad from which the relationships between parents and children take their meaning and form.

Against this background we devised a project which would take account of clients, workers and the setting in which they came into contact with each other.

THE AIMS OF THE PROJECT

The literature which has had the most influence on social work has been written mainly by practitioners. If not offering exact prescriptions for action, it has been concerned with ideas and values, remained close to action, and has arisen out of attempts to 'change the world' rather than out of abstract scientific enquiry. We ourselves believe that we can only develop useful ideas by maintaining our own practice.

In our original proposal we described our aims: 'to develop methods of marital casework which could be applied by local authority workers, with local authority clients, in a local authority setting'. The emphasis was on application. We wanted to test ideas developed in our own and other clinical settings and see how far they needed to be adapted; we knew they could not automatically be transferred into what we understood was the hurly-burly of a social services department. The best way to find out about their relevance, we believed, was to go into a department and try them out. A related aim, and one which is embodied in this book, was to try to understand what went on between us and our clients in the context in which we were working. Many books on casework take little account of the setting, and others on social work management ignore the precise nature of the task for which the organization is set up and the effect this has on the worker, and, therefore, on the organization. It seemed to us that what we had to contribute was our understanding of the interactive component in marital problems, in the relationships between clients and workers, and between workers in the organization; we aimed to try to bring these three components together.

WHAT WE DID

The project was set up with a social services department of an inner London borough, geographically compact and not too far from the

IMS. Its senior management was known to be committed to high standards of casework as evidenced by the fact that it recruited only trained social workers or workers on limited appointments who were willing to be seconded for formal training.

We opened negotiations in the beginning of 1973 and learnt something of the department's structure. Organizationally it was divided into four divisions: one dealt with administration; one provided residential care, and one, known as community services, was responsible for day care, home helps, transport and provision of various aids and benefits; the last, known as the social work division and in which we were to be based, was closely involved with the others and, in particular, with community services. The social workers, alongside many other referrers, screened clients for services, although they did not usually have final responsibility for whether these were received or not. The primary responsibility of the social work division was social work with individuals and families. It was organized into three geographical areas, each under an area officer. (During the course of the project the reorganization of the health services took place and hospital social workers joined the social work division of the department.) In the two areas in which we later came to work, the social workers were divided into teams, each of which dealt with cases from the whole area and took it in turns to be on duty for new cases coming in on a particular day. (These two areas differed from a third which operated a special intake team and allocated some workers to a particular geographical district within the area.) In rare times of staffing abundance a team would have a senior social worker, three or four trained social workers, a trainee social worker, a social work assistant and a group clerk.

By the end of 1973 we had made sufficient advance in the negotiations and planning with some members of the management team for it to be appropriate to discuss the proposal with the field social workers. As might be expected, their reactions were mixed.

Some welcomed the project as a potential method of increasing their skills. Others modestly felt that the type of skills to be learnt were beyond them or, more robustly, that the skills were irrelevant to the type of work they had time to undertake and to the clients with whom they were working. Yet others felt that even if casework were relevant, it was only one function of the department and there was danger that the department would be reorganized to facilitate casework as opposed to dealing with its other responsibilities. Some objected to what they saw as the political overtones of the project and to the way it had been introduced, arguing, for example, that the project was a Trojan horse introduced by management in order to stifle radical social work. Even those most friendly to the project were worried about the amount of time it might involve.

Thus we embarked on a project embodying a set of values and ideas that were by no means unreservedly accepted in the department and which were under attack in the outside world.

We started in 1974, which was defined as a pilot year, and spent a day and a half a week in the department. In 1975 and 1976 we worked two and a half days a week on the project, in 1975 approximately two of these days actually in the department, in 1976 approximately half a day, using the rest of the time for assembling the material. In 1977 and 1978 we maintained regular, but less frequent, contact with the department. We had previously decided that the project could use two full-time workers, but we thought it best to employ four workers half-time. We needed to be 'of' and 'not of' the local authority department, and we needed to maintain the ways of working we brought from our own setting if we were to be helpful in another. For this reason we carried between us a caseload comparable in size to those carried by the full-time workers but heavily weighted by families with multiple problems.

Two of us were based in one area, two in another and the two pairs did not attempt to follow identical programmes. In one area the two of us were invited to become members of different teams, and like the other members were accountable to the team's senior social worker. We picked up cases from team allocation meetings and participated in team events, doing intake duty and covering for other members. In the other area the two of us worked more independently, were not part of a team, circulated more freely, and were asked to take cases and used as consultants by some members of all teams. In addition to working cases on our own, all four of us shared cases with other social workers at their instigation. We introduced ourselves to the clients and others involved with them as social workers and carried the usual written authority to this effect.

In addition to our work with cases, we began a series of weekly seminars. These were held in both areas, led by ourselves, and open to any social worker who wished to come on a regular basis. Initially these seminars were not restricted to the discussion of marital cases and the aim was to create some form of common language and understanding.

At the beginning of 1975 these seminars reconstituted themselves as the project groups and we concentrated entirely on cases in which married or cohabiting couples were involved. By this time the discussions were seen to be useful. In the pilot year we sometimes had only a handful of social workers with us, but by 1975 it was rare to have less than ten and the average size was probably fourteen. Some of the original members had left the department, some had decided that this type of work was not for them; others, newcomers to the department, had joined. The area officers and the seniors were members alongside the basic grade workers. In one area, trainee workers were also invited to join.

We studied the interaction of the families, the relatives, the workers and other professionals involved in the case and what we believed were the underlying and interactive processes operating between them. At the end of each meeting we allowed time to look at the behaviour of the group in relation to the material we had discussed and the feelings with which we were left. Sometimes we felt filled up with the depression the worker had described and noted how muted and slumped we had become. Sometimes the fight between the clients was imported into the group and an argument, as opposed to a discussion, took over. Sometimes men sided with men, and women with women. Sometimes the men, sometimes the women, were silenced. We used this information to help us understand what was happening in the marital war and in the work with the clients, and we tried to become more aware of the uncomfortable and less conscious feelings with which we were left, so that, once identified, they could be handled and not intrude inappropriately into work with other cases during the remainder of the day.

In accordance with our original plan, we also held meetings with the management. We scheduled weekly meetings with the area officers, monthly meetings with them and their senior social workers, and monthly meetings with the management team of the social work division which constituted the project management committee. We held occasional meetings with the top management team of the department. The purpose of these meetings was to try to formulate some of the institutional issues involved in working with marital and family problems.

In 1975 in one area, and in 1976 in the other, we began to work with the seniors on the problems involved in their supervisory role. It was felt that these meetings were fruitful, and they were extended to the third area which, apart from its area officer, had not previously been involved in the project.

Finally in 1977 and 1978, we worked with the project management committee on the text of this book and discussed some of the issues raised in it.

The fact that we worked only part-time in the department meant that we avoided some of the strains imposed on other social workers, as, for example, the unremitting nature of the work. At the same time we acquired other strains — the need to switch ourselves chameleon-like from one setting to another; the need to leave worrying cases unattended without being able to comfort ourselves that we would be about if they 'blew up'; and the realization that we were not completely members of the department with the support, as well as the limitations, that this involved.

Our two-day week highlighted the dilemma which both we and the social workers faced and which came across clearly in some of the earlier meetings. Were we, as they saw it, highly-trained creatures whose esoteric concerns had no relevance to their mundane tasks, or were we, by contrast, just another set of social workers without experience of their particular setting and, therefore, with nothing or, at least, nothing different, to contribute? For our part, we were sometimes tempted to see our local authority colleagues as a somewhat harassed group of individuals with whom we had little in common, whereas at other times we ourselves felt like fish out of water and admired the skill with which they operated in their own setting. In any event, the difference between us and the local authority workers was helpful in enabling us to think about what was going on.

Our time spent in the department, in casework and in project meetings yielded us three types of data: the observations we were able to make during the course of our work; a sample of cases; and the reaction of the department to our discussion of structural and organizational issues.

PARTICIPANT OBSERVATION

As part of our research plan we kept notes of our days in the department and experienced, like other so-called participant observers, the guilt induced by this spy role. Our work, however, differed from most participant observation in that we were at least as much participant as observer, and we had to apply our insights to our own behaviour as well as to that of our colleagues, clients and other contacts.

In many ways our participant role gave us access to data which otherwise would have been denied us. In our contacts with the hierarchy we reacted with dismay to the way they appeared to perceive the situation of the social worker and we became trapped in a somewhat juvenile, or even paranoid, stance as we urged our views upon them. On occasions we became involved in shouting matches with the homeless families unit when its staff would not do what we, or our clients, wanted. Initially we reacted with anger and dismay to the way we felt general practitioners and psychiatrists treated us, and we experienced a wide range of emotions as we strove to find the appropriate way to the bureaucratic hearts of the Department of Health and Social Security (DHSS).

These reactions were of value in so far as they gave us insight into the way a social worker might instinctively react in a particular situation. They were dangerous in that they tended to cloud our judgment and also deny us access to data, which, for example, a better relationship with the homeless families unit might have enabled us to get. We were also in danger of feeling that, as we reacted in this way, other social workers would do the same. Despite these dangers, however, we feel that our experience gave us access to data which we could have obtained in no other way.

One side-effect that may still be visible to the knowledgeable reader relates to language. We quickly picked up the shorthand used in the area offices, saying, for example, 'Take a place of safety' or 'Section' rather than using the more prosaic terms of the Children and Young Persons Act 1933 or the Mental Health Act 1959. In some parts of the text we have deliberately kept this phraseology. Language expresses emotion as well as legal niceties. The short, active verb in '*Take* into care', a phrase often used by the workers, carries a feeling of aggression and responsibility which the more prosaic and accurate phrase, '*Receive* into care' (Children Act 1948) lacks. We have tried to use legally accurate phraseology in our analysis while keeping the more expressive phraseology in the examples.

THE PROJECT CASES

Much of this book is based on a sample of sixty-eight 'project cases'. This sample includes all the cases with which we worked ourselves and all the cases involving married couples which social workers brought to the weekly project group. The cases, therefore, entered the sample by diverse routes. Some are there because we ourselves asked for them in allocation meetings. Others we were asked to take either because we were thought to have appropriate skills or because no one else was available or willing to take them, or, we suspect, because it was hoped to show we were as ineffective with them as anyone else. Social workers had similarly diverse motives in bringing cases to the project group. Some brought cases because they did not understand what was happening and felt very stuck with them; others brought cases with which they were doing particularly well; others, public-spiritedly, volunteered to bring a case because no one else was offering that particular day. As far as we could see, however, no one brought a case with which he or she was not heavily involved.

Clearly this method of selection ensures that the sample is quite unrepresentative of cases, even cases involving married couples, in contact with a social services department. However we wished to pick up a sample of cases in relation to which we or the other social workers in the project group were thought to have something to contribute. We wanted also a sample with which social workers were heavily involved, partly because these were the cases which were most difficult and on which they spent most time, and partly because their involvement gave us access to data which would have been missed in more superficial contacts. Our method of selection achieved both these ends.

In order to get a yardstick of comparison for our sample, we carried out a survey of all the current cases in one area which involved married or cohabiting couples. This survey is described in the next chapter and, among other things, highlights the fact that whereas many cases take up very little social work time, others are extremely demanding of it, often over long periods, and have a marked influence on the operations of the department. We found that the time-consuming married clients shared four major characteristics and we used these characteristics to define a core sample of thirty-two of our sixty-eight cases. We have made the work with this core sample the focus of this book. With the social worker's dislike of neat classification, however, we do not confine the text to the core or total samples, but we let the reader know whether a case is in either sample by the pseudonym. Names of cases in the core sample start with a letter from A to M; those in the larger sample from N to W; those not in the samples start with the letter Y.

Our core sample enables us to employ the methods of clinical description and analysis which have long been used in the field of medicine. The doctors who developed the concepts relating to schizophrenia, for example, did not begin with random surveys. On the contrary, they began with patients who were referred to them for help and, seeing some order in the symptoms presented, they developed systematic concepts which could be used by other clinicians in their work. In the same way we make no claim that the ideas presented in this book apply to all the varied clients with whom social workers are involved, or even to all the cases in our sample; only that they apply to some of them, that we suspect that these cases would tend to be among the more difficult and demanding, and that we hope that the ideas will prove helpful in the practice of others as they have in our own.

This clinical model may help to explain a second feature of our approach — our lack of a control group. A control group enables one to say whether or not one class of individuals differs from another in particular ways. For example, one well-known study has shown that urban mothers who are depressed are more likely than the less depressed to have unsupportive marriages, three or more children under fourteen, poor housing and no outside work.[6] A social worker influenced by such a study might attempt to improve a couple's marriage and housing and put the younger children into a day nursery so that the wife could go out to work. He might then find, as did one of us on the project, that a temporary improvement in the marriage led to a further pregnancy which, in its turn, led to more stress; apparent improved housing led to rent arrears and increased anxiety; and the placement of a child in a day nursery, far from enabling the wife to go out to work, increased her sense of

[6]   Brown, G.W., Bhrolchain, M.N., and Harris, T. (1975), 'Social Class and Psychiatric Disturbance Among Women in an Urban Population', *Sociol.* 9.

inadequacy as a mother and hence her depression. (Implicit in this example is the degree of responsibility the worker felt for what happened to the clients. We refer the reader to Chapter 3, in which many of the quotations illustrate this point.) In this particular case a control group study failed to suggest various dynamic features which the worker's attempts to help can reveal. We believe that a clinical approach has a respectable logic of its own and that, as in this case, it can supplement control group studies and deepen the understanding they provide.

DEPARTMENTAL REACTION

The sixty-eight project cases were also useful in understanding the workings of the department. In one way or another clients try to get a department to react to their plight or need; social workers in contact with them try to get reactions from them but also from other sections of the department and from the outside world. The results of these efforts were often highly revealing in the same way that attempts to operate a piece of machinery are often highly revealing of its mechanism. It was through observing these efforts and attempting to get reactions from the department ourselves that we came to formulate a hypothesis about the suitability of a social service department for handling the problems of the kind of cases we encountered.

A particular aspect of our role was that we wished to be helpful to the social workers and their managers. We decided to try and develop ideas which would clarify the social workers' situation both in relation to their organization and in relation to their clients, and we strove to create an atmosphere in which these ideas could usefully be communicated. One of the benefits of doing this was that, as in casework, the exchange of ideas produced further clarification.

OUR ANALYSIS

We began this project with a question: How far is marital casework facilitated in a local authority setting?

In exploring this problem we have used some of the standard methods of social science, for example participant observation, but, with some exceptions, we are not reporting facts unmarked by selection and interpretation. We are, in fact, presenting an analysis of our practical experience, sometimes only painfully gained. Some readers will recognize from their own experience many of the conflicts and difficulties we attempt to analyse. But, if they are to integrate our experience with theirs, they will need to share in the pain, anxiety and misery we describe. We have attempted to grapple with some fundamental and painful issues. Often in social research apparent certainty is bought at the price of relevance. We believe our interpretation to be relevant, if not proven.

3   The Scope of
the Problem

Joshua, the son of Nun, and Caleb, the son of Jephunneh,
Were the only two that ever got through to the land of milk and honey.
                                                                    Anon.

Local authority social workers deal with a variety of clients and do
equally varied work with them. However, while some of these
clients are similar to those encountered in other settings, some are
characteristic of local authority work and particularly important in
the influence they exert upon it. It is these clients, or at least those
amongst them who are married or cohabiting, for whom we have
been striving to develop an appropriate treatment rationale and
about whom we are writing.

Our justification for this choice of client group is based on a
rough survey of cases in one of the areas in which we looked at
referrals, caseloads and high-priority cases. Our survey of cases at
the intake stage gave us an idea of the range of problems with
which social workers came into contact and the proportion of those
which were seen to involve marital problems. However, many of
those seen at intake were found to have a very brief contact with the
department. (To judge — rashly — from the figures collected in
another area, 40 per cent of the cases would have been expected to
be closed on the day of referral and a further 26 per cent within six
weeks.)

We therefore needed to supplement our study of referrals with an
examination of caseloads. Here again we found that social workers
were carrying some cases whom they saw rarely or even not at all.
So, in addition, we needed a particular study of cases to which
social workers gave priority.

In discussing these surveys we use the word 'married' to include the cohabiting, and the phrase 'married cases' to cover any case in which the family included a married or cohabiting couple.

We use the surveys to show the concentration of effort on relatively few priority married clients, the characteristics that seem to define these couples, and the apparent problems in attempting marital work with them.

REFERRALS

Our survey of a year's referrals involved 1198 cases, only 22 per cent of which involved a client who was either married or had married parents. The details of this are in Appendix I. Here we quote only the conclusions.

> From the study of 1198 cases two things are clear. Firstly, at the intake stage, the number of cases having an overt marital problem was very small. In only 3 per cent of the total did the social workers think it worth while mentioning a marital problem on the referral sheet.
>
> Secondly, with negligible exceptions, those who had overt marital problems neither referred themselves, nor were referred with an overt request to deal with the marital problem for its own sake. 'Battered' wives required accommodation and deserted husbands day care facilities on the grounds of their marital difficulties, but this was a far cry from requesting the social worker to intervene in their marital affairs. Two or three cases within the 1198 could be seen as requests to the social worker to carry out marital work as a means of reducing other problems (depression or alcoholism) and other cases left the social workers scope for deciding whether or not they would consider working with the marital problems. In these latter cases it seemed that the social workers often chose to concentrate on the immediate practical difficulties.

It appeared that social workers were not seen as a community resource for dealing with marital problems and this fitted with our general impression. With very rare exceptions, general practitioners did not refer marital problems to social workers even when, as a result of these, one partner was depressed or ill. The stated policy of the citizens' advice bureau (CAB) was to refer marital problems to the department only in exceptional cases which seemed likely to involve child care difficulties. The headmistress of a local primary school, with whom an IMS worker discussed a case, remarked that the clients needed 'professional help' and 'should go to the marriage guidance council'; she said this without any apparent sense that the worker would regard this remark as a slight on his professional expertise. It was thus a central difficulty of doing marital work in a local authority department that the social worker was rarely accorded the right to do it.

CASELOADS

On our second survey in 1976 we interviewed the seventeen basic grade social workers and social work trainees in one of our areas. We asked them, firstly, how many cases they carried, secondly, how many cases involved a more or less stable marriage.

These questions proved more slippery than we had predicted. In the first instance, the notion of caseloads was unsatisfactory. Most social workers said that their caseloads contained a number of quite inactive cases and one apparently contained some clients who were literally dead. Further, as the supplementary benefits commission have found, the definition of cohabitation is itself a matter for fine judgment. Whom does one count as cohabiting — couples who have frequently separated and reunited in the past and have now been apart for two months, couples who have never previously separated but are now apparently set on divorce, couples who are currently separated only for alleged practical reasons, or only the stably married? What about a young homosexual man who was cohabiting with a female old age pensioner with whom he had an emotional relationship?

The social workers, however, were usually clear about whom they considered to be, in our terms, married and, on their definition, the number of married couples they carried on their caseloads varied from 13 per cent to 45 per cent. Overall they carried 667 cases, of which 206 (31 per cent) were said to involve a married couple — an average of twelve per worker.

The workers were asked to say how many of their married cases exhibited marital problems. The definition of marital problems was difficult. Sometimes they had no doubt that such problems existed: 'Oh Lord, yes.' At other times it was a matter of doubt and suspicion: 'Well, it's a matter of a weak dad ...', '... There used to be ...', '... It's a cockney marriage, based on grumbling about each other', '... I guess it's there, but I don't really know'. However, in 62 per cent of the married cases the worker was prepared to say that there was a marital problem, in 12 per cent that there might be and in only 26 per cent that there was not one.

The sharp difference between apparent incidence of marital problems on caseloads and those noticed at the referral stage must have arisen in part because social workers knew their own cases better than they knew new referrals; and they were, in any case, more likely to mention marital problems when questioned about them than when given latitude over whether or not to mention them on an intake form. The second part of the explanation was that marital problems were associated with cases to which social workers gave 'priority'.

DEMANDING AND PRIORITY CASES

At the beginning of the interview, the workers were asked to name five cases on their caseload which they regarded as priority in the sense that it was most important that they were kept open and given active supervision, and the five cases which they considered most demanding in terms of time. There was a marked overlap between these two categories, 74 per cent of the demanding cases being considered priority and vice versa.

The same proportion (46 per cent) of priority and demanding cases involved married clients. 87 per cent of the demanding married clients and 88 per cent of the priority married clients were said to have marital problems.

This gives a picture of the importance of marital problems in local authority work very different from the one we obtained in the sample of referrals. On these figures, slightly more than four out of ten of the cases on which social workers said they were spending most time and to which they gave priority involved marital problems.

Demanding and priority cases obviously took up more time than suggested by their numbers. Among the married cases, 58 per cent of those assessed as demanding as against 18 per cent of the non-demanding and 55 per cent of those assessed as priority as against 19 per cent of the non-priority contained a family member who had been seen by a social worker in the previous week. These cases were also open longer; 58 per cent of them had been open for more than two years as against 27 per cent of the remainder.

These figures became more significant in the light of the fact that many cases were not seen very often. The workers were interviewed at a time of relative staff stability and none had been on leave the preceding week. They said that in the previous seven days they had had face-to-face contact with 53 of the 206 married cases, an average of just over three per worker. The following table gives the intervals since they had last seen a family member in all the 206 married cases.

Intervals since family member seen

Intervals	Number of families
Less than 7 days	53
8 to 14 days	31
15 to 21 days	24
22 to 28 days	19
29 days to 2 months	34
2 months plus to 3 months	17
3 months plus to 6 months	18
Over 6 months	6
Never	4

At first sight these figures are impressive; in approximately a quarter of the cases at least someone had been seen within the past week. However, this figure includes those who will not be seen again for two weeks, three weeks or more. The number who are being seen weekly is, therefore, far less than fifty-three. If one were to assume that social workers see their clients regularly and that in any one week they see half their two-weekly clients and a third of their three-weekly clients, etc., one would estimate that these workers were seeing twenty-two married clients on a weekly basis or, in other words, an average of slightly more than one married case per worker. On the same assumptions, the number of married cases the average worker can see at regular intervals of three weeks or less is three.

This picture is consistent with the findings of research on the amount of time social workers spend with clients.[1] These studies suggest that social workers spend only 30 per cent of their working time (twelve hours out of a forty hour week) in 'contact related to clients'. This 'contact' includes escort duties, telephone conversations and meetings with others concerned with the clients as well as face-to-face discussions with the clients themselves. The number of different client-families who can be seen more than briefly in any one week must, therefore, be small and the problem is made more difficult by the fact that many cases are split into two or more units and workers are sometimes ill and go on holiday. We have assumed, therefore, that it is only the priority cases that have much chance of sustained and regular contact. (For further discussion see Appendix II.)

We wanted to know the characteristics of the married cases which were receiving this sustained contact.

SEVENTEEN PRIORITY CASES

Each social worker was asked to select the married case which he considered to have the highest priority. The cases selected appeared to fall roughly into two groups.

The first group could be called, 'Young mother under stress', with the social workers' emphasis on youth.

> She was a West Indian girl who came over to England at the age of twelve after having been brought up by her grandmother. She quarrelled with her parents after her grandmother's death and became pregnant at the age of seventeen. She then left home and had a continuous housing problem with eleven changes of address. After a violent liaison with the father of her child had broken up, she formed another. This also broke down and the social worker supported her through her depression and feelings that she should part with her child. On a recent visit he found she had rent arrears of £300 and was again living with her last boyfriend.

---

[1] Grey, E. (1969), *Workloads in Children's Departments* (HMSO).
Carver, V., and Edwards, J.L. (1972), *Social Workers and their Workloads* (National Institute for Social Work Training).
Walker, R., Goldberg, E.N., and Fruin, D.J. (1972), *Social Workers in Northern Ireland and their Workloads* (National Institute for Social Work Training).

Many of the children in this group had been notified as being 'at risk'.

> The couple were referred by a neighbour for leaving two children under four on their own. Both partners were described by the social worker as 'very deprived' and the husband, a Moroccan, as 'ignorant of the customs and laws of this country, wanting guidance and very dependent on his wife'. They lived in grossly overcrowded accommodation and the wife drank and kept on leaving home without the children, who were then inadequately cared for by the husband.

The second group contained eleven cases all of which could be described as 'problem-families'.

> The family was Irish with parents in their thirties and having six children ranging in age from sixteen to five. The marriage had been violent and unstable and there were financial problems. The wife was currently in prison awaiting trial and four children had been received into care. There was anxiety about how the father was caring for the other two.

The two groups differed in the average number and age of children, the length of time the case had been open, the professionals involved and the treatment resources used. Although the second group numbered only eleven families, it included fifty-six children, an average of 5.1 per family in contrast to 1.1 in the first group. In the second group, no case had been open for less than two years (one had been open for fourteen years), and 75 per cent of the fifty-six children had used expensive treatment resources such as residential care (children's homes and special schools) and child guidance clinics as well as those supplied by the social work division. In the first group no case had been open for two years. And while in this group contact with the department seemed to relate to relatively recent and acute crises, the second group seemed to have maintained contact through a series of never-ending emergencies.

Despite the differences between the two groups, the seventeen cases shared some common features. We isolated four characteristics which were shared by fourteen of the seventeen families and we later used these characteristics to define the core sample of the project cases. They were:

1.   Ambivalent marital bonds
2.   Lack of success in parental roles
3.   Lack of constructive support from families of origin
4.   Continual threat of separation from one or other members of the family.

AMBIVALENT MARITAL BONDS

From the point of view of the project, the most important common feature of these cases was the ambivalent marital bond. This was described by one of the social workers:

> The parents are locked in a kind of marriage where they can't live without each other and yet their interaction isn't satisfying and doesn't meet each other's needs. They're deprived as people, so they haven't very much to offer. She was one of fifteen and he spent long periods in care. Neither has much affection to give.

Fourteen of the seventeen marriages involved chronic ambivalent bonds characterized by quarrels with a greater or lesser degree of violence. Things had clearly been bad for a long time or from the beginning of the marriage in all of the fourteen except two, in which it was not clear when the trouble started. In thirteen of them, one or other spouse had at one stage left home and in some of them coming and going had become a way of life.

The remaining three marriages were not satisfactory. One faced an acute crisis and the husband was contemplating leaving. The other two did not apparently involve excessive quarrelling but were described as follows:

> She's killing him. He used to be a big healthy man two and a half years ago. He's had three strokes since and a heart attack and his prognosis is very poor ... He's a poor thing now. ... He can't escape. He took a major overdose, I don't think I mentioned that.

In the second case the social worker had never seen the present husband. She said:

> She thinks of him as some kind of god. She's seen so much dirt that I think she wants a little bit that's all right for herself.

This wife was still in some sort of contact with her previous husband, with whom she had a stormy liaison and to whom the social worker thought she was in some ways still attached.

LACK OF SUCCESS IN PARENTAL ROLES

The histories of the women involved in the seventeen cases would render them liable to feeling bad as mothers. Seven of the seventeen had at some stage abandoned their children, six others had accused themselves or been accused by others of neglecting them, and two others had felt so unable to manage that they had asked for their children to be received into care (under the Children Act 1948). Of the remaining two, one had two children of whom one was subnormal and the other a former drug addict and possibly alcoholic.

In almost all cases the fathers had difficulty in providing for the families' material needs on the scale demanded.

> There are heavy debts, housing problems and they're threatening to split up.

And so it went on. Only one of the seventeen families had not involved their present or past workers with housing or monetary problems. Eleven of them had at one time been in homeless families accommodation. This situation seemed unlikely to increase the self-respect of either spouse.

Irrespective of the accusations they may have levelled at themselves, many of the families would seem to have been quite realistic in regarding themselves as subject to the disapproval of others.

> It's the kind of case where from time to time you get a flurry of telephone calls saying what is happening about that awful family and those poor children.

> They have been judged as failures. ... They had a dog with some trouble but, although they took the dog to the vet, they were afraid to take the dog out because of what people might say about it. In the past the welfare department has said some very judgemental things about them. [Of a couple with educationally subnormal children.]

LACK OF ALTERNATIVE SOURCES OF SUPPORT

Of the thirty-four husbands and wives involved in the seventeen cases, eleven came from Ireland, Scotland, Mauritius, the West Indies or Morocco and were therefore probably cut off from their families of origin. A further fifteen came from backgrounds about which the social workers expressed reservations, often major ones. None had backgrounds which were described positively. Therefore, in the event of marital break-up, the clients had dubious support available to them from their families of origin; and the number of children involved would often add to the difficulty of making use of support that was available.

CONTINUAL THREATS OF SEPARATION

A central issue in the handling of the seventeen cases was that of separation together with the related question of who should live with whom.

> We decided that the child who was fostered had to go to boarding school and this is a fraught situation that I've got to sort out.

> The department has a history of involvement in this case. The mother buggered off to Ireland and for two years they tried to reconstitute the family under the father. Then it became obvious that this wasn't going to work and they sent a telegram to the mother asking her to come back.

> There was the episode where she wanted to get away and it was quite obvious that I supported her in this.

> At the moment we are trying to establish who should have the kids and what place they should be.

The issue of separation had usually been around since the beginning of the contact but a striking reminder of its continuing importance came from an examination of the agenda covered in the social workers' most recent meetings with their clients.

In all but the last three interviews, issues related to separation were on the intended agenda. However, similar issues were also involved

Agenda	Number
Feelings about actual or proposed marital separation.	2
Financial matters and legal proceedings about eviction of cohabitee.	1
Social worker visited to say goodbye.	1
To check or arrange baby-minding arrangements consequent on wife's recent departure.	2
To arrange meeting between separated siblings.	1
To explain to children in care about mother's situation in prison.	1
To discuss leaving foster home and going to boarding school.	1
To discuss new placement, social worker's policy of limiting home visits, and recent expulsion from school.	1
To discuss arrangements for husband while wife goes on holiday.	1
To discuss rehousing (wife threatened to leave if husband did not accept).	1
Grandmother anxious about young mother. Husband threatening to leave, baby neglected, housing problems.	1
Follow-up to family interview in office (one child recently received into care, two older children recently left mother).	1
To check up on unregistered baby-minding.	1
To check up on family situation and unpaid gas bill while husband in hospital.	1
To check up on family situation including non-attendance at school.	1

in the last three. The mother who was engaged in unregistered baby-minding was having difficulty in allowing her children to leave home. The social worker visiting about the unpaid gas bill found two children aged five and six on their own. And the visit to check up on the family situation was partly to ensure that the children were safe enough to be allowed to remain there and included a discussion of another child separated from his parents in another part of the country.

In thirteen of the seventeen cases, one or other spouse had at one time left home. In fourteen of them there clearly was, or had been, an issue over whether the children should be received into care. In eleven cases, children had actually been removed. In two more cases the department was actually or potentially involved in separating the family, in one case by accepting the wife as homeless without her husband, in another by encouraging her to become so. In the seventeenth case the department had no statutory reason to be involved in the temporary splitting of the family, although, interestingly, the clients had involved the social worker in arranging a holiday in which the husband and wife would, in fact, be separated.

These findings are not, of course, remarkable, since social workers are involved in these cases precisely because it is feared the relations between parents and children will become intolerable, the children become delinquent, or one or other parent desert, with the result that the children are received into care. The resources which the department has or is connected with — children's homes, homeless families accommodation, recuperative holiday homes, psychiatric hospitals, etc. — are not only havens for the isolate and 'at risk', but also provide means whereby people can be removed from each other. By a similar token, Section 1 monies (under the Children and Young Persons Act 1963) and domiciliary services may be used to prevent this happening.

THE PROBLEM OF DOING MARITAL WORK WITH THE SEVENTEEN CASES

The fact that fifteen of the seventeen couples had overt marital problems and the remaining two had certainly experienced them in the past did not necessarily mean that marital work was being attempted with them. Various priorities and difficulties militated against such a plan of action.

The first main group of difficulties related to motives and the contract between client and worker. At the IMS, clients seek treatment almost always with the jointly professed aim of working at their marital problems. The local authority social worker is often in a position where he has to seek out the client in relation to aims for which a client may profess no agreement.

All but one of the seventeen cases involved children in some sense 'at risk'; in only three of these cases were the social workers operating with authority confirmed by a court order. In these two facts lay a dilemma, for while it was obvious both from conversation and from the nature of the cases chosen that the workers were ordering their priorities in terms of risk rather than of the clients' amenability to treatment, their social control function was not usually backed by explicit authority. Although about half the children involved had been in care at one time or another, less than one in seven had been subject to care orders or rights and powers resolutions. Even these legal measures seemed to have less bite in them than a layman might have expected. For example, one father had refused to return four children on a care order to their placement and, although the social worker objected, it proved impossible to get the children back. More common were situations in which

> There are no grounds for a place of safety order — at least we do not think so.

This lack of authority was sometimes felt as a problem:

> We're hoping that the court will make a supervision order as a condition of divorce which will make our lives a bit easier.

This, however, did not lessen the feeling of responsibility:

> I've got responsibility for the children. I've got to visit regularly and see them.

> At the moment we are trying to establish who should have the children and what place they should be.

Nor did the lack of authority necessarily lessen the expectations of others involved in, or knowing of, the case:

> I feel I am being asked to 'demand feed' people. I feel I am continually standing between people. I could be more active, but there does not seem enough to go on yet. Still, as long as they can say it is our fault a lot of people seem to be satisfied.

And inevitably the situation of many of these families resulted in a number of clients who were either hostile or whose motives were at cross-purposes with that of the social workers.

They were very suspicious at first — in fact, downright un-cooperative.

She wants me for financial aid. She wants help with a nursery place, but she occasionally rings up when things are going very badly, not in a manipulative way, just to talk things over.

In the last quotation, the social worker made it clear that talking things over was a better use of her time than the various other uses this client had at times proposed to her. However, the fact that the social workers operated within a nutcracker of conflicting expectations meant that what they did could not be determined solely by what they or their clients wanted. In this kind of case, there was a necessity to maintain contact and one way of doing this was to avoid, at least for the time being, the question of the client's motives — the awkward question of whether the worker could be concerned with emotional matters of any kind, let alone with marital ones.

Certain features of the social worker/client relationship helped in this respect. Only two of the last meetings between social workers and the seventeen clients had taken place in the office, so the client's motives were not necessarily clarified. Although meetings had been frequent (an average of 4.5 in the last month), only four of them had been arranged at or before the previous meeting. And twelve of the meetings had left the social workers with some practical task which they had contracted to perform on their client's behalf. By taking on practical tasks, the social workers acquired an excuse for further contact. Some social workers acknowledged that they were using practical means to further emotional ends:

I was trying to work through the housing problem and the day nursery and trying to find out what was going on. I kept chasing her to find out. You've got to hang on to them by their passive consent. It's very manipulative really.

I was supposed to be meeting them to collect payment in order to discuss marital things.

We worked out that it was important that I should give them something. And I got the day nursery place which they both wanted, and that made a big difference to my relationship with them.

Nevertheless, although a limited supervisory and welfare role could be maintained by this type of strategem, it could be exceedingly uncomfortable for the social worker. For example, one worker was trying to keep in touch with a hostile family, where the mother had been convicted of the manslaughter of one child and there were five children, including an eighteen-month-old baby, 'at risk'. Another social worker described the dilemma clearly.

> What I am trying to ascertain is if, in general, things are good enough for the children to stay there .... One has times of wanting to run away — it's all a bit much .... One feels very vulnerable and rather naked. It's very difficult in the situation here to give it enough time and thought. Outsiders turn to you as the person who knows what is happening in the family and you have to turn round and say you don't really know what's happening. Perhaps, I feel inexperienced too. What is so dispiriting about it is this kind of living with no growth .... It feels as if it takes up a big lump, and yet I can't allow a big lump stopping me from doing other things.

The lack of motive for marital work was often more pronounced in one partner than in the other:

> I used to try and do marital interviews with them, but last time he had a fix and was bland. ... And also I found that when I tried to do marital interviews I was told so many lies by each of them that it was definitely not worth the trouble. I think they've got a lot to hide. He's involved in a lot of criminal activities anyway and he is not going to confide in a social worker. [And there is the difficulty] that I had been involved in her leaving and I'd fallen back on the belief that all I could do was try and support her. The fact is that in so far as I've got a relationship, it is actually with her. I don't believe her for a minute when she says she is leaving him, but it's obvious I'm more her person than his anyway.

> I have never tried to see them alone as a couple. He would not agree, of course. He doesn't want to have anything to do with anyone in authority. What can they help him with?

There were also emotional rivalries. Husbands could be said to feel that the social worker was threatening their 'dictatorship' and the problems of jealousy and exclusion which affected the clients' families equally affected their relationship with their social worker:

I am not sure what marital work would be with these two. She would probably come along on her own and say, 'We can get on best without him'.

For quite a period he wouldn't speak to me and she used to come round and talk about what a pig she lived with. She wanted to keep the situation as it was.

He was more resistant for he saw me partly as a competitor.

These jealousies and rivalries accentuated the problem of focusing on the couple. In fact, they formed part of a second main group of difficulties in doing marital work. This group includes the variety and number of problems presented, the size of the families, the dispersed nature of many of them, and the lack of available time. These constraints often resulted in a concentration on individual members of the family, either child or adult. Some workers thought it more appropriate to concentrate on the children rather than on the marriage of the parents:

> I say, 'Mr Young, I suggest you take your troubles to your solicitor, because there is really nothing I can do about them'. I do not think it appropriate to do casework with Mr Young, his marriage or his cohabitation. It is a hopeless thing to do. It has been tried for a very long time without any conspicuous success. Most of the work I do is with the kids, because to me they are the ones who are suffering most apparently, more than they should. I suppose I am setting myself up as a substitute mother for them until they are placed on a long-term basis. I am the only stability they've got.

Altogether three workers made it plain that their main focus was on the relationship between themselves and the children. The clearest example was provided by a social worker dealing with a large delinquent family where several of the children had had incestuous relationships with each other and were now placed in various residential establishments:

> What do I think my role is? It's not a word I like to use, but I think that it is controlling the situation and giving stability to the children as a whole. There's no stability within the home, just constant drinking, smoking and sex .... You have to be very firm [with the mother], give her an inch and she will take a mile. She never says

'No', and gives the eight-year-old cigarettes and drinks — not that dad is all that responsible. They are irresponsible parents.

A further four workers clearly had their main relationship on a one-to-one basis with the mothers, all of whom had voluntarily sought help (even though two of them were thought to be at risk of 'battering' their children). All of these cases fell in the 'Young mothers under stress' group.

> I see my role as the first-line alert, being close to mother if things get very bad because that is our contract. She is honest with me and can come to me. She can in no way approach the psychiatrist or the GP, ... and so I try to strengthen my relationship with her so that if anything did happen I could receive the child into care or get a place of safety order and it would not be in any jerked way but almost cohesive.

Seven workers tried to have the whole family as their focus, although usually they had a closer relation with one of its members than with the others:

> What I do is to make it quite clear to the parents that I visit to see all the family members and I visit regularly to see everybody. I have made one or two visits without appointments when I have called and they were not in and I've called back in a week or so. The sort of thing I discuss is the children, economic situation, mum and dad, schooling.

'The family', however, could prove rather an unwieldy focus, and lead to an almost frantic concentration on one member after another.

> It's a case that worries me, because you can't put it into neat packages and you're not sure what you're doing with it. It's very difficult to deal with all their schooling at the same time. There are endless problems all over the place. It's not a crisis case, you can hold up dealing with it. It's not a success story at all, it's untidy. All you can do is to busy yourself with little bits of it. Like getting the kids to school. And yet you manage. Delinquency isn't too much of a problem. Wally's not been caught yet.

> She explodes about financial problems, violence, delinquency, "Will you take Peter into care?' Or she asks why the kids are truanting ... Peter is very much a scapegoat for the rest ... I like her, she's a nice woman. She goes on. 'Doreen's in court again; now it's Dave; would you like a cup of tea?' Finding a focus is so difficult.

The same worker stressed the lack of time.

> In social services, if they're not presenting crises, they tend to get pushed into the background. You tend to deal with things to keep them quiet. There is probably a lot that could be done. And there's the fact that you have to visit them in the evening. They could be a full-time job.

Despite these difficulties, three couples had received quite intensive help focused on the marital relationship. Two were project cases and all three had received previous help of the rather opportunist nature described above. It was clear, however, that marital work with this type of case in which the marital difficulties were so intertwined with housing, financial and child care problems could be negotiated only with difficulty:

> It changed from being a holding procedure to a situation of actually trying to resolve something in it. Initially it was just going along with what was happening and trying to keep the family going. Now it feels more like looking at what is happening in the family and trying to decide what is in the best interests of them all — whether to stay together or to part.

Another worker had survived a period of severe acting-out. She said that she had got to the point where either she or someone else could now do marital work:

> They came together and for the first time they could acknowledge a real problem that anyone could discuss with them. It was a question of whether they could split up and go.

Although two of these latter cases might be described as successes, the predominant feeling roused by surveying the priority cases as a whole was one of burden, anxiety and failure:

The case doesn't please me very much because they are a constant source of failure ... I don't like the way they operate. I don't like that sort of psychopathic plausibility and I am concerned about the children. They are used to it. They live with it.

Another worker voiced the sense of carrying a load.

The burden of this sort of case is quite an important element, I think. It can affect one's way of working, a feeling of very little possibility of achieving a great deal, and having to carry things, because that is what the department is about really — keeping things going. And there is a lack of time and a feeling of things creeping up behind you. One gets all involved in the dynamics of the family and being caught up in it like another member of the family almost.

THE CHOSEN FEW

In the area in which we studied the incoming and outgoing work, few overt marital problems were referred and, if they were, it was not usually for marital help. However, marital problems were much more common in caseloads and said to be almost universal among the married clients to whom social workers were giving priority. These priority cases seemed to be the only ones likely to receive sustained help.

The central concepts underlying the work with these cases were those of 'risk' and 'emergency', 'responsibility', 'supervision' and 'monitoring'. The job of social work was seen as exercising oversight and 'keeping things going'. If cases were not presenting crises, they got pushed into the background. Out of monitoring, emergency contact and holding off society's creditors and policemen, a supportive relationship was seen to grow, but not too much was expected of it. In this situation the kind of casework which might perhaps deal with fundamental problems and get the cases off the books was seen either as alien or as a desirable, but unrealistic, extra.

The job of holding off the gas board, conciliating the schools and courts and hoping that nothing too terrible would happen was, however, an uncomfortable and, in the long run, not a very satisfying one. For this reason alone, it seemed worth struggling with the possibility that more might be done.

Within our total of sixty-eight project cases, we found we had a core sample of thirty-two cases which could be defined by the same four major characteristics as the seventeen highest-priority cases studied in the survey:

1. ambivalent marital bonds
2. lack of success in parental roles
3. lack of constructive support from families of origin
4. continual threat of separation from one or other member of the family.

These were the cases which tied down the departmental resources. Of the thousands who approached the department and the many more thousands who might do so, these few were the ones which consumed a disproportionate share of the social work time, and gave the area office its image and its sense of burden and threat. It was as if the intake system operated as a sort of gigantic sieve designed to select the clients who, on the face of it, were the least amenable to treatment.

It is these clients about whom we have chosen to write and for whom we need appropriate theories. In the final chapter of this Part we outline the theoretical base we have used in our analysis.

4　Four Theoretical Themes

*One could as little catch the psyche in
a theory as one could catch the world.
Theories are not articles of faith; they
are either instruments of knowledge and of
therapy, or they are no good at all.*

　　　　　　　　　　　　　　　C.G. Jung

To a 'pure' research worker, a theory is something to be stated
tentatively and then to be tested, if necessary, to destruction. A
social work practitioner, however, cannot afford to take quite such
a cavalier attitude. Faced with disorganized and disturbing
behaviour, he needs theoretical ideas to help him understand his
experience. As Dr J.D. Sutherland has said, 'There's nothing so
practical as a good theory'. Having found a 'good theory' which
both makes sense to him and supports his therapeutic optimism, in
itself vital for the job, the practitioner is less likely to want to
destroy either theory or optimism; but he does need to keep
questioning his theory if he wants to keep thinking.

On this project, as in all our work at the IMS, we are practitioners and concerned with improving our practice and helping
other workers to improve theirs. We write as practitioners and our
attitude, which is reflected throughout this book, is made up from
a mixture of ideas, some of which at present we feel certain about
and some of which we are more tentative about. All of them,
however, are ones which we have found useful in understanding the
behaviour of our clients, ourselves and our colleagues in the
working situation of a social services department.

For our practical purposes, our theories need to cover four main
areas: the individual personalities of the clients; the interaction
between the clients; the interaction between clients and workers
(including referrers); and the influence on all these interactions of

the organization in whose context they take place and, conversely, their influence on it.

The interviews in chapter 3 contain frequent allusions to all these factors:

> They are very deprived as people, so they haven't very much to offer. She was one of fifteen and he spent long periods in care. Neither has much affection to give.

Or speaking again of the same case:

> The parents are locked in a kind of marriage where they cannot live without each other and yet the interaction is not satisfying and does not meet each other's needs.

These two quotations refer to personal pathology (deprivation and its consequences) and also to marital interaction. Other quotations refer to the situation of the social workers within their organization (in particular to the pressure under which they work) and to the effect of the client families upon them:

> And there is a lack of time and a feeling of things creeping up behind you. You get all involved in the dynamics of the family and being caught up in it, like another member of the family, almost.

The description of the work with Mr and Mrs Jafferji reveals the same factors at work, perhaps in a more dramatic way. There is the disturbed and deprived behaviour of the husband and wife, their fraught marital interaction, the mutual recriminations and provocative behaviour of the professional workers, and the bureaucratic and at the same time pressured context within which they were working.

We have used four theories which relate to these four main areas. They are:

John Bowlby's theory of *Attachment and Loss.*[1] This is predominantly a theory of individual personality and seems to us particular-

---

[1] Bowlby, J. (1969), Vol. 1 'Attachment'; (1973) Vol. 2 'Separation — Anxiety and Anger', *Attachment and Loss,* (The Hogarth Press and the Institute of Psycho-Analysis).

ly relevant to clients with the kind of background of those in our core sample.

The theory of *Marital Interaction* developed at the IMS.[2] Although it has been developed in relation to marital problems, this theory can also be applied to other interactive systems.

The theory of the *Reflection Process*.[3] This was originally developed by Harold Searles and later applied by Janet Mattinson to casework supervision.[4] It is concerned with the effect of client disturbance on the workers, not all of whom may be in the same organization.

The theory of *Institutional Defence*.[5] This was originated by Eliott Jaques and elaborated by Isabel Menzies in a classic paper.[6] It is concerned with the way organizations, which are not closed systems, deal with events likely to arouse unpleasant emotions such as anxiety.

In this chapter we give a brief outline of the relevant parts of these theories. Throughout the rest of the book we apply them to our illustrative material and extend some of the ideas.

[2] Pincus, L. (ed.) (1960), *Marriage: Studies in Emotional Conflict and Growth* (Institute of Marital Studies).
Institute of Marital Studies (1962), *The Marital Relationship as a Focus for Casework* (Institute of Marital Studies).
Bannister, K. and Pincus, L. (1965), *Shared Phantasy in Marital Problems* (Institute of Marital Studies).
Guthrie, L., and Mattinson, J. (1971), *Brief Casework with a Marital Problem* (Institute of Marital Studies).
[3] Searles, H.F. (1955), 'The Informational Value of the Supervisor's Emotional Experience', in (1965) *Collected Papers on Schizophrenia and Related Subjects* (The Hogarth Press and the Institute of Psycho-Analysis).
[4] Mattinson, J. (1975), *The Reflection Process in Casework Supervision* (Institute of Marital Studies).
[5] Jaques, E. (1955), 'Social Systems as a Defence Against Persecutory and Depressive Anxiety', in Klein, M., *et al., New Directions in Psycho-Analysis* (Tavistock; and New York, Basic Books).
[6] Menzies, I. (1960), 'A Case-Study in the Functioning of Social Systems as a Defence against anxiety.' A report on a Study of the Nursing Service of a General Hospital, *Human Relations,* Vol. 13, No. 2 (May).

ATTACHMENT AND LOSS

Understanding the response of a child to separation from, or loss of, his mother figure turns on an understanding of the bond that ties him to her in the first place. Bowlby believes that attachment has a biological basis and is to be found in primates of all species. He defines attachment behaviour as 'seeking and maintaining proximity to another individual'. Speaking of its place in nature, he says,

> In the countryside in springtime there is no more familiar sight than mother animals with young. In the fields, cows and calves, mares and foals, ewes and lambs; in the ponds and rivers, ducks and ducklings, swans and cygnets. So familiar are these sights and so much do we take it for granted that lamb and ewe will remain together and that a flotilla of ducklings will remain with mother duck that the questions are rarely asked: What causes these animals to remain in each other's company? What function is fulfilled by their doing so?

The two main features of this behaviour are firstly the maintenance of the proximity and its restoration when it has been impaired, and secondly the specificity of the other. 'Parent and young usually behave towards each other in ways very different from the ways they behave towards other animals. Individual recognition and highly differentiated behaviour are ... the rule ...'

As regards humans, Bowlby believes that attachment behaviour varies in the readiness with which it is elicited over an individual's lifetime, and he provides a chronological account of its development. According to him, it is present only incipiently during a child's first half-year and becomes manifest and effective at about seven months. It is then exhibited readily and regularly until the end of the third year. During this period the child's behaviour is very much influenced by the presence or absence of the mother. When he knows she or a familiar mother-substitute is around he displays much more confidence. As long as he is sure she is nearby, so that he can periodically check her whereabouts, he can explore and increase his skills and independence. At first the toddler cannot determine what is influencing his mother's movements towards or away from him; but later he acquires some idea of her motives and his own. 'Once that is so,' Bowlby says, 'the groundwork is laid to develop a much more complex relationship with each other, one that I term a partnership.' By the age of three most children are secure enough to accept their mother's absence for limited periods, trust in her return and use a substitute attachment figure.

Throughout childhood the attachment figure remains important as a base from which to explore the outside world and to which to retreat. Bowlby provides a list of factors which promote heightened attachment behaviour (retreat to base) in children. Some of these factors relate to the condition of the child: 'fatigue, hunger, ill-health, pain and cold'. Other factors relate to the environment: 'occurrence of alarming events, rebuffs by other adults and children'. Finally, others relate to the attachment figure: 'mother absent, departing, discouraging proximity'.

Adolescence sees further changes in attachment behaviour, although during this period of seeking and finding adult autonomy, the young person often displays extreme swings of behaviour, one moment fiercely independent, the next clinging and uncertain.

Marriage gives the opportunity for reattachment to a specific figure and legally sanctions attachment behaviour.

> Provided the couple meet their new obligations, pay the rent, care for the garden, no one is going to find it regrettable if, in their newly-found attachment, the young marrieds cannot bear to be out of one another's sight. And, if the neighbours are amused at the clinging on the front doorstep, they will also be touched, and may even feel sad, to realise how soon this phase of re-enacted attachment behaviour will give way to a state where a perfunctory wave will do. No one will find their behaviour pathological nor dream of suggesting that the couple should 'pull themselves together and snap out of it'.[7]

Attachment behaviour can be heightened again at times of sickness, the birth of a child, or when prolonged separation is threatened. (The leaver, as well as the left, may manifest anxiety.) However, presuming the environment is not too frightening and there is a degree of basic trust that help will be available when required, it normally continues at a comparatively low level until old age. The fact that attachment behaviour is less obvious when attachment is

[7] Lyons, A. (1973), 'Therapeutic Intervention in Relation to the Institution of Marriage', in Gosling, R. (ed.), *Support, Innovation and Autonomy* (Tavistock).

felt to be secure does not mean that the underlying affectional bonds are any the less.

From this very brief account, it is clear that once the capacity to attach is developed, attachment behaviour is most readily aroused when a person is comparatively helpless on his own and that it is accentuated at the beginning of a person's life, at the birth of a baby and in old age. It is these periods of life with which the majority of social services clients are involved. The situations which provoke heightened attachment behaviour — sickness, calamity and rebuff — are also characteristic of the situations of many of these clients; for example, threats of separation are a defining characteristic of our core sample. These considerations provide the first of our two main reasons for using Bowlby's work.

Our second reason relates to the similarity between the behaviour which we observed among our adult clients and that which Bowlby described among young children suffering from separation anxiety. He describes the typical reactions of a young child separated for a period from his usual care-giver:

> At first he *protests* vigorously and tries by all the means available to him to recover his mother. Later he seems to *despair* of recovering her but none the less remains preoccupied with her and vigilant for her return. Later still he seems to lose his interest in his mother and to become emotionally *detached* from her. Nevertheless, provided the period of separation is not too prolonged, a child does not remain detached indefinitely. Sooner or late after being reunited with his mother his attachment to her emerges afresh. Thenceforward, for days or weeks, and sometimes for much longer, he insists on staying close to her. Furthermore, whenever he suspects he will lose her again he exhibits acute anxiety.

In prolonged separations children can remain compulsively independent (detached), rejecting as far as possible human relationships, putting their trust in objects. Others exhibit a form of anxious clinging to an alternative attachment figure and find it difficult to let that person out of their sight. Others appear highly ambivalent, swinging from one type of behaviour to the other, sometimes approaching, sometimes rejecting a possible attachment figure.

Bowlby brought together a great deal of evidence concerned with the behaviour of young children separated from their attachment figures. Of the many studies he used we quote from Burlingham and Anna Freud's[8] recorded experiences of caring for infants and young children in a residential nursery during the Second World War. This behaviour illustrates the strength of feeling that attachment and loss can invoke and, therefore, the degree of ambivalence.

> Not only did children in these nurseries become intensely possessive and jealous of their 'own' nurse, but they were also unusually prone to become hostile towards her, or to reject her, or else to retreat into a state of emotional detachment, as the following record illustrates:

> 'Jim was separated from a very nice and affectionate mother at seventeen months and developed well in our nursery. During his stay he formed two strong attachments to two young nurses who successively took care of him. Though he was otherwise a well-adjusted, active and companionable child, his behaviour became impossible where these attachments were concerned. *He was clinging, over-possessive, unwilling to be left for a minute, and continually demanding something without being able to define in any way what it was he wanted.* It was no unusual sight to see Jim lie on the floor *sobbing and despairing.* These reactions ceased when his favourite nurse was absent even for short periods. He was then *quiet and impersonal.*'

> 'Reggie ... formed two passionate relationships to two young nurses who took care of him at different periods. The second attachment was suddenly broken at two years eight months when his "own" nurse married. *He was completely lost and desperate at her departure, and refused to look at her when she visited* him a fortnight later. *He turned his head to the other side when she spoke to him, but stared at the door which had closed behind her after she had left the room.* In the evening in bed he sat up and said, *"My very own Mary Ann! But I don't like her."* ' [our italics]

There are many points of similarity between the behaviour of Jim and Reggie and that of Mr and Mrs Jafferji. Mrs Jafferji was clinging and over-possessive of Mr Jafferji, unwilling to be left when he was at work or out with his friends, but hating him when he was there. She seemed to be desperately asking him for

[8] Burlingham, D., and Freud A. (1942), *Young Children in War-time.* (Allen & Unwin).

something, for what he was not sure, but whatever it was he was unable to meet the request. Mr Jafferji was even less able to define what he wanted. His behaviour was either 'impossible', twisting her nose or throwing a chair through a window, or he was quiet and impersonal and wanted no marriage at all. When she had finally departed, a departure on which she had insisted, she wanted him back again. It is not hard to see in Reggie's remark, 'My very own Mary Ann! But I don't like her', a clue to the ambivalent marital bonds characteristic of our core sample.

MARITAL INTERACTION

Most people feel that marriage should be a committed and intimate partnership which involves togetherness and in which each partner complements the other.

The IMS is primarily concerned with the difficulties some people experience in handling their feelings regarding attachment and separation. Its working experience provides grounds for questioning the belief that 'monogamous marriage provides either the most practical and comfortable or the easiest way in which to live and rear children'.[9] Other people wonder that the institution survives at all.

One reason for the survival of marriage may be the fact that it has a second biological purpose over and above a purely sexual one. In Western marriage there is an emphasis on the specificity of the chosen partner who, in Bowlby's terms, is, therefore, a 'suitable object for attachment'. Therapeutic experience in the IMS, however, suggests that marriage may also serve two psychological purposes, one concerned with psychological development, the other concerned with the avoidance of psychological pain.

From the developmental point of view, the opportunity to reattach and, therefore, to be in touch with feelings associated with attachment holds the promise of being able to make better what was felt to be wrong in the past and to make partnership more satisfying than is dimly remembered from childhood. The likelihood of being able to do this is heightened by the unique combination of the responsibilities of family life and the opportunity to behave childishly within the intimacy of an ongoing

[9] Lyons, A., op. cit.

sexual relationship — as expressed in the quotation on page 49 above.

Furthermore, the partners may choose each other as complements to express what they cannot express for themselves. Some of these different characteristics may be valued; others may be feared, but, if they can be handled within the current situation and experienced as less destructive than previously, old ghosts can be laid to rest.

These two factors endow marriage with hope and provide it with a psychological purpose. In these terms it can be seen as a vehicle which can be used for development and it offers an opportunity to carry the child (within us all) forward, as opposed to 'dragging it unconsciously behind'.[10]

With this in mind, we can then use Jung's vision of marriage as an 'emotional container'.[11] Just as a young child needs to be contained and given a base from which to explore and to which to retreat, so too may an adult develop more of his fullness of nature if provided with an emotional container.[12]

Sometimes, however, the containment is used defensively to ward off conscious and unconscious anxieties of both partners and to prohibit development. We have found that often these anxieties are shared, so that both partners have the same vested interest in trying to avoid particular situations which they feel might be disastrous. This may be so even when at first sight their ways of handling their fears are quite different. For example, if one partner displays compulsive detachment, the other compulsive attachment, it is likely that both have suffered from separation anxiety and continue to have difficulty in trusting an attachment figure.

This theory of defensive containment can be applied to couples with varying preoccupations. For example, one couple may have a common concern with madness, another with delinquency, another

---

[10] Jung, C. (1940), *The Psychology of the Child Archetype,* Vol. IX *Coll. Works* (Routledge & Kegan Paul).

[11] Jung, C. (1925), *Marriage as a Psychological Relationship in the Development of Personality,* Vol. XVII *Coll. Works* (Routledge & Kegan Paul).

[12] Lyons, A., and Mattinson, J. (1977), *Individuation and Marriage* (unpublished), public lecture given for the Society of Analytical Psychology, London, Jan.

with control. In this book, our task is to apply the theory to couples in which both spouses are concerned about their own deprivation, by which we mean an unsatisfactory experience of attachment in childhood. The pictures deprived spouses carry in their minds may, indeed, be very different: some may remember violence, others their vain attempts to attract the attention of a depressed, despairing or withdrawn mother, others the ambulance which carried their mother away.

Each of these pictures relates to a different kind of deprivation, but whatever the particular cause of the original pain, human reactions against such pain, although still containing their own individualized flavour, have certain psychological characteristics.

The IMS account of reactions to emotional deprivation uses the concept of defences which we define as the techniques the ego uses when the conscious mind is under greater strain that it can bear. Such strain can be caused, for example, by pain, anxiety or conflict. The notion of defence owes more to Freud and classical psychoanalysts than to Bowlby (although later in this chapter we show that the two theories are not as distinct as they might at first appear). In this respect Freud suggested that the defences of repression, denial and splitting of the ego could all be traced to experiences of loss.[13] At the age when attachment behaviour and the anxiety aroused by actual or threatened separation is greatest, the mind is not strong enough to bear the mixture of feelings aroused by loss — the anger and the wanting — and so defends against them.

Of these three defences that Freud related to loss, that of splitting is particularly important in IMS theory and it looms large in this book. As different authors have used the term in varying senses, it is important to clarify what we mean by it. We use the word to describe the mechanism whereby, when a person has conflicting feelings towards another, either the positive or negative ones become unconscious. We believe that this occurs when the mind cannot tolerate the painful conflict between opposing feelings. Those that are made unconscious are then sometimes displaced or projected on to other people. Typically, but not

---

[13] Freud, S. (1893-95), *Studies in Hysteria,* Stand. Ed. 2; (1926) *Inhibitions, Symptoms and Anxiety,* Stand. Ed. 20 (The Hogarth Press and the Institute of Psycho-Analysis).

always, in the situations concerning attachment and detachment with which we will be concerned, the yearning and love is unconscious, the anger and hatred conscious. The unconscious nature of one side of the split does not mean, however, that there is no evidence for its occurrence. In fact, the inconsistency between the behavioural and verbal evidence provides grounds for believing that a split exists. For example, a person may claim to love another while apparently behaving in an angry and sadistic way. Or he may behave as if he yearns for the other, seeking out his presence while quite truthfully saying that he hates that person.

The rigidity of a split can be measured by the degree to which mixed feelings towards another cannot be acknowledged. There are few greys in the world of the person prone to compulsive splitting; it is seen in extremes of black and white. Some people are seen to be all bad, some are idealized until they too fall, as they must, from grace.

When two people both use this type of splitting mechanism as their predominant defence, their marriage becomes a useful vehicle by which the conflict can be externalized either between themselves (one spouse expressing one side of the split, the partner the other), or between them as a strongly identified pair on the one hand and the outside world on the other. If we assume that each partner embodies two sides of the split of which only one is conscious, there are four possible combinations. The married partners can both defend against the anger so that only the need and yearning are expressed between them. In this case they may feel that everyone else is against them. Such a pair often leave the impression of 'two babes in the wood', clinging together in the face of impossible odds. On the other hand, both partners may express only anger and rejection but still fail to part. In such 'cat and dog' marriages, the rest of the world may be idealized.

In yet other cases the split is retained between the partners. One or other of the partners expresses anger and denies any need or yearning for the other, relying on the other's expression of need to keep them both together. We call this combination 'the net and the sword' after the gladiatorial combats in which a man with a net strove to encompass another wielding a sword. In such marriages either partner can wield the net, but if he or she becomes more openly rejecting, the previously rejecting partner is likely to become less so. Thus it is not surprising that Mrs Jafferji, who initially broke her marriage, wanted her husband back at the precise moment when he had had enough of it.

To put the four possible combinations in tabular form:

1. 'Babes in the Wood' Conscious yearning   Conscious yearning
                       Unconscious rejection   Unconscious rejection

2. ⎫   Conscious yearning   Conscious rejection
   ⎪   Unconscious rejection   Unconscious yearning
   ⎬ 'Net and Sword'
   ⎪
3. ⎭   Conscious rejection   Conscious yearning
                       Unconscious yearning   Unconscious rejection

4. 'Cat and Dog'   Conscious rejection   Conscious rejection
                       Unconscious yearning   Unconscious yearning

Although one of these combinations may often be predominant, we do not think of them as types of marriages. They are systems of splitting behaviour which can be employed by the same couple in a variety of mixtures. Much of the time both Mr and Mrs Jafferji denied their need of each other and were only angry and rejecting toward each other. Only after she had gone did his need become more apparent, and only after he had gone did hers. Before that, however, both seemed to be fighting as to who should be allowed to be the baby, furious with and rejecting the other for not allowing them to be so. They could not ask each other in a way which invited the response they wanted, perhaps because they were even more afraid to have it. (Subsequent rejection might then have felt worse.)

THE REFLECTION PROCESS

The idea of the reflection process is also concerned with a shared defence — shared by clients and workers. In chapter 1 we described the behaviour not only of Mr and Mrs Jafferji but also of the workers. We used the word 'mirrored'. The workers mirrored the clients' behaviour. In their modified and more sophisticated version of the fight, those who apparently identified and sympathized with Mrs Jafferji said in words or action: 'Make him a patient', 'Punish him', 'Give it to me', 'Do' something, or 'I'll report you'. The male statutory day-worker, the only one who attempted to relate to Mr Jafferji, was outnumbered and became, like him, a bad object. Eventually, feeling as hounded as Mr

Jafferji and, by the time of the injunction, as untrusting, he fell into the role and said, 'No, I won't give you anything', not even an explanation of why he was working in that way in an attempt not to anticipate or precipitate any more violence. Despite his years of experience as a caseworker, which were considerably more than those of the majority of basic grade workers, he apparently forgot that Mrs Jafferji was also his client and in his fury with her and the numerous workers supporting her (and only her) could make no move towards her when she was no longer in the marital home.

The behaviour of the workers in this case suggests that they had been uncomfortably near primitive (infantile and strong) feelings against which they had had to defend themselves. At the IMS, emphasis is laid on the strength of the unconscious feelings and processes to which social workers are subjected in the course of their daily work with disturbed clients. And it is also taken for granted that social workers, like their clients, are human beings and have an unconscious and feelings about which they sometimes cannot bear to know. It is assumed that if they did not have an adequate set of defences they could not endure the work, but that their potential strength lies in their ability to try to understand these defences and relinquish them when appropriate.

In the IMS book, *The Reflection Process in Casework Supervision,* Janet Mattinson developed the idea that *the responses of workers which are out of character with their normal behaviour and which are defensive in quality give an important indication of the strength and type of disturbance to which they have been subjected.* In this book she was concerned with the effect of the client/worker relationship on the relationship between worker and supervisor. She described how the one relationship affected the other through what Searles called 'the reflection process'. Obviously she was also conerned with the client/worker relationship itself, and therefore with the psychoanalytic concepts of transference and countertransference.

The concept of transference was first developed in clinical situations and applied to the transfer on to the physician of feelings which had arisen in past relationships. A strong transference on the part of a client is 'characterized by a distorted perception of the stimulus, an over-extended or inappropriate or untimely and often repetitive reaction, provoked by the underlying need to make the present relationship fit into the psychodynamic structure of a previous one'.[14] The client does not respond to the worker as he is, but rather to a stereotype that has more to do with the past than with the present. The worker's countertransference (as opposed to his own transference on to the client) is sometimes a conscious reaction to the client's observed behaviour — an objective counter-transference — sometimes an unconscious reaction to behaviour which he has not consciously understood.

When the worker is subjected to a strong unconscious message which, for some reason, he cannot translate into consciousness, he will also act defensively. Usually he either identifies with his client and uses the same defence, or recoils and uses the opposite one. Similarly, if two or more workers are involved in a case, one will often adopt the client's predominant defence and the other the opposing one. This is particularly likely to happen when the predominant defence to which the workers are subjected is that of splitting. In the IMS we normally work in pairs, so that both partners have their own worker. We then try to make conscious use of the workers' joint enactment of the clients' defences; the workers have to solve their quarrel before they can help the clients to solve theirs. If the workers continue to enact the defence over a lengthy period of time, they reinforce the clients' despair and belief that nothing can change.

Janet Mattinson argued that lack of conscious involvement with the client does not automatically protect the worker from this phenomenon but in fact has a paradoxical effect of getting the worker unknowingly more deeply involved in the client's most negative projections.

> His conscious decision not to be involved will further blunt his capacity to look at the collusive nature of his behaviour. Action supposedly based on an 'objective' decision, because of the distance from which it has been made, is often a horrifyingly accurate reflection and confirmation of the client's worst fears.

It is therefore important to recognize the power of unconscious transactions and the fact that workers do get caught up in the clients' defensive systems rather than to deny that this occurs. The problem is how to work with this phenomenon.

This argument is obviously in keeping with Jung's belief that

[14] Mattinson, J. (1975), op. cit.

'You can exert no influence if you are not susceptible to influence'.[15] By actively allowing himself to get involved and be open to influence and then standing back to see what has happened, a worker gains important insights into what his client does to his spouse and other people in close relationships. Even more important, by understanding how he has been drawn into the difficulty, the worker is on the way to doing something about it.

> The worker is then perceived by the client as a creature not so different from himself actually doing something about the difficulty which they have been in together and in which they have both been human beings. Perhaps it is this, alongside the more practised understanding of the anguish, and the times when the worker does not collude, that really affects the course of any helping process.

The term reflection is used when the worker's countertransference is carried over into an adjacent situation, for example, supervision session or case conference, or in his dealings with other workers.

THE ORGANIZATIONAL DEFENCE

During the 1960s when we were developing our ideas about the reflection process we became increasingly aware that these individual reflections could be amplified by the working environment. We were supported in this by Isabel Menzies' study of a nursing service in a general teaching hospital. Her specific purpose was 'to consider and account for the high level of stress and anxiety chronic among the nurses'. As her study proceeded, it became increasingly important to 'understand the nature of the anxiety and the reason for its intensity'.

The actual work of nursing — constant contact with people who are physically ill, the 'threat and reality of suffering and death', intimate bodily contact and the carrying out of distasteful tasks — is likely to arouse anxiety and strong feelings: 'pity, compassion and love; guilt and anxiety; hatred and resentment of the patients who arouse these strong feelings; envy of the care given to the patient'. The direct impact of the situation is intensified by the similar impact on other people in or near that situation. The patient

[15] Jung, C. (1931), *Problems of Modern Psychotherapy,* Vol. XVI *Coll. Works* (Routledge & Kegan Paul).

himself is affected by his suffering, his enforced dependency and the intimate bodily contact. Relatives are often relieved to be free of the responsibility of care and at the same time guilty and jealously resentful at having relinquished the intimate contact. They can be demanding and critical. Colleagues are similarly affected by both patients and relatives, whose depression and anxiety are often projected into them.

'By the very nature of the work the nurse is at considerable risk of being flooded by intense and unmanageable anxiety' because, Menzies suggested, 'the objective situation bears a striking resemblance to the (unconscious) phantasy situations that exist in every individual in the deepest and most primitive levels of the mind.' She queried, however, whether that fact alone could account for the height of the persisting anxiety, and, in doing so, was led into a study of the organization itself. In her view, the culture and patterned behaviour in any organization is influenced by a number of interacting factors. These include not only the nature of the primary task, the technology and prevailing political and social pressures, but also the psychological needs of its members. She believes that the influence of the primary task and technology can easily be exaggerated and prefers to regard them as limiting factors. 'Within these limits, the culture, structure and mode of functioning are determined by the psychological needs of the members.'

When the need of the members is to defend against what is felt to be intolerable anxiety, the organization will be used for this purpose.

> The needs of the members of an organization to use it in the struggle against anxiety leads to the development of socially structured defence mechanisms which appear as elements in the structure, culture and mode of functioning of the organization.

> An important aspect of such socially structured defence mechanisms is an attempt by individuals to externalize and give substance in objective reality to their characteristic psychic defence mechanisms.

> A social defence system develops over time as the result of collusive interaction and agreement, often unconscious, between members of the organization as to what form it shall take. The socially structured defence mechanisms then tend to become an aspect of external

reality with which old and new members of the institution must come to terms.

From the point of view of the new member, the social defence system already exists as an aspect of external reality to which he must 'react and adapt'. Menzies emphasizes, however, that defences can, in fact, be operated only by individuals. A social system itself cannot operate a defence. The behaviour of the individuals is the link. If an individual is to continue membership of an organization there must be an adequate match between his own attitudes and behaviour and those exemplified by the social defence system.

In studying the nursing system, Menzies found that much of the work was characterized by certain features: the denial of the significance of the individual and the depersonalization of the patient ('the liver in bed 10'); attempts to eliminate decision-making by ritual task performance; the reduction of responsibility in decision-making by checks and counter-checks; purposeful obscurity in the formal distribution of responsibility; reduction of the impact of responsibility by delegation to superiors; and the avoidance of change. These features failed to help the nurse to face anxiety and develop her capacity to tolerate and deal more effectively with it. Instead, they helped her to avoid it. In fact, because of the actual demands of the task, a compromise was inevitable. The anxiety could not be completely avoided, but, because it was not faced, the individual's underlying phantasies were not brought into contact with the reality, she was not reassured, and she was denied the satisfaction that a developing capacity to tolerate the anxiety would have provided. And failure to alleviate primary anxiety can arouse 'a good deal of secondary anxiety', as can the social defence system itself. For example, the ritual task-list makes it difficult to adjust workloads when necessary by postponing or omitting less urgent or important tasks.

Social work is concerned with anxieties similar to those raised in nursing. As in any organization caring for the rejected (both young and old), the disturbed, the ill and the dying, socially structured defences will, on Menzies' theory, develop particularly against the inevitable sadness and pain of these conditions and the anxiety, doubts and guilt aroused by them.

One function of the field social workers in the area offices is to work with some very deprived and disturbed married clients who, although numerically few in number at the intake stage, are, as we showed in the last chapter, high-priority cases, demanding and extremely time-consuming on the long-term caseloads. They might be expected, therefore, to have a disproportionate effect, compared with some clients, on the individual workers and, therefore, on the social defence system.

If the workers are continually subjected to the splitting mechanisms of these clients, they too may become predisposed to this mode of behaviour. And as the individual worker can reflect his client's defence, so too may some of the organizational practices which the worker is expected to perform. The problem is that whereas the individual worker may eventually use his reflection constructively in understanding the client's emotional problem, it is much more difficult for the organization as a whole to do this once a particular practice has become institutionalized. Unfortunately, just as the resistance to change is believed to be greatest in clients exercising the most primitive psychic defences (and splitting is a very primitive defence), so group resistance to social change may be greatest in social systems also dominated by this mode.

COMMON THEMES

Our four theories have certain links. This is not surprising in that all four had their originators or proponents in the Tavistock Institute of Human Relations.

The first and most important characteristic is that all of them accept the basic precept of the existence of an unconscious that influences behaviour. All of them derive partly or wholly from psychoanalytic thinking for which the Tavistock Institute and Tavistock Clinic have traditionally stood.

Bowlby's work stems partly from ethology and partly from psychoanalysis. Although his theoretical position differs in its starting-point — he relied on observational studies rather than the reconstruction of the patients' history from their own accounts — many of the central concepts of his schema are, as he says, 'plainly stated by Freud'.

Firstly, Freud's theory of the causes of neurosis is centred on trauma. Bowlby similarly argued that separation of a young child from his mother can be as traumatic as Freud suggested and that this is particularly so when the separation occurs during the period of childhood which Freud saw as crucial to the child's development. Secondly, both have stated that the psychological changes that occur after prolonged distress can be seen as defences against pain and anxiety. Thirdly, both of their theories are based on instinct.

The two main points of difference relate to their models of instinctive behaviour. Freud used one of psychical energy. Bowlby used one based on control theory with its concept of feedback; he gives as much attention to the conditions that terminate an act as to those that initiate it. Secondly, Bowlby has been influenced by later developments of Freudian theory, particularly object relations thinking expounded by Klein, Balint, Fairbairn and Winnicott, who all emphasized the strong and natural tendency within the individual to seek relationships as a primary principle of psychic life.

The thinking of the IMS regarding attachment in marriage is wholly psychoanalytic and, with its emphasis on the particular need to seek relationships, it is also indebted to the object relations school. It has been particularly influenced by the Balints, Enid Balint, a former member of the IMS, having succeeded Michael Balint as a unit consultant and over several years having led the weekly case conference which all members of staff must attend. It has also been influenced by the wider perspective of Jung, who in 1925 wrote on *Marriage as a Psychological Relationship*.[16]

In relation to our last two theories, Searles, who initiated in America the use of the term 'Reflection Process', is a psychoanalyst. Janet Mattinson, who developed this theory in the social work field, is a Jungian analyst. Jaques and Menzies are also psychoanalysts who applied their analytic insights to the behaviour of organization.

Another common characteristic of our theories, with the possible exception of part of Bowlby's, is that they are what we call 'clinical theories'. Research in the field of the natural sciences and of some parts of psychology has traditionally been concerned with measurement, prediction and control. It is useful to people who are concerned with what can be measured and with the control of

[16] Jung, C. (1925), op. cit.

events. As implied by the quotation at the beginning of this chapter, it is less obvious that such theories can be useful to those concerned with understanding persons and liberating more creative behaviour. Typically, clinical theories, as we use the term, do not set out to predict what will happen in every instance. Rather, they alert us to what to look for and provide ideas to help us understand events when they do occur. As Bowlby says,

> Why some individuals should recover, largely or completely, from experiences of separation and loss while others seem not to is a central question, but one not easily answered. In living creatures variation of response is the rule, and its explanation is hard to fathom. Of all those who contract poliomyelitis, less than 1 per cent develop paralysis and only a fraction of 1 per cent remain crippled. Why one person responds one way and another another remains obscure. To argue that because 99 per cent recover, polio is a harmless infection would obviously be absurd. Similarly, in the field under consideration, to argue that because most individuals recover from the effects of separation or loss these experiences are of no account, would be equally absurd.

Similar comments could be made about all the theories we have used. Our ideas about marital interaction and the reflection process do not enable us to predict how a marriage will develop or a worker behave with a particular client. Nor can we say what form a social defence will take in any one organization nor how massive it will be. These ideas, however, help us to read the situation, just as, for example, the idea of a 'fork' helps us in a game of chess or the idea of jealousy helps us in dealing with children.

Finally, despite the different emphases of these theories — on deprivation, marriage, casework and the organization of workers — there is a strong common thread to do with interaction and feedback; feedback between mother and child; feedback between husband and wife; feedback between client and worker and supervisor; and feedback between many clients and many workers within an organizational structure. As we stated in the introductory chapter, ideas about the interactions which we observed between married clients, between them and their workers (including ourselves) and between field workers and other members of the organization are the substance of this book.

PART TWO

The Clients

Edward: *I'm beginning to feel very sorry for you, Lavinia.*
You know, you really are exceptionally unloveable,
And I never quite knew why. I thought it was my fault.

Reilly: *And now you begin to see, I hope,*
How much you have in common. The same isolation.
A man who finds himself incapable of loving
And a woman who finds that no man can love her.

Lavinia: *It seems to me that what we have in common*
Might be just enough to make us loathe one another.

Reilly: *See it rather as the bond which holds you together.*

T.S. Eliot

5   The Corpses in the Graveyard

I loved him not; and yet now he is gone
I feel I am alone.
        Walter Savage Landor

The weariest and most loathed worldly life
That age, ache, penury, and imprisonment
Can lay on nature, is a paradise
To what we fear of death.
        William Shakespeare

Although we have stressed our interest in feedback and interaction, we concentrate in this part of the book on only one element in our analysis - the clients. By doing this we run the risk of making a misleading extraction. However, the problems the clients pose to each other have much in common with those they pose to the social workers, and their reactions to each other have a similarity to the reactions of the social workers to them, and to some of the institutional practices we observed. If, for the sake of clarity, we choose to focus initially on one element in our constellation of clients, workers and institutions, the clients are the ones with whom to begin.

All analysis begins with questions and the one with which we start is why, when our clients were evidently so unhappy with each other, did they find it so difficult to separate on a permanent basis? One worker spoke despairingly about this in the survey:

One hopes to work with the marriage, but without much hope. The only hope would be if they could separate, but there does not seem to be much hope of that. She's actually said that 'history is repeating

67

itself'. She had an idle, hostile father who abused her and an absent mother.

[Why doesn't she leave him?]

What she says is, 'I can't stand up to him'. Sometimes she puts it down to physical fear, but sometimes she says she desperately needs his approval. Also she cannot do with being alone. She would feel redundant. She has very little concept of what she could do with the kids.

The answer to our question implicitly contains answers to three related questions.

What is wrong with the outside world that the woman does not prefer it to this sort of marriage?— She cannot do with being alone. She is afraid of managing the children.

Is there anything that is attractive to her in her husband?— He is like her father. She needs to be needed. She needs his approval.

Does her husband do anything to make her stay?— He is said to use physical force.

In this and the next three chapters we deal with these explanations: the fear of being alone, the need for the spouse and its paradoxical expression, and the techniques for managing the partner so that he or she does not leave. We are also concerned with the inability of each to meet the other's need when their own was so overwhelming. As always, our emphasis is on the interaction between the partners and the effect of one of them on the other.

We start with a chronological account of three cases which would formerly have been classified respectively under the headings of child care, welfare and mental welfare. The accounts illustrate the range with which we worked and the repetitive crises characteristic of many of them. Two of the couples, Mr and Mrs Buzzard and Mr and Mrs Flimsby, were in our core sample. For contrast, Mr and Mrs Papcastle were not. They illustrate the relevance of much of our thesis to the less flamboyant clients who, although less time-consuming, also figure on the long-term caseloads.

We describe the course of events with the minimum of comment.

MR AND MRS BUZZARD

Mrs Buzzard referred herself by telephone saying she was afraid her husband would beat her up when he returned from work. She wanted to leave home but had nowhere to go. The social worker on duty gave her the address of a refuge and told her someone would call as soon as possible. A letter was posted to her saying that a worker would visit on the following day.

When the social worker arrived, Mrs Buzzard (from Trinidad) was in the middle of some very disorganized and aggressive sewing, ironing and packing. As Mrs Buzzard piled things in the cases, took them out again, ironed them and put them in another, she said she was leaving that evening with the baby, David, aged seven months. She would never desert him. She complained vociferously that her husband had beaten her and expressed fear that he would do so again. Yet her other main complaint was of his passivity both in and out of bed. She expressed great jealousy of his sister — he was a 'sister's boy' — and she asked for confirmation of her stance by saying 'Right?' at what seemed like the beginning, middle and end of every sentence. Thump went the iron on the board. 'Right?'.

When the worker, feeling as thumped as the ironing board, could get a word in, she offered to visit regularly and to come the following evening to see them both together. Mrs Buzzard was sure she did not want a reconciliation (thump) and the worker acknowledged the force behind the thump and said that if the marriage was really at an end the discussion would be centred on how they could part. Mrs Buzzard grudgingly threw out some of the clothes from a case. David lay listlessly on his cot with a streaming cold.

However, Mrs Buzzard did not wait for a second visit. The worker found Mr Buzzard in a state of shock and incomprehension, having arrived home from work to find David and the seven and eight-year-old boys on their own. Mrs Buzzard and the eldest boy of fourteen had left.

After two weeks Mrs Buzzard seized the seven and eight-year-olds from school, returning them back to their doorstep six days later. During these weeks and the next few months she played a 'cat and mouse' game with the worker, telephoning her from various parts of London, demanding immediate rehousing, accepting appointments and then failing to keep them. She ensured that several complaints of ineffectiveness were lodged by a variety of statutory and voluntary agencies against the worker, who now felt it might be true that her apparently passive husband had been goaded into hitting her. By this time the worker would have liked to do the same.

When the worker first met Mr Buzzard he was in a state of collapse and unable to accept the fact that Mrs Buzzard might not be back in a day or two to look after himself and the children again. He appeared quite helpless and saw the worker's role as that of 'wife-recoverer'. She experienced him as fitting half his wife's description — apathetic and ineffective. It was difficult to imagine his fitting the other half — aggressive and violent.

Gradually he pulled himself together. He took a holiday, then unpaid leave from work and as he nursed the baby back to health he obviously derived increasing satisfaction and comfort for himself. It appeared that for much of the first seven months of his life David had been left on his back in his cot. He was backward in sitting, moving, reaching for things and responding either happily or ill-temperedly. Within two months of being looked after by Mr Buzzard his condition and demeanour became quite normal for his age. When the worker visited, Mr Buzzard was often feeding him and the activity obviously gave them mutual enjoyment, David on Mr Buzzard's knee and both of them wielding a spoon. David spent more time on the floor and was learning to crawl. Mr Buzzard proudly took him to the clinic to have his progress recorded.

He was eventually able to make satisfactory arrangements for getting the other two children to school and David to a daily minder of his own finding, but it was several more weeks before he could put these plans into action and actually get himself back to work. Then his life was hard, working in the day, caring for the children morning and evening, and earning no overtime. He and all the children appeared to thrive; all were in good health and became increasingly lively.

After some months Mrs Buzzard applied to have a separation order and custody of the children, but her case collapsed in court when she went into hysterics. The custody was awarded to Mr Buzzard, who had counter-petitioned. She then failed to use the access which she had been granted.

Mr Buzzard impressed his solicitor with his stability and honesty and obtained the custody of the three youngest children on the firm

assurance from them both that his sister would move in and keep
house. However, various delaying excuses were given which were
perfectly reasonable; the sister had to work out her notice and pack
up her house; an assurance from Mr Buzzard's firm was needed
that when it moved out of London she would be formally
considered as part of his household. When the worker went on
holiday, the sister was due the following week. Instead, Mrs
Buzzard moved back and shortly afterwards instituted divorce
proceedings.

When the worker returned from holiday and made her regular
visit to Mr Buzzard she found Mrs Buzzard installed on the top
floor with the eldest boy, the three youngest children and Mr
Buzzard on the floor below. Mrs Buzzard said she was pregnant by
her husband and was about to seek an abortion. She gave four
reasons for her return: She did not think her husband was looking
after the children properly; he had not fulfilled the conditions of
the custody order and she was going to get it reversed; she was
afraid he would move out of London and take the children with
him; and, with the greatest emphasis, she said she could not stay in
her lodging because of 'the corpses in the graveyard opposite.
Right?'

She immediately went into a tirade against her husband; he
passively shrugged his shoulders and tried to leave the interview.
The worker's report continued:

> I reinstated fortnightly visits to try and work with them to help them
> to be more comfortably separate on their separate floors. The
> situation was extremely confused and I could never make head nor
> tail of the rows nor what was going on between them. I made no
> headway at all. I saw Mr Buzzard become more apathetic, all his
> aggression, previously used to prove that he was better at looking
> after the children, now expressed passively by not doing anything.
> He became more and more evasive. His biggest weapons were
> delaying the divorce and the hiding of David with 'his' baby-minder,
> who now kept the child from Monday to Friday. Mrs Buzzard
> resented the secrecy, but seemed surprisingly unperturbed by not
> knowing where her child was, perhaps because the arrangement
> enabled her to go to work. Many of the rows were about food and
> money and Mr Buzzard's lack of provision, but Mrs Buzzard, while
> complaining there was not enough food, refused to spend any of her
> earnings as she was saving them for equipping a new house.

The marital war between Mr and Mrs Buzzard resembled a game of 'catch as catch can'. The more she tried to control from the top floor, the more Mr Buzzard escaped out of the front door, and the more he evaded her, the more she tried to control, eventually moving down a floor. From this he fled even further and became even more devious. He also wanted the divorce, he said, but he held up the proceedings for months, refusing to sign the papers and failing to keep appointments with his solicitor, who now became as confused as the worker as to what his client wanted.

After six months of this the children were showing signs of deprivation and disturbance. Mr Buzzard's ability to love, cosset and stimulate the children had been shown to be greater than that of Mrs Buzzard, but when they were together this could not be known or used. Mrs Buzzard could not admit in any way that she was worried about her ability to care for children, even though she had an older illegitimate child in the care of another local authority. Her anxiety only became apparent over a period of time and it was only when the worker discussed the problems with the project group that she could see that one of the difficulties in this marriage was Mrs Buzzard's conscious or unconscious fear that Mr Buzzard might be a better parent than she, and his feeling that she might be right.

One Friday evening when the worker was at the Buzzard house, Mr Buzzard brought David home for the weekend. She had seen him the previous week in the minder's home and by this time he was walking. His gait was uncertain, but he was a confident and adventurous explorer, calmly picking himself up from a fall and looking towards his minder for praise and encouragement. Arriving at the Buzzard house he staggered in and immediately started to swing the wheel of a bicycle lying on its side on the floor. Mrs Buzzard scooped him up in her arms. He wriggled free. By the time he had been told ten times 'not to touch' and ten times more had been scooped into her arms in a strangulating hug, he was a confused and cantankerous infant sitting bawling on the floor, the poise with which he had entered quickly slapped away 'for being so naughty'. An accusing baby confronted an accusing mother who had tried to meet her own need first and to display to the worker and her husband her 'motherly love'.

David not only failed and disappointed her when he refused to respond to her enveloping hugs, but his clean blue clothes and his fuzzy hair immaculately plaited in tiny knots all over his head may have been felt as a further reproach. Her primitive fury was released and turned back on her husband. He in his turn (and as one equally deprived) seemed to resent the caresses heaped on the toddler, but was quite helpless in getting any of these directed towards himself.

Clearly the baby had not done for Mrs Buzzard what she had hoped. He had a life and purpose of his own for which at that time she could not give space within the ambit of a caring, loving and watchful eye. In search for an explanation for this sad scene, she launched into an attack on Mr Buzzard and 'his' baby-minder for not having looked after David better during the week while she had been working so hard. Mr Buzzard, standing by the door, at first smiling with triumph but soon angered by her attempt to take over the mothering, refused to help and support her, and thus provided a target on which she could vent her mixed feelings about the baby. He shrugged his shoulders and went back to the car.

Eventually Mrs Buzzard obtained a divorce, custody of the children and a Council flat. And then she asked for first one and then, in turn, the other children to be received into care.

MR AND MRS PAPCASTLE

Mr Papcastle was in his early seventies, Mrs Papcastle in her sixties, when he had a stroke which left him severely disabled. Up till then their marriage had worked well for them. As Mrs Papcastle said, 'I married him for better, for worse. We had lots of better, so now I must take the worse'. Their two married daughters retained good relationships with them and during this difficult period were loving and kind, visited regularly and provided gifts of things which Mr and Mrs Papcastle could not afford. They provided holidays by having them to stay, and careful organization on their part enabled Mr Papcastle to attend important family functions such as one of the grandchildren's engagement party.

The first social worker who took the referral arranged, with the help of the occupational therapist, various practical services — a telephone, an attendance allowance, appropriate aids and a place one day a week at a day centre. She maintained regular contact as Mr Papcastle refused to stay at the day centre without Mrs Papcastle and this defeated one of its purposes of giving Mrs Papcastle a break and an opportunity to get out on her own. He then refused to go at all. The tension between them mounted rapidly as they became confined together in the flat, sometimes for seven days a week. They would not use the daughters as 'sitters-in'.

When she was leaving, the social worker wrote in her handover report:

> Mr Papcastle gets frightened when left alone in the flat and only allows Mrs Papcastle to go out for an hour to shop. It is obvious that the marriage has always been dominated by Mr Papcastle. He has proudly stated that he used to go off for weekends on his own and that he preferred women's company to that of men because they didn't argue! This attitude makes it hard for him to bear the complete dependence for washing, dressing, moving, etc., which he now has on Mrs Papcastle. He cannot conceal his resentment any more than she is able to conceal her anger at him for being so ill. She feels that his working so hard and never being able to rest caused his illness in the first place.

A second worker was given a similar picture of the past, but learnt that Mrs Papcastle had been overtly dependent on Mr Papcastle and had had great difficulty in leaving him for two weeks to go into hospital in middle age. She said they always went out together. Both of them, however, expressed satisfaction with themselves and what they had achieved.

During the next twelve months Mr Papcastle's physical and emotional condition deteriorated.

> His fears and depression (?) increased and it seemed as if, with less controls, he was crying not only for his present condition, but for all he had never cried for earlier. But as he got physically weaker, he still maintained he would get better and walk again. I imagine denial must have been his main defence in health. Mrs Papcastle continued to look after him well, and often very lovingly, but was very impatient with his tears. Then he became angry and abusive towards her and it seemed as if forty years of pent-up anger was launched forth. Alternately he swore at and abused her, and cried if she was not there. During the worst part of this spell she became, not surprisingly, less tolerant, and was often sharp and unkind to him.

Then Mr Papcastle got pneumonia and appeared to be dying. He was rushed to hospital and saved. On his return he was more decrepit and even less mobile, incontinent, and his anger was at its most extreme. He had been a 'bad' patient in hospital, always crying for Mrs Papcastle. Even with the help of the district nurse on twice-daily visits, the strain of caring for him was great. 'Intermittent admissions' were arranged and twice he went back into hospital for fourteen days, which gave Mrs Papcastle a rest. Mrs Papcastle had great difficulty in letting him go on the first of these admissions, felt extremely guilty and visited twice daily, only to be abused for leaving him there.

By the autumn his anger seemed spent and the last three months of his life were a time of loving and peace between them. A week after what was experienced by them both as a good Christmas he died.

When registering his death, and having 'bought her black' as she told the worker a week later, Mrs Papcastle had a serious heart attack and was rushed to hospital. Apparently getting better, she expressed a determination to get well enough to go to the wedding of one of her grandchildren. Two days later, when walking up the ward for the first time, she collapsed and died.

The worker had been expecting that Mrs Papcastle would need some further help when finally separated. Having become very fond of them both, she was shocked by the double death. In retrospect, however, perhaps this was not so surprising and, in fact, is not an uncommon phenomenon when a long marriage has throughout been based on a pattern of mutual identification and strong attachment behaviour. When discussing the case some time later, it was suggested by one worker that perhaps the tears and the anger were unconsciously about their not being able to be more separate in life or in the face of approaching death. The loving calm at the end suggests an acceptance of the inevitable.

MR AND MRS FLIMSBY

Mr Flimsby's first contact with the department was in 1972, when he asked and received support for a housing application on the grounds that his wife was mentally ill.

Two years later Mrs Flimsby was referred by her GP who wanted her 'persuaded' towards the psychiatric services. He gave a daunting history. Two workers agreed to share the case but, before they had taken any action, Mr Flimsby rang one of the workers and demanded the immediate compulsory removal of his wife to a psychiatric hospital.

He said his wife was in no fit state to be left on her own. She took drugs and was drowsy most of the time ... her room was like a child's, filled with toys. She bombards him with telephone calls at work and rings the Samaritans at all hours of the day and night. He has to act as nurse. She is under the control of her mother who is an 'aggressive, neurotic woman'. He tells his wife that she is mentally ill and should go into hospital, but his mother-in-law countermands this. His wife keeps him awake at night by walking the floor. His temper is at breaking point and he has recently hit her. He can take responsibility no longer.

The worker refused to respond to Mr Flimsby's immediate request for his wife's compulsory admission, but after further negotiations with the GP the second worker wrote to Mrs Flimsby offering help. Mrs Flimsby telephoned. She did not want to see any social worker. Her mother had forbidden her to see any social worker or psychiatrist and would be very angry with her if she did. She put the receiver down, but rang back the next day to apologize. She seemed anxious that in that mood she had also written 'rude and degrading things' about her husband to the doctor. She insisted she loved her husband and he had furnished the whole flat for her. She accepted the offered appointment.

Following these telephone calls the Flimsbys were seen together twice, once by one worker, once by the other. This was not what had been planned, but the history of the whole contact was one of plans endlessly made and seldom fulfilled. At the beginning the Flimsbys intruded into each other's interviews. For example:

Mr Flimsby came back into the room and commented that someone in the flats opposite had committed suicide. While drawing the curtains across the window and then moving over towards his wife, he suggested it would be a good idea if *she* committed suicide too and stopped bothering everyone. She laughed nervously and said she couldn't as she wanted to go to Heaven to which he responded that undoubtedly she would go to Hell.

Even after death, it seemed, there was to be no way out.

The early contact was dominated by Mrs Flimsby's openly expressed fear that she would be forced into hospital by a conspiracy between her husband and the social worker. Despite this, the role of patient was not unattractive to her and she dominated these interviews with her problems. Mr and Mrs Flimsby withdrew from contact and subsequently Mr Flimsby persuaded Mrs Flimsby to go into hospital where she was compulsorily detained.

Three months later she was discharged and after returning to her husband she brought their son, Paul, to live with them. This produced an immediate crisis. Mr Flimsby arrived dramatically in the office announcing that an orgy involving his wife and another woman had taken place and that the worker must return with him to the flat if murder were not to be done. The worker went back with him and helped Mr Flimsby to leave and took into his own custody what Mr Flimsby grandly described as a cutlass — which was, in fact, a carving knife.

Five months' intensive work followed. For most of this time Mr Flimsby, who had previously commanded quite a big salary, was out of work and had spectacular debts. He was a man who in the grip of strong emotions would sweat and writhe in his chair. He felt he was a poor father and did not understand children. He bought a dog to have 'something for himself'. His feelings of helplessness in the face of his mother-in-law and of what he experienced as his wife's insatiable demands were reiterated. He demanded that the social services department set limits by writing down how much money she should be given. He stated sadly that he was a middle-aged man and that sex had little attraction for him. This, however, did not prevent him from returning again and again to the subject of his wife's infidelity and to his insistence that she had endless pregnancy tests. Sometimes he would tell his worker that his wife needed to be beaten and that, if he were man enough, he would do it; at other times he would confess how ashamed he had been when he had struck his wife.

Mrs Flimsby paraded her helplessness no less than Mr Flimsby, endlessly seeking advice and help from GPs, parsons, psychiatrists, Samaritans, lay counsellors, and religious sects. Her telephone calls so alienated the doctors that it became difficult to find one who would accept her on his panel. Her intense, extreme and unremitting demands intensified her husband's feeling that he was unable to satisfy a woman.

Both Mr and Mrs Flimsby spent a lot of time proving the other one was to blame. Mr Flimsby endlessly returned to the subject of his wife's 'filth' and madness. They described nightly scenes when he would shout at her that she belonged only in a mental hospital, and she would reply, also at the top of her lungs, 'Wife beater! Get out! Get out! Get out!' A note in the record says:

> Mrs Flimsby called at the office. She left some dog dirt to prove what a filthy beast her husband is for not looking after his dog and that he is to blame, not her.

Another shared characteristic was their inability to separate. Both denied that they cared for each other. Mr Flimsby described himself as callous and explained his marriage to her on the grounds of getting money out of her family and sex out of her. She explained her marriage to him on the grounds that she had been too high on drugs to know what she was doing. They had left each other on numerous occasions in the past and during this five months he was usually on the verge of leaving her, using the social services office as left luggage department to signify his intention of doing so. Yet somehow, there was always a practical reason why this should not happen, just as she never managed to go ahead with the divorce proceedings she had initiated. It was only at the end of the work that each was able to admit that at some level they had cared for each other (and incidentally for the workers). Significantly, it was at this point that they were able to separate for more than a few days.

However, apart from the outwardly strange love they may have had for each other, there was also the question of alternatives. Mrs Flimsby had little, if any, confidence in her ability to look after her son. She would try and get the worker to tell her whether she should change his clothes after he got wet. When removing the child from her, her own mother had apparently remarked, 'What chance has he got with a drug addict for a mother and an alcoholic for a father?' Mrs Flimsby's role as a daughter was as dubious as her role as a mother. She had quarrelled with her stepfather and was doubtful of her welcome in that home. She had been unable to hold down a job and her confidence had been further undermined by her numerous hospital admissions. On one occasion she remarked that it was 'just easier to be a patient'.

Mr Flimsby also did not face an easy situation if the marriage broke up. He was middle-aged, had ill-health, debts and a drinking problem. He had been previously married and he would then have a past of two broken marriages to two psychiatric patients. His future gave him no certainty of employment, friends, or place to live.

Eventually Mr Flimsby did leave Mrs Flimsby and went to his mother's house in Wales. In his telephone calls he said he was happy enough, but he could not get work and was having to take tranquillizers. Feeling he did not belong in Wales, he returned briefly to London; but finding he did not belong in London either, he soon went back. Mrs Flimsby also returned to her mother in Cornwall and on a visit to London about practical matters saw her worker again. The last note in the record reads:

> We had a long talk. Mrs Flimsby is finding it difficult to manage without Mr Flimsby. When I mentioned that he had been in touch and had asked how she was, she eagerly asked whether he might really want a reconciliation and showed me a letter (very calm and friendly) which she had written to him.

> While she recognizes to some extent the problem of trying to manage in London, she obviously has reservations about settling where she is. She talked about feeling superfluous as her mother and stepfather are so good with Paul and of the difficulties of fitting into an organized household where she has no positive place.

THE FEAR OF BEING ALONE

We believe two different sets of reasons made it difficult for our clients to part. The first concerned their fear of the alternatives; the second, their need for each other. In this chapter we deal only with the first.

The practical and financial difficulties facing any parents who are left on their own with children or who want to leave their spouse taking the children with them are obvious. Except for the very wealthy, material hardship normally ensues. In the face of such difficulties, anyone is likely to be hesitant.

The clients in our core sample, however, had particular reasons for hesitation. By one of the definitions of the core sample, they did not have supportive families of origin. Neither Mrs Buzzard nor Mr Flimsby had parents to whom they could easily retreat. Mrs Buzzard felt herself to be very rejected by her widowed mother, who already fostered one of her illegitimate children. There had been no contact for a long time. Mrs Flimsby had had an ambivalent relationship with her mother and stepfather over years and, although she did return there, she felt undermined, rather than supported, in her role as a mother and with no 'positive place' in the household.

Also, by another definition of the core sample, our clients had difficulties in parenting and were likely to be afraid of looking after their children on their own. Their fear of acting as single parents was usually obvious. Mrs Flimsby showed her uncertainty about the care of Paul to the social worker. When she and Mr Flimsby finally parted, she lasted only three weeks on her own before going back to her mother. Mr Flimsby was quite explicit that he was a poor father. Mr Buzzard managed for a limited period on his own, given regular encouragement from a social worker. Mrs Buzzard, however, when finally divorced, rehoused and with the legal custody of the children, asked for first one and then, in turn, each of the other children to be received into care. She was not atypical - we know of four cases in the core sample where the children were taken into care for extended periods following the break-up of a marriage or cohabitation, and only one where this occurred while the partners were still together. Some of the receptions took place after the project had ended, when our knowledge of the sample was partial. Our evidence is, therefore, suggestive, not conclusive. It would be useful to examine the association in a larger sample prospectively. If real, it may, of course, reflect social work attitudes as well as client behaviour.

To these two reasons we add a third — that they were afraid of being alone. Our emphasis on this fear is in keeping with our use of attachment theory. This fear plays an important part in Bowlby's thesis, for he believes that those who have never had a secure attachment are, for that very reason, afraid to venture out into the world on their own.

Loneliness in our clients seemed to arouse different emotions from those it produces in the more fortunate, who may, like Coleridge, be

> ... grateful, that by nature's quietness
> And solitary musings, all my heart
> Is softened, and made worthy to indulge
> Love, and the thoughts that yearn for human kind.

Or with Andrew Marvell, say

> Fair quiet, have I found thee here,
> And Innocence thy Sister dear!
> Society is all but rude,
> To this delicious solitude.

Our clients' feelings about this state seemed to be more akin to terror and to what some poets have seen in the fear of death. We suggest that Mrs Buzzard's phrase, 'the corpses in the graveyard opposite', depicts the underlying terror of being alone when the feelings of badness, madness or helplessness become more menacing.

Although Mr and Mrs Flimsby were middle-aged, on separation they both returned to their parents despite difficult relationships with them. Even when living together, Mrs Flimsby's continual telephone calls to all and sundry and the IMS worker's struggle for forty-five minutes to end such a call suggested that she found it difficult to be on her own even for a few hours. Mrs Flimsby was afraid of her madness and both she and her husband displayed extreme helplessness.

The helpless Mr Papcastle was overtly fearful of being left on his own even in the sitting-room. If Mrs Papcastle and the worker chatted for a few minutes in the hall when the worker was leaving, he called angrily and imperiously for his wife. He found it as difficult to go into hospital as his wife had done fifteen years earlier. Her personal experience of this fear must have added to her difficulty in letting him go. Mrs Papcastle had a serious heart attack two days after her husband died and another which killed her a week later.

Mr Buzzard was in a state of collapse for a few days when Mrs Buzzard left him, although with the worker's support he was then able to marshal his resources. However, even when he had found a baby-minder and made arrangements for the other children before and after school, it was another three weeks before he could get himself back to work. Mrs Buzzard developed several nervous symptoms when she left Mr Buzzard, including alopecia which was bad enough for her to wear a wig. When she moved back, her own hair started to grow again.

In practice, it seemed, being alone raised even more anxiety than

being together. This faced our clients with an intolerable dilemma.
Their presence occasioned no delight. Neither Mrs Buzzard's work
nor her pregnancy won her husband's support when she returned to
him. Her children flourished with him and the baby-minder, but
not with her. She needed her husband's support, but, unable to
admit her doubts about her ability with the children, she could not
ask her husband to help her to put them to bed. He might refuse, so
instead she accused him of being late home and of getting on too
well with his workmates. But away from home were the 'corpses in
the graveyard'.

The combination of lack of alternative sources of support,
doubts about their own ability to manage parental roles and a
terror of facing the world on their own created a dilemma in which
it was difficult for one spouse to leave the other, despite their
threats to do so and the misery of their life together.

6   Dilemma and Demand

Their tongue is as an arrow shot out.
                                    Jeremiah

That shaft of slander shot
Miss'd only the right blot.
I see the shame
They cannot see:
'Tis very just they blame
The thing that's not.
                        Coventry Patmore

Did our clients' reluctance to part arise only from their fear of alternatives, or were there other reasons, and, in particular, had they any need of each other? If so, they seemed to have a peculiar way of showing it. Despite this, a careful examination of the common features of their behaviour suggests they had an insistent need for each other together with an equally insistent wish to disguise this.

We look at three of these common features before attempting to analyse what underlies them. We take our evidence from the behaviour of the three couples we presented in the last chapter together with that of Mr and Mrs Jafferji described in chapter 1.

The most obvious common feature is the *ambivalent behaviour* of each partner towards the other and to other members of the family. Mrs Jafferji obtained an injunction to get her husband out of the house; three weeks later she wanted him back. Mrs Buzzard said she would never leave the baby; less than twenty-four hours later she did so; she seized two other children; a week later she returned them; she left her husband; she returned to him; she started divorce proceedings. Mrs Flimsby yelled at her husband: 'Get out!' She wanted a reconciliation; she started divorce proceedings; she stopped them. Mr Buzzard said he wanted a divorce but drove his solicitor to distraction by delaying tactics, just as Mr Flimsby confused his worker. At one stage Mrs Papcastle found it almost impossible to live with her husband, yet found it equally difficult to let him go into hospital.

As we suggested in our theoretical summary in chapter 4, the fact that husband and wife shared the ambivalence enabled them to take turns as to which part each would enact. When Mrs Buzzard had deserted, Mr Buzzard wanted the worker to get her back. He was agreeable to a joint interview as long as, it seemed, she could be relied upon to refuse. When, finally, she was willing, he would have nothing to do with it; he had 'given up' he said. Mrs Flimsby always seemed to ask for a reconciliation just when Mr Flimsby did not want one.

A fact which both exemplified and exacerbated the shared ambivalence was that although the partners apparently felt helpless and terrified on their own, and therefore might be thought to need the support of their spouse, they had great difficulty in asking for it in ways that were likely to be successful. When Mrs Jafferji was crying and at her most vulnerable, she told her husband to go away. Her efforts to get him to spend more time at home took the form of complaints. Mrs Buzzard explained her return to her husband in terms of needing to control him rather than a need of his company. Mr Papcastle continually harked back to the time when he did not need his wife and often tried to force her rather than ask her to meet his needs. Mrs Flimsby posed continual demands on her husband, pursuing him at his work and even, according to him, when he was on the lavatory; but in most moods it was also important to her to maintain that she did not need him.

The partners who evaded this control appeared, when the couple were together, to resent the closeness, and it was easy to miss that the need was often reciprocated. Mr Jafferji, Mr Buzzard, Mrs Papcastle, and Mr Flimsby spent a great deal of time evading control, but their collapse after a separation belied this feigned independence.

A second feature, but this time not characteristic of the Papcastles, was the *obsession with blame*. Mrs Jafferji tried to put her husband in a bad light in front of the worker at every possible opportunity. Mrs Buzzard asked again and again for confirmation that she was right and, by implication, that her husband was wrong. The story of the Flimsbys was full of accusations and counter-accusations involving wife-beating, filth, dog-dirt, and promiscuity.

Another feature was the *difficulty about third parties* and alliances. Mrs Jafferji sought to ally herself with the worker against her husband and, failing this, sought other workers for the same purpose. She felt threatened by her husband's relationships at work. Mrs Buzzard objected to her husband's sister, his relationships at work, his baby-minder, and probably to 'his' social worker — as the worker, in *her* mind, became. Mr Papcastle was consciously afraid of being 'pushed into a corner' and fiercely jealous if his wife and the worker had a conversation apart from him. Mr Flimsby objected to his wife's relationship with her mother, her female friend, her male friends and her other associates. He reacted in a very extreme way to the arrival of his son. Mrs Flimsby objected to Mr Flimsby's dog and was always very suspicious of his social worker.

These features are linked to the defining characteristics of the core sample. Ambivalent marital behaviour is, of course, itself a defining characteristic and is linked to the constant threats of separation. The obsession with blame and the difficulty with third parties is linked to another defining characteristic - the inadequate performance of parental roles. The inadequacy of one partner gives the other the opportunity for attack and provides an excuse for his own inadequacy. The need for a tight alliance often leads to the formation of one with a child or another person (sometimes the social worker) at the expense of the spouse. Both the provocation and the expression of jealousy enables the partners to undermine each other as parents.

Our suggestion is that, in these couples, ambivalence, jealousy and blame have common roots. We argue that they are linked to the kind of split we described in chapter 4; on the one hand, to the yearning for needs to be met, and, on the other, to fear and anger at the possibility that they would not be. We look more closely at the basis of this split and at the same time introduce some other couples.

HELPLESSNESS AND LACK OF TRUST

The dilemma in which our clients found themselves — on the one hand their misery in their partnerships, on the other their terror of being alone — drew our attention to their apparent helplessness. They were helpless in the most basic sense of the word. They did not feel able to rely on themselves or others. In part, this helplessness was a product of their present circumstances, but with some it seemed to have been learnt from an early age.

Mrs Whiteside, for example, had always been considered 'stupid' by her parents and she had virtually not been allowed out on her own until she was married off at the age of seventeen to a middle-aged man whom her mother had designated to look after her. She was able to get out of that marriage, but she and her second husband came to the attention of the department when they were not able to manage the usual problems of daily life in earning regular money and in bringing up a young family.

Some of their difficulties were occasioned because they were not able to tolerate a normal daily separation. It was as if they felt incomplete apart, even for a few hours. Both of them were quite explicit about how their anxiety mounted when the other was missing. Mr Whiteside would pace the room if Mrs Whiteside was out longer than he expected when she was shopping round the corner. More often they shopped together. When Mr Whiteside was working, which was not very often, Mrs Whiteside would take herself and the three children, two of them then of toddler age, one still a baby, out on the coal lorry with him.

When life became too difficult — the debts and other problems too defeating — Mr and Mrs Whiteside, or both of them, became ill. While one was ill, the other would look after the children, or they would both retreat to bed together. The worker, let in by the eldest child, would raise a sympathetic and enquiring eyebrow at the two heads only just visible. One Whiteside would groan with pain and huddle further under the covers and the other would raise a languid arm and with a pained expression explain the latest injury, which invariably had gone septic. Never had the worker known a couple who 'went septic' quite so often. At the beginning of the work with them, spells on the coal lorry usually lasted about two months, those in bed and limping septically around the flat about four.

It may be that the Whitesides behaved as they did because they had never experienced a secure attachment figure and could not trust each other out of sight. An alternative explanation is that their parents had discouraged them from self-reliance and they themselves simply felt they could not manage on their own.

It appeared to us that both these explanations applied to the clients in our core sample whose heightened attachment and detachment behaviour provided the extreme examples of ambivalence described in the last chapter. We think many of them had been kept helpless and at the same time deprived of the opportunity of developing trust in a reliable figure who could give them the help they needed in lieu of a belief in their own ability.

The histories of our clients (when we could obtain them — some were amnesic, some found memories too painful to relate, some considered them quite irrelevant) provided one source of evidence. Mrs Doggart could describe what had happened to her.

> She told me her mother died when she was three and her only memory is of her being carried out on the stretcher saying, 'I'll be back'. Her father soon remarried and she sees the rest of her childhood as having been the slave of her stepmother whom she could never please. She said she lost all initiative and could only sit in the chair waiting for the next order.

Another source came from our observation of the behaviour of the children of our clients.

> At six o'clock one evening I visited the Briggs. I found the two girls, one aged six, the other thirteen, alone in the house. They told me their mother had left again, having gone without announcement four days previously, and that their father would be back soon. The eldest girl, small, pasty, and listless, talked of the uncertainty they faced over whether their mother would be at home to let them in on return from school, and of evenings spent hanging round the streets for their father because they had no key to the house.

> Obsessed with the misery of the situation and the ineffectiveness of all the adults, including myself, within it, I suggested that the oldest girl should ask her father for a key and that, as it was now holidays, the two of them should go to a play centre to get them out of the house. The oldest girl responded that they were better off spending their days in the house and that outside they might be murdered or raped.

This fear of the outside world had in part been fostered by her parents, who discouraged her from using the bus and going out with her boyfriend, and sometimes from going to school. Mr Briggs often locked Mrs Briggs in to prevent her from deserting and she, in her turn, kept the children in with her. Even when not locked in, Mrs Briggs would at times refuse to go out for weeks on end and she remembered with guilt the occasion when the oldest girl, then aged four, had been left unattended outside and been involved in a car accident. In these ways the parents gave a clear message that the outside world was fearful.

The paradigm implicit in these circumstances is an important one and impossible for the victim. The girl, who looked much younger than her thirteen years, was being kept comparatively helpless, erratically educated, and afraid to use public transport and, as such, was in need of her parents' help and support. At the same time, any support which might have been offered was apparently unreliable, sometimes completely missing. It was, in fact, untrustworthy.

The combination of helplessness, need of support, absence of reliable support and subsequently a lack of trust in help being available has already been illustrated in the description of the Jafferjis, the Buzzards and the Flimsbys, and, to a lesser extent, the Papcastles. Each spouse needed the other for the help they needed. In these circumstances they attempted to avoid vulnerability by denying their need, but much of their behaviour suggested otherwise, and in this duality they depicted the type of split we described in our theoretical summary. The underlying longing for a reliable and trustworthy attachment figure was apparent in the anger they expressed when their partner did not offer the support they wanted and in the control they attempted to exert over the movements and behaviour of that partner.

DENIAL, ANGER AND CONTROL

After Mrs Arncrow's early marriage at the age of sixteen to the middle-aged Mr Arncrow, her behaviour veered between anxious attachment — doing his bidding — and periodic rebellions against his attempts to keep her in the house. Mr Arncrow boasted of his independence and spent evening after evening 'helping' his friends and 'doing deals' with his associates. At the same time he wanted his pretty child-wife to be 'always there' and he would not allow her to have friends (who, he believed, would take her away from him) either in or outside the house.

When she finally deserted, his behaviour, like that of many of our clients (and of the children separated from their mothers described by Bowlby), alternated between protest and despair. He was either violently angry (he had a conviction for grievous bodily harm against his first wife) or in a state of maudlin collapse. On one telephone call to the department — and he made many such calls after her desertion — he threatened to shoot the worker, he wept, he threatened to kill himself, and he asked the worker to supply him with blankets to keep him warm.

Mr Garstang's behaviour was even more extreme. His wife left him when he battered the baby, who was admitted to hospital on a place of safety order.

> He came into the office and twice attempted to commit suicide by hanging himself with his tie, all within the space of three-quarters of an hour. *We could not leave him alone.* These attempts were very much gestures, but, on the other hand, they said a lot about how desperate and distraught he was. He cried a great deal and it was difficult to talk to him. He was all over the place emotionally and in one sentence he was going back to Egypt and he didn't care; in the next he was going to take his baby away whatever anyone said or did; in the next all he wanted was his wife back; and in the next he would find another flat and she could keep the baby. [In the light of our later discussion it is interesting that he mentions every possible family combination except the threesome of husband, wife and child.] And all these suggestions came up in the space of five minutes; he was just all over the place.

The behaviour in these examples is needy, angry and controlling. By telephoning or coming into the office, Mr Arncrow and Mr Garstang made it clear they wanted assistance. Deserted and alone, Mr Arncrow wanted warmth, but at the same time made it extremely difficult for the worker to respond in a warming way when he threatened, in the same breath, to shoot her. And her response was, no doubt, also coloured by the fact that a few weeks previously he had reported her to the CID for breaking and entering the house. (She had accompanied his wife when collecting much-needed clothes for the children.)

Need was sometimes expressed directly, but usually only in relation to material things; Mr Arncrow asked for blankets. Most of our clients felt, often quite consciously, that the expression of emotional need rendered them too vulnerable. In the words of one of them, it was better 'to cut off'. One wife explained that she would steal from her husband rather than 'beg' from him.

Clearly, Mr Arncrow and Mr Garstang could not believe that the workers would respond and give help unless forced into doing so. Mr Garstang's suicide gestures were, in the short term, highly successful in controlling the proximity of the workers. In the long run, however, this behaviour undermined his position with them and was counterproductive in getting him the comfort and support he needed. His and Mr Arncrow's actions aroused fear, anger, exhaustion and eventually, through their repetition, contempt. These attempts to control the attachment or substitute attachment figure were particularly self-defeating. If they succeeded, it could not be known whether the person stayed voluntarily, as was desperately wanted. Even more important, they only succeeded in eliciting equally ambivalent and rejecting responses.

A facet of the lack of trust and subsequent attempt to control the behaviour of the other was a need for predictability. This was expressed in attempts to create a predictable image of the spouse. If, in the course of the work, there was a shift in the behaviour of one of the partners, the other seemed unable to perceive it. They were often unable to hear, let alone consider, a point of view other than their own and would attempt to drown it in a repetition of their own saga and complaint. At the same time, however, the rigidity of their own behaviour invited a predictable response, but not the one they said they wanted — only the one about which they complained. In the following example we illustrate the combination of the lack of trust, the underlying panic when left, the attempt to control, the creation of a predictable image and the denial of need.

Mr Levens worked as a suburban train driver. Mrs Levens not only insisted on his telephoning her several times a day, but pushed the pram two miles and back to take his mid-day sandwiches. She was comparatively content when he was on regular shift and she knew the time of the end of a run and, therefore, when to expect the telephone call and when to take the sandwiches. When he was on stand-by, however, she was beside herself with anxiety, not knowing when he would be sent off on a train, on which route, or how long he would be.

What Mrs Levens did not know she often assumed. On one occasion she arrived on her own for what had been planned as a joint interview. A relative had died and Mr Levens' mother had been expected for the funeral later that day. Mr Levens had gone to meet her at the station, had missed her and spent several hours looking for her.

Mrs Levens went into an over-detailed account of the missing mother and expressed her fury that Mr Levens had telephoned only after he had found his mother. He had said he would be back in time for the interview. She knew he must be drunk. Having made baby-sitting arrangements so that she also could go to the funeral that evening, she had now cancelled these.

At this point Mr Levens arrived and apologised for being late. He said he had been ordering flowers and had had to wait twenty minutes for a bus. Yes, he had had one drink.

'You're drunk', screamed Mrs Levens. 'That's all you've been doing. I know you'. Mr Levens exploded, said he had had enough and asked me to make arrangements for a divorce. Mrs Levens continued to say he was drunk, he was aggressive, he was foul. I said I did not understand her panic. When she did not know where he was, when she had not got exact 'tabs' on him, she had prematurely cancelled the baby-sitting arrangements. But Mr Levens was here and he was clearly not drunk. Mrs Levens said *she knew him:* he was.

Obviously Mrs Levens felt helpless and out of control when she did not know where her husband was, and in a worse panic than usual either because a mother-figure was missing, or because she feared her husband had gone off with his mother and left her out of the expedition — the odd one out.

After another interview with Mrs Levens the worker reported:

She talked non-stop and I could hardly get a remark in until five minutes before the end, and even then I had to make a huge effort to do this. I asked her when she had last had an evening out. 'Two years ago'. I wondered why she could not ask her husband to take her out or for something she wanted. Mrs Levens ignored this, as all my previous remarks, and again talked of what her sister could ask for.

I interrupted and said Mrs Levens had done with me what she was always doing with Mr Levens. This at last caused her to pause. I said she had talked and talked and talked and filled me up with words and had hardly allowed me to get a word in. I had just made one very big suggestion about her asking Mr Levens to take her out or to give her something she wanted, but she had not even been able to consider it. She had gone on talking about her sister's being able to ask, but had refused to think about why she could not ask.

THE OBSESSION WITH BLAME

Mrs Levens perceived Mr Levens as 'drunk, aggressive and foul', none of which he had actually been in the interview. Most of our core sample clients were obsessed with trying to prove how bad their spouses were. One was at times almost unintelligible on this theme. She answered simple and innocuous questions with irrelevant accusations or statements to the effect that many others were worse than she.

We believe this obsession can be explained partly in terms of the clients' need for excuses and partly by their previous experiences of attachment and loss.

Many of them were, in one sense, 'in the dock'. Mr Garstang, Mr and Mrs Arncrow and Mrs Flimsby had been suspected of battering a child and at least three of them knew this. Mrs Jafferji, Mrs Buzzard and Mrs Briggs were thought by the social workers to be neglecting their children. The husbands of these women had all been accused of using violence on them and were defending themselves against these accusations, sometimes in the presence of the social worker. A concern with accusation and what and who was good or bad had, therefore, social implications for them.

Blame was also endemic in situations where a spouse had rebelled against his parents by marrying someone of whom they disapproved. For example, Mrs Flimsby married a man who fought her mother's influence at every turn. She blamed him for this and played him off against her mother; as long as she was with her husband, she maintained that her mother was 'an angel'. At the same time she excused flouting her mother (or refusing to see her social worker) on the grounds of her husband's wishes; and, similarly, she displaced on to her husband's shoulders much of her anger against members of her family of origin.

'Rebellious' marriages of this kind were quite common in the sample (only marginally less frequent than marriages made out of loneliness and 'to get away from home'). These marriages allowed the 'good' spouse to live vicariously through the 'bad' spouse and at the same time to uphold parental standards by attacking the partner for his 'badness' and, if necessary, to excuse lapses of her own behaviour on the grounds of the subversive influence to which she had been subjected.

Mrs Mothersill, small and red-faced, as if scrubbed with carbolic at regular intervals, used these tactics. After a period in an orphanage exercising a strict regime, she was, in her teens, cared for by an equally strict fostermother who had exploited her, forcing her to spend an inordinate amount of time keeping the house immaculate. Part of her fostermother's teaching was that gypsies were, beyond all others, to be mistrusted. Mrs Mothersill married not only against the wishes of her fostermother but a man who, it turned out, came from a gypsy family. This might have suited her well, since her accounts of her early history included unnecessary, but exciting, walks by gypsy encampments. However, she vilified her husband for gypsy origins and excused her own drinking, swearing and standards of housekeeping on the grounds of his influence.

In relation to previous experience of attachment and loss, the reader will remember that in Bowlby's view children separated from their parents express anger on their return at the way they have been treated. 'Sometimes it is the anger of hope; sometimes the anger of despair'. The clients with whom we were dealing often seemed to us to be stuck in a state of despair. In this situation, there were two reasons why they were likely to resort to blaming. Firstly, many of them had had childhoods in which they were dumped from one place to another and in which it was natural to develop the view that other people were more powerful than themselves and therefore to blame for whatever happened to them. Secondly, all the clients we have so far been describing were in situations where separation from an important attachment figure was an ever-present possibility. In these circumstances, protest in the form of verbal attack would, according to Bowlby, be common.

The blame seemed to serve both sides of a split. Superficially it sounded simply like a rejection of the spouse, but if listened to carefully and in context it could be heard as the expression of need. This was evident in the tone and content of the accusation. The tone often changed from a roar of fury to a whining plea. The content often related to separation or unpredictability and lack of control. Mrs Jafferji attacked her husband for spending long hours at work, to such an extent that her worker found himself wondering whether she wanted her husband to go to work at all.

Not surprisingly, in view of our clients' difficulty in asking, the blame often took the place of a request. 'You never do anything for me'. 'You never take me to the pub'. 'You never come home and help me'. These statements were used rather than 'Will you take me out?' or 'I cannot manage on my own; will you help me?' The worker's suggestion that the hurling of accusations was counter-productive was seldom heard.

We soon came to realize that the habit of blaming, fulfilling as it did so many functions, could not be easily relinquished. The implied rejection arose from ties which kept the partners together. The reader will remember that Mr Flimsby was unable to give up his wife for more than a few days until he had for the first time spoken kindly and sadly about her. Blame, by its own logic, denies a need, yet, at the same time, allows its continued and indirect expression.

Our analysis suggests that blaming, like other actions intended to control, is likely to be both a stabilizing and self-defeating form of behaviour. It is likely to lower the self-confidence of those exposed to it and from this point of view may make them less likely to leave. On the other hand, the hostility created by blame is likely to make the relationship yet more insecure and hence increase the lack of trust which helped to give rise to the blaming in the first place.

THIRD PARTIES

Blaming was often connected with third parties.

> Mrs Dockeray said that she sometimes shouted at her child, 'Why won't you let me love Daddy?' She felt that this little boy came between them and that she found that she shouted at him when her husband was around. Similarly, her husband was always 'at him'.

Three associated individuals can be regarded as three isolates, three related individuals, or two related individuals and one isolate. Our clients seemed to operate on the assumption that the last was most likely. Because of their needs and lack of trust, a third party was immediately seen as a threat or an ally. Any mutual love or rapport between two of the three was unbearable for the third and left him feeling a complete outsider and more on his own than before.

Intense jealousy and the provocation of jealousy were both rife.

Mrs Boothroyd, for example, was described by Mr Boothroyd as jealous and certainly many of her most painful concerns could be explained in this way. She was deeply angry that Mr Boothroyd, although cohabiting with her for twenty-five years, had never married her; and she believed this was due to his continuing attachment to his first wife. She remembered with bitterness the presents he had given the daughter of his first marriage on their first Christmas together. Mr Boothroyd confessed that he was equally jealous. He had ripped Mrs Boothroyd's clothes to pieces with a knife after he had seen her with another man and, in his own words, 'half-killed' her when he believed she had been unfaithful to him.

Jealous quarrels centred most frequently on the children, but relatives, animals and lovers were also objects of jealousy. The affairs, arousing strong passions within the family, were often fleeting and apparently sexless. Even when a real affair had taken place, intense suspicion continued long after. Forgiveness was something which did not come easily to these couples, so strong was the hurt if their spouse was not felt to be their exclusive property. For five years Mrs Mothersill harped on the fact that her husband was in love with a schoolteacher with whom he had once had a brief affair. Following this the woman had moved out of the area and no one knew where she was.

The provocation of the jealousy was often apparent. The recipients of the jealousy often made an exclusive, or would-be exclusive, alliance with a child, and the eliciting of jealousy was part of the marital war. Mrs Briggs, who had an affair openly, told her husband that her lover was a better man than he. She threw her family into consternation when she made her frequent departures and said, 'It's only when you're gone, that you are missed'. Mr Entwhistle said that he valued the berating his wife gave him because it meant that she cared. Mrs Calder described an incident in which she kissed a man with the precise intention of getting her husband to stop her. Mrs Entwhistle remembered with pleasure the occasions before her marriage on which her fiancé had beaten up men who were interested in her.

One evening Mrs Hardknott told Mr Hardknott that she wanted to live with another man. She timed this to tell him just before I arrived at the house. We shared the shock. I was not at all convinced that it was true and Mrs Hardknott immediately denied that she had meant it, saying she had said it because she 'wanted something to happen'. This seemed to be true, whether the other man was reality or fantasy. Mr Hardknott was very white, angry and abusive, and Mrs Hardknott responded by shouting counter-allegations.

According to Bowlby, intense jealousy and possessiveness are symptoms of deprivation. It is not clear, however, from his account whether the intense jealousy displayed by children in a nursery was the result of the deprivation *per se* or the fact that in addition to being deprived of their mothers the children were competing for the attention of nursery nurses who inevitably had to divide their concern among a comparatively large number of children.

We believe the deprivation *per se* gives rise to an envy which underlies much of the behaviour we have described in the last three sections of this chapter. Envy can, perhaps, best be summarized as the pain occasioned by seeing someone else occupy a position one wants to be in oneself. For example, an adult who would like to be a baby may envy a real one.

We believe that the jealousy, as opposed to the envy, relates to the competition which is intrinsic in a situation of deprivation, and arises from the need to compete for scarce resources and the fear of losing out to someone else. Both these factors seemed to underlie the difficulties our clients had with third parties, and probably were engendered by heavy competition either with other children when temporarily or permanently separated from their parents, or with siblings within the family.

Mr Arncrow was the twenty-first of twenty-six children! When the worker exclaimed and asked if he got lost in the crowd, he replied, ' "Crowd" is the wrong word. It was more like a gooey mass'. He was an exception in that his family was quite so huge, but many others came from large families (Mr Levens one of nine, Mrs Levens one of six) and talked of their jealousy of their siblings. The following account of a potential breeding-ground for jealousy is taken not from a history but from the worker's observations of Mrs Mothersill and her three children.

I called and found Mrs Mothersill on her own with Patrick (twelve months), Kevin (four years) and Simon (eight years). Mr Mothersill was out. At the previous interview he had groaned audibly when I had reminded Mrs Mothersill that she could ring me up. This may have been his way of indicating his displeasure at a potential alliance between Mrs Mothersill and me.

The interview began with Mrs Mothersill trying ineffectively to get Simon out of the room, saying that he knew much more than was good for him and had betrayed the family by telling their secrets at school. As Simon had until very recently slept in his parents' bed and also witnessed several violent scenes, it was very doubtful whether he could learn anything that he did not know already. It seemed to me that Mrs Mothersill wanted to enjoy my exclusive attention without the interruptions from the sidelines that Simon was inclined to provide.

In the event, Simon could not be banished and attention shifted to Patrick, who set up a wail from the playpen. Mrs Mothersill went over and stuffed the dummy in his mouth and returned to talk to me. Patrick stopped crying but immediately restarted when Kevin snatched the dummy from his mouth and put it in his own. Mrs Mothersill removed the dummy from Kevin's mouth and put it back in Patrick's, and Kevin promptly and angrily removed it. This process happened two or three times until Mrs Mothersill smacked Kevin hard and he retired howling to a corner.

In this case the desired goods were the worker's attention, Mrs Mothersill's attention or, failing that, the dummy. All of these goods were in short supply and subject to competition. Whenever the worker gave his attention to Mrs Mothersill, or Mrs Mothersill gave the dummy to the baby, somebody else butted in and attempted to get the attention or the dummy. Similar situations are found in many families, but the Mothersills and other families in the project were marked by the number of transactions which were dominated by this type of rivalry and the degree of intense feeling underlying them. Such feelings are likely to be more intense and frequent in deprived families in which there are not enough material and emotional resources to go round.

Feelings of jealousy were often brought into prominence by the birth of a baby and compounded the envy occasioned by the reality of that baby. For example, just before the birth of her little boy, Mrs Dockeray went to bed for a week and Mr Dockeray refused to feed her. When the baby was born, Mr Dockeray went straight out and got himself arrested for carrying housebreaking tools.

Some of the women seemed to feel that marriage and parenthood were quite incompatible.

> Mrs Izatt felt that her own mother had been so caught up with married quarrels that she had had no time for her. Her own first marriage came to grief with the birth of the first baby. Subsequently she left her husband and had three abortions. She now said that as long as she had her son with her she could never remarry. Her reason was that her son became very attention-seeking whenever she had a man with her and the man objected to him.

She acted on this assumption when she finally did marry again, first aborting her second husband's child and then sending her son of the first marriage back to her former husband.

The next example demonstrates threesome difficulties not only in day-to-day transactions but also in major life decisions, and the interpretation given to them.

Mrs Calder, a careworn mother of three in her thirties, was married to a delinquent man. She felt burdened by debts and her husband's mistreatment of her, which included occasional violence. One of her predominant characteristics was the favouring of one child, who had to be ill to get favoured. As one child became ill and received all the attention, the others were emotionally neglected. Another would get ill and replace the first and so it would continue. One or other of the neglected children would raise child care problems turn and turn about.

At one stage in her contact with the social worker, Mrs Calder talked of her past history which was, indeed, traumatic and littered with broken relationships. She described how she had broken with her parents, left her first child when he was two years old with her first husband, been divorced, lost an important boyfriend and then a lover. It was noticeable that she believed all these relationships had been going well until the intervention of a third party. Her sister was said to have ruined the relationship with her parents, her child that with her first husband; the court had given her husband the custody of the child, the boyfriend had two-timed her and the lover's wife had demanded him back.

It is unlikely that these relationships were as perfect as she described before the intervention of a third party. However, as well as this being used as the explanation, it was clear that all present transactions within the current marriage were dominated by a fear shared by both of them that in any threesome they would be the odd one out. Mr Calder blamed his drinking, firstly, on their housing situaion, and, secondly, on his jealousy of Mrs Calder's previous marriage and the fact that she had been raped at the age of fifteen, so that he was 'not the first'.

Two examples of their jealous interaction concerned one of the children. In the first example a fierce argument arose while the worker was present; it involved James, the eleven-year-old.

> Another source of disagreement was that James was always around. Mr Calder said he shouldn't be, because how else could the parents sit down and have a decent conversation? He seemed to be blaming James for this. (Incidentally, James slept in his mother's bed when his father was away.) Mrs Calder seemed to justify her actions and defend James at the same time by saying that he only came in to see what was going on when Mr Calder was drunk. 'He's worried about me'. James sprang to the defence of his mother and spoke defiantly to his father.

The second example suggests that Mrs Calder was not just the innocent victim of this situation. On this occasion she was more reflective.

> Mrs Calder said that Mr Calder had helped James with his fractions one evening. The two of them sat together while she went out to the kitchen. I asked her if she was pleased and she said she was 'quite put out'. She was used 'to being the centre of attention'.

Jealous behaviour, like the other controlling behaviour we have described, maintains a vicious circle. It makes it more difficult for the recipient to leave (although in the end it may drive him to do so), but it also tends to deprive the jealous person of the certainty that the other stays of his own free will. Thus it breeds the uncertainty which is in itself its origin.

Our clients operated on the basis that 'One is terrifying, two ought to be company, three cannot possibly be'. They were caught in a dilemma between, on the one hand, their helplessness and need to be supported by another, and, on the other hand, their lack of trust, envy, jealousy and need to control, all of which effectively sabotaged their efforts in attachment. Some of the sabotage, however, fulfilled the need to keep an omnipotent and infantile hope alive that some time, somewhere, an all-giving, all-loving attachment figure would come to heal.

This is a very different story from that recounted by Dodie Smith in her book on her Manchester childhood, *Look back with Love.*[1] Her first memory of using her imagination was when the family was moving house. It was getting dusk and she had been put to sit on the piano. She suddenly got concerned that she had been forgotten, but almost instantly she knew that she was far too 'valuable' and, knowing this, allowed herself to play with the idea of 'scaring herself pleasantly'.

It is difficult to imagine our clients ever feeling valuable enough to be able to scare themselves pleasantly.

[1]   Smith, D. (1974), *Look back with Love* (Heinemann).

7 Meeting Demands

In my heart it has not died,
The war that sleeps on Severn side;
They cease not fighting, east and west,
On the marches of my breast.

Here the truceless armies yet
Trample, rolled in blood and sweat;
They kill and kill and never die;
And I think that each is I.

None will part us, none undo
The knot that makes one flesh of two,
Sick with hatred, sick with pain,
Strangling — When shall we be slain?

When shall I be dead and rid
Of the wrong my father did?
How long, how long, till spade and hearse
Put to sleep my mother's curse?
                                    A.E. Housman

Obsessed with their need to be attached but, at the same time, afraid of being attached, and veering ambivalently between these extremes, our clients were unlikely to be effective attachment figures themselves. It was difficult for them to respond to the demands of their partners when these were expressed as paradoxically as we have described. Moreover, their own unassuaged needs made it difficult for them to listen to those of others, let alone to start to meet them.

A vicious circle was set up. Failure in getting themselves more comfortably attached and in acting as attachment figures fed their own doubts about themselves and their partner's mistrust of them.

101

Failure, doubts and mistrust increased, in their turn, the obsessions, the fear and the paradoxical behaviour of both partners.

This vicious circle was exacerbated by stress. In the interview with the Flimsbys described below, Mr Flimsby's need for support came partly from the fact that he was out of work.

> Mr Flimsby said he was now being paid £35 per week by social security and that he could not manage on it. Apart from this, his main aim was to prove how filthy his wife kept the place. I was just trying to do some work about this when Mrs Flimsby came in. She was immediately dragged into the game of defending herself against the charge that she was extravagant, showing me before I could do anything about it the contents of her shopping bag. She then left the room to return a moment later with a glass of water to tell me how difficult for her was her life with Paul which, in turn, got into an attack on Mr Flimsby for hitting the child and threatening her.

In effect, Mr Flimsby complained that his wife did not look after him and financially demanded more than he could provide. His wife's need for support arose from the fact that for the first time for over a year she was trying to be a mother to her child. However, her cry for support, hidden as it was under her complaint of not getting support, could not be heard by her husband, who felt he had troubles enough of his own.

Obviously everyone does not respond to stress in this extreme way, so this on its own cannot be a complete explanation of Mr and Mrs Flimsby's behaviour. Whilst recognizing that stress exacerbates behaviour characteristics, we need to look further. In doing so, we discuss the model, or mental picture, our clients used to interpret events and predict the future. The pictures were dismal enough in the first place and current events reinforced the gloom. A major element in these pictures was the clients' view of themselves.

MODELS OF ATTACHMENT

Many of our clients carried with them from their families of origin what amounted to a self-fulfilling prophecy about how their lives were likely to turn out. We were unable to check their accounts of their past histories but, to judge from what they said, only about a quarter of the core sample could be said to have anything but appalling backgrounds. Even those who had experienced something more stable usually seemed to feel they were the black sheep or that they came from families with so many children that they themselves had got 'lost'. From this stemmed the lack of support from their families of origin which was one of their defining characteristics.

Few of them had experienced good attachment relationships of any kind and, not surprisingly, their doubts about the reliability of attachment figures affected them both when they were turning to others to fulfil this role and when they were trying to play it themselves. Some of them expressed a feeling of doom, as if, somehow, they belonged among inadequate people and the question was only which unsatisfying role they could play in an unhappy company. Mrs Dockeray, for example, was hesitating over whether to marry a desirable suitor on the break-up of her first marriage to an apparently unreliable delinquent.

> She has now met an older man who gets on with the children. This man is bothering her by ringing up too much. She feels 'inferior' and this man is not 'inferior'. She feels she has to put on an act with him. She feels that if she married this man she would always miss her husband, with whom she can be herself. It is only right for her to marry an 'inferior' man.

Need, like inferiority, appeals to the needy as well as frightening them. Mrs Ahmad wondered why she returned to her violent Middle-Eastern husband.

> She was clearly having second thoughts, but she acknowledged the appeal he made to her, especially when he behaved like a deprived infant, crying for his mother. This alternated with his ill-treatment of her.

The ill-treatment, it seems, was also paradoxically attractive.

> During this time she expressed guilty feelings about her rejection of her own mother when she had asked to be taken into care. She also recalled an occasion when she had attacked an older brother, one of twins, with a red-hot poker, causing severe burns on his shins. This

was linked with sadness for the other twin who had been mentally subnormal and had then died. From the way she talked it seemed that she could deal only with unkind treatment and that kind treatment for herself elicited only her sadism.

This feeling probably had a curious logic to it. When a child, Mrs Ahmad had been very badly treated by her mother and she may have somehow associated the state of being attached with receiving cruelty. When adult she had ill-treated and abandoned her children by a previous marriage. If she felt her choice of roles to be limited, it was not surprising that she preferred to receive ill-treatment rather than give it.

Mrs Boothroyd was another client who expressed the view that it was important to occupy a particular role because failure to do so would lead to her occupying a much less attractive one.

> She talked of her father's drunkenness and cruelty and his attack on her mother with a hammer. Yet following his death, her mother, whom she described as 'sweet and kind', had had only 'six lousy months of life'. She said she had cursed her father every day of her life and, when she is drunk, she sees his face in those of others and attacks them. It is at such moments that she feels her father 'coming out in her' and this makes her worse. She drinks and fights because she is not going to be pushed around like her mother.

The two roles in this woman's repertoire were those of the drunken aggressor and the abused saint. More often she played out the former, but sometimes the latter, washing her family's laundry at all hours of the day and night and at times asking her husband to beat her. Her cursing, like the blaming described in the last chapter, ensured her continued involvement with this ancient history and its continued influence upon her.

Clients like Mrs Ahmad and Mrs Boothroyd seemed to view life as if there were only so many roles to go round and it was important to select the least undesirable one as a defence against getting one of the others. This meant in part inducing others to accept particular roles. Mrs Dockeray, for example, saw not only that it was 'only right' for her to marry an 'inferior' man (she was a bank clerk and her previous husband largely illiterate) but also that

she deprived him of responsibility and kept him, in her terms,
'inferior'.

> She felt guilt because she had never responded to her husband as a
> person with needs and his mother never had either. Somehow she felt
> that her needs had blinded her to his.

The difficulty in recognizing some of the needs of others was often
exacerbated by the fact that they triggered off old feelings of
deprivation and loss in the supposed attachment figure. Mrs Izatt,
separated from her husband, put this process into words shortly
after she had returned her seven-year-old child to his father.

> She went on to talk in a rather detached, ironical way about Luke.
> She thought she was very confused and not very maternal and not
> very good with Luke. She said that she had been damaged by her
> upbringing and did not want Luke to grow up like her. She suffered
> from a terrible fear of being alone and, when Luke felt lost, this
> touched off feelings in her which were unbearable.

Mrs Izatt dealt with the situation by sending her child away and by
keeping 'a stiff upper lip'. For example, she falsely told her child
that she had not cried for him, although she had. Other clients dealt
with a similar problem by denying the reality of the other's needs.

Other clients attacked needy behaviour in the spouse, although
often encouraging it in other ways. As we showed in the last
chapter, this was usually coupled with a denial of their own need.
Sometimes they had been exploited in childhood, having been used,
for example, as a skivvy, a caretaker of other children, or even a
breadwinner. Such clients associated attachment with exploitation.
Their own needs led them to accept exploitation, but at the same
time they saw their partner's needs as an excuse for exploitation.
This, of course, our clients resented.

In their quickness to sense exploitation, our clients were alive to
themes from their childhood which had to do with attachment. Just
as needs reminded them of exploitation or deprivation, so family
situations were perceived as providing a choice between exploiting
or abandoning those attached to them, or being exploited or
abandoned themselves. If this was the legacy from the past, what
did the present offer them?

ATTACHMENT ROLES

In our culture, the most socially supported marriages are probably those between people of similar class and racial background, marrying for the first time and with their parents' consent. It is commonly believed that racially or religiously mixed marriages, or second marriages, are less likely to survive. It is, therefore, interesting that just under half our core sample were mixed marriages between people from different countries. And again, in just under half the couples, one or other spouse had been married before or had had a liaison which produced a child. Among the ten cases where neither of these things applied, at least five of the marriages took place against a background of parental disapproval. And hardly any of the core sample had their parents on hand to support them. When, exceptionally, there was frequent contact with parents, the involvement was invariably a source of trouble rather than support.

If the circumstances surrounding the marriages were not of the kind traditionally thought to endorse a marriage, the circumstances surrounding the adoption of parental roles were often less encouraging. At the end of the project we looked at the outcome of the last known pregnancy of the women in the core sample. Seven out of ten of these either resulted in an abortion or in a birth the surrounding circumstances of which could only be described as traumatic. A further one out of ten remembered previous traumatic births. The birth of other children in the sample may have been happy events, but we doubt it.

It may not seem surprising that women in touch with an agency concerned with the protection of young children at risk should have had traumatic pregnancies. However, even when the children were quite old, the events surrounding the pregnancy were often remembered with acute distress.

Both Mr and Mrs Ingledow seemed to feel very guilty about the seventeen-year-old daughter's handicap and there was some issue about whether Mr Ingledow's drunkenness and violence towards Mrs Ingledow during the pregnancy was responsible for her condition or whether it might have been a consequence of some neglect by Mrs Ingledow, as the condition did not become apparent until some time during the first year.

Some of the women recognized their depression or despair:

> She told me she first became depressively ill after John was born. She couldn't bear the fact that he cried so much and she felt she couldn't satisfy him or look after him properly. She went to hospital and her mother-in-law looked after John and did so again when they separated.

More commonly the depression or despair was not recognized and was disguised by shame.

> Mrs Ahmad had married and been quite happy until the birth of her first child, when she seems to have become very depressed. This depression was both unrecognized and untreated and became even worse with the birth of the second child. She couldn't seek help and was somehow denigrated by her mother-in-law, who implied that women should be able to overcome such feelings.

The last two examples illustrate the problem of validating the insecure mother. In the first example the woman was treated as incompetent and her mother-in-law took over. This did not help. In the second example Mrs Ahmad was given the opposite treatment and told to snap out of it. This did not help her either. The problem of the mother-in-law was no doubt related to the ambivalence of the younger woman, part of whom probably wished to give up the role and collapse, part of whom probably did not want to do this at all. Whichever part the mothers-in-law responded to, they were likely to be accused of doing the wrong thing. This type of ambivalence was reflected in the relationship with the social workers. Either the clients thought they could be mothers, in which case they did not need any help, or they could not, in which case the social services should remove their children. They found it difficult to conceive that they could be supported *as* mothers.

It would normally be expected that the most important figure in validating the young mother would be her husband, but, because of the difficulties described in this chapter and in the last one, this was not so. In this respect the husbands were less explicit about their feelings about the baby than their wives, although some referred to the feeling of (awful?) responsibility of being a father, or to the feeling of being pushed out. Their unexpressed feelings had to be guessed from their behaviour — increased drinking, crime, violence or promiscuity — which appeared to coincide with the pregnancies. They were more undermining than supporting.

This undermining, arising partly from their general hostility, partly from their envy and jealousy of the mother and the baby, also seemed to be occasioned by a common difficulty of both partners in conceiving that the same person could be wife, mother and sexual partner, or husband, father and sexual partner. Crudely put, many spouses seemed to operate on the assumption that women could be virgin mothers or sluttish prostitutes and men violent brutes or mewling babies.

Mr Ahmad, for example, apparently found his wife living as a prostitute and bought her for £2 on the understanding that she was never to get pregnant. This she did, and the worker commented:

> He never really forgave her for this dereliction from their agreement. Characteristically, he never felt he had any responsibility for what happened. Sex, pregnancy and its avoidance were a woman's problem. This attitude seems to have been related to a cultural attitude towards women in which wives are seen as degraded and sexually depraved as compared with mothers, who are idealized and non-sexual.

The worker felt that Mr Ahmad wanted both a prostitute and a mother, but the latter was to be for himself rather than his children:

> There was some evidence that Mr Ahmad was very muddled in his attitude to his wife and in some sense seeking to make her into a mother for himself to replace his own unsatisfactory mothering, which had been interrupted by the birth of successive children — twelve of them — and by violent parental quarrels.

The split between sexual and mothering roles was important not only because of its influence on family structure, but because it meant that love and tenderness could not be conveyed through sex. The possibility of enacting and validating attachment roles was therefore reduced. In Bowlby's theory, the behavioural system concerned with sex is different from that concerned with attachment. We deal with sex in this chapter partly because of the conflict our clients saw between sex and attachment, and partly because, paradoxically, sexual failure was also used as evidence of lack of love.

SEX

Among our core clients the story of sex is sad and drab. In approximately one in seven families one or other spouse described the sexual relationship as good. In approximately two out of three it was said to be poor, spasmodic or non-existent. In one in five families we had no information, but our guess is that in most of these it was also poor.

The couples who described the sex as good were all involved in spasmodically violent relationships with each other.

> The worker was also made anxious by the primitive nature of their interaction which, she reported to the group, was apt to be chaotic and often violent. She gave the impression of a couple who related intensely primitively and demanded fierce bodily gratification which, if denied, exploded into rape or violence.

The connection between sex and violence was even more explicit with the Cabassis. Mrs Cabassi frequently referred to an incident in which her husband had beaten up a man with whom she was walking arm in arm, and, while her complaint was one of outraged innocence, it barely concealed her excitement. In their frequent and violent quarrels Mr Cabassi would call Mrs Cabassi a whore and on one such occasion she apparently tried to castrate him with a pair of scissors.

Mrs Doggart implied a similar connection when she proffered three pieces of information at the same time: her husband had probably been involved with the murder of a prostitute, they had sex twice a year, and 'he always gets more violent at that time'.

In other violent couples, the violence concealed the drabness of the sex. 'We're not very sexual people', said Mr Entwhistle. 'She's not much of a hand at it and nor am I', said Mr Mothersill, who, in drink and violence, had much in common with Mr Entwhistle. 'You mustn't mind for us', said Mr Gilcrux. 'We don't want it. We're better off without'. Yet sex still troubled the Gilcruxes and the Mothersills. One of the Gilcruxes' most dramatic rows occurred over a double bed which Mr Gilcrux wanted to purchase when he was trying to become 'lord of his own castle'. And Mr Gilcrux and Mr Mothersill both infected their wives with VD when they were pregnant.

For Mrs Doggart the association between sex and disgust was quite explicit:

> She said that for many years she had known that her husband had had numerous encounters with women but the preceding Saturday he had had a woman in the lavatory, which to her was the final insult. She thought he had a split personality and was so guilty about his sexual encounters that after each one he went on for days washing himself 'as if to wash the dirt away'.

Sometimes the disgust was associated with a split-off excitement:

> Mrs Calder said that when Mr Calder gets nasty he keeps on reminding her that she was not a virgin when they married and how much this distressed her ... She said that she was raped when she was fifteen by a man with whom she had been going out for about six months. She went over the event in some detail and, although the facts were pretty traumatic, her tone of voice was more one of enjoyment than of horror.

Sex between the Calders sometimes followed the row 'to keep the peace', a milder version of the earlier rape.

> Mrs Calder was very angry with Mr Calder. He had been at the Play-boy Club till three o'clock ('men can go anywhere') and had been drunk on many other nights although his sobriety at a recent darts match proved he could control himself if he wanted. In his drunkenness he had called her a whore, a prostitute, a cypriot cunt and other choice phrases. She had been watching a television programme on horse breeding and he had told her she ought to 'get a stallion to cover her' and that she cared more about the TV than getting his dinner. She told him to 'grow up', whereupon he slapped her face. All this was in front of the children! Ten minutes later he was apologizing and they'd gone to bed. She'd only agreed to intercourse to keep the peace.

We may assume that Mrs Calder made a point of the fact that 'all this was in front of the children', illustrating the distinction between the sexual playboy and the good parent. Similarly Mr Calder emphasized the contrast between a housewife who would care for him and get his dinner and the 'depraved' Mrs Calder.

The drama of this interaction covers the sexual insecurity and obscures the question of who wants sex. Mr Calder's performance was often impaired by his alcoholic intake. He described her as the one who needed the stallion, which he may well have envied. She, suffering from various gynaecological complaints, put the demand on to him.

Gynaecological complaints were common in the marriages, like that of the Calders, in which alcohol and violence and poor or non-existent sex coexisted. In the core sample almost as many women as not were known to have received medical attention in respect of abortions, venereal disease, hysterectomies or cervical cancer. The meaning these women attached to these medical interventions obviously varied, but they were often given as a cause of complaint and self-denigration. For example, Mrs Hardknott attempted to kill herself in her despair that her boyfriend had been unfaithful to her, but she succeeded only in aborting her baby. Such events could only add to the degradation associated with sex. The shame with which these couples regarded sex was often as marked as the physical difficulties.

Mrs Briggs described her arrival at the hospital after the overdose. She had been living rough, but her husband had learnt of her admission and had removed drink and dirty underwear from the bedside locker. Mr Briggs laid stress on the underwear and Mrs Briggs then told us defiantly that she had been having her period. She cried bitterly and genuinely that these things were brought out 'in front of social workers'. We acknowledged the awfulness, angry at Mr Briggs' sadism, but, surprisingly, he saved the day by remarking that, 'If there was no washing, there would be no point in families'. Mrs Briggs then remarked that, 'Even the Queen must have dirty underwear sometime'. This thought comforted us all.

Sex was rarely a vehicle for the communication of love; firstly, because it was mainly experienced as unsatisfactory, and, secondly, because, satisfying or not, it was usually divorced from tenderness. And this is not surprising in a group of marriages in which the main unconscious obsession and quarrel enacted by the partners was who would mother whom and, therefore, who could be the baby. The adult, genital sex act, when it was practised, was in these terms irrelevant, although its failure added to the despair.

TOKENS

Sex for our couples was often a sideshow, part of a sub-plot somehow split off from the central drama of deprived infants and uncaring mothers. Other props, which we call 'tokens', were, however, more centrally connected with the main theme of mothers and mothering.

'Tokens', as we use the word, are objects such as food, drink, houses and money which hold both conscious and unconscious significance. They may be valued for themselves, as, for example, money is of value to a man in debt; or they may be valued for what they signify, as when the offer of tea denotes hospitality; or they may hold an unconscious symbolism as when a person seeks some primitive comfort in alcoholic liquor; and they may be used in any combination of these ways.

In terms of attachment behaviour we are most interested in the meaning given to these objects in the context of family relationships and their status as objects of attachment in their own right and as evidence of ability to meet attachment needs. Obviously we are not denying the fact that houses and money were in themselves of central importance to our clients, many of whom had housing problems or debts. However the unremitting nature of some of their demands on each other and on the social workers and the way they related to these objects at times suggested a significance far beyond their obvious practical use.

The clients' houses sometimes reflected their own dismal picture of themselves, as if they had no right to make them better. Mr and Mrs Gilcrux's small and just adequate flat was cheerless and dirty. During the course of the work with them it seemed as if they felt more hopeful about themselves. They decided to decorate, but the wallpaper remained in its roll for many weeks and then only went up in erratic stages, trimmed only at the bottom. One wall remained unpapered for two months, but was finally completed when news of a long-lost son of a previous marriage had been obtained. The worker offered a carpet she had acquired and this was proudly laid and cleaned for the reunion. Mr Gilcrux, still working hard to become 'lord of his own castle', bought a chair with arms; a 'father's chair', he called it. But the carpet remained the weathervane of their feelings about themselves, and perhaps the worker, at times allowed to get dirtier and dirtier, spottier and spottier, and at its most spotty when the work was ending with them. During the period of decoration one massive row was occasioned by Mr Gilcrux's insistence on painting the lavatory what he called 'bulrush brown'. But only one wall *got* bulrushed.

Although the state of the house often signified the current state of the marital relationships it was probably particularly significant to the woman. One, pointing to the indescribable chaos around her, described herself as a slut but took no action to remedy the matter apart from attempting to exclude people from the house. She said that because of her husband she had no heart to put the place in order. However, the correspondence 'neat house equals good state of the marriage, untidy house equals bad state' was by no means exact.

Mrs Entwhistle, in contrast to those mentioned above, kept an immaculate house filled with highly polished pseudo-antique furniture. Periodically she reported that her husband smashed the furniture and spewed sick over the walls, but the worker, visiting the following day, could see no trace of these violations. The wife would not allow her husband to paint the place because of the mess he made. The house showed her dominance and her husband's position in it as a clumsy bull in a china shop, just as the small bed belonging to Mr Beattie emphasized his position in contrast to the large bed occupied by his wife and teenage daughter.

The house was often used as an explanation of the family's unhappiness. This added to the problems of rehousing. Moves, of course, carried their own stress — breakdown of old ties, fear about the reactions of new neighbours, the strangeness of everything, the fact that the children would now have a room on their own, and increased financial responsibility. Often these worries were denied and attention was still focused on the ideal:

> She kept going off into the realms of fitted carpets and completely new furniture. It was difficult to focus on the debts, rent arrears, gas bill, etc.

And not only was the furniture going to improve. The report on this family after rehousing read:

> In this interview she was able to say that she thought the reason she had been so depressed lately was that she had come to realize that no

matter where they lived, even out of the area, Jim wasn't going to change.

Mrs Redhead could go one stage further:

I know its not the flat any longer. It's me.

It was difficult to estimate the strength of the emotional, as opposed to the practical, significance of a new house or flat and, not surprisingly, the timing of moves rarely seemed to be right.

> The Whitesides were able to accept a flat, very adequate for their needs, but very different from the idealized picture they had previously painted of the type of accommodation which, they had said, would be the only thing they would accept. Great as their despair had been in their previous accommodation, their behaviour regressed dramatically just preceding and after the move two streets away. Mrs Whiteside managed to get one child with no symptoms into hospital where, as she was later able to say to the worker, she herself would have preferred to retreat. Although they were fully aware of the number of hours their much-loved deep freeze could be disconnected, they managed to leave it unconnected three days and lost vast supplies of food. Within three days they had a fire but wanted to stay enough to put it out with great efficiency, although they almost got evicted for throwing a burning mattress out of the window. But, as Mrs Whiteside said, she did look to see there was no one below. Debts, previously reduced, leapt to alarming new heights and septicaemia, which had been relegated to the past, broke out again.

We sometimes related the request for a house or the fear of occupying one to the woman's need for recognition as a wife and mother coupled with her fear of taking on this role. The provision of a house (or expensive kitchen fittings) might, it was hoped, soothe her doubts over whether her husband would provide her with the necessary equipment.

> Mrs Capstick refused to return to her husband in the flat following the birth of her baby unless he provided her with a house. He failed to do so and she went into homeless families accommodation instead.

Mrs Capstick had had a sad history since her father had forced her to give up an illegitimate baby when she was sixteen. Her insistence on a house — in the circumstances a request almost as difficult as those made to suitors for the princess in fairy stories — may have been an excuse for getting rid of her husband. It may also have been a desperate request for him, in contrast to her father, to validate her as a mother by providing her with the tools for the job.

Mr Capstick made a different interpretation to the one we have made, complaining that his wife wanted him only as 'a provider' and feeling powerless to satisfy her. His insight was in some ways correct, if limited, for tokens, including houses, have significance for the capacity of the attachment figure to provide as well as the likelihood that the person attached will have their needs met.

Food was a good example of this, and it and its serving assumed a great deal of significance, sometimes conscious, sometimes unconscious.

> Mrs Entwhistle told me: 'We don't talk much when you're not here. When we are getting on, I give him his meal there by the fire. When we are not getting on, I say to him, "It's on the table. Go and get it." '

Mrs Entwhistle laid stress on the significance of food as a recognition of Mr Entwhistle's status in the household and also his need for comfort. This helped to explain why when Mr Entwhistle, product of an impoverished home and a denigrated father, returned home from the pub to find his dinner cold, he went berserk, throwing his meal out of the window into the courtyard for all to see.

Sometimes the fury aroused by food, spoilt or unspoilt, suggested an unconscious significance of which the aggressor was quite unaware. Mrs Arncrow left Mr Arncrow after he had accused her of poisoning him, thrown his lunch in her face and threatened to stab her. Two other clients thought they had been poisoned by their spouse. Others attributed sinister qualities to their spouse's cooking. 'You ought to taste fish and chips when it has been cooked by a Persian.'

'It's all about food', said one member of the project group in a seminar when the worker on another case had described the compulsive eating of the eleven-stone teenage daughter and the scraps of food and faeces lying in the hall of the house. 'Food and shit', another member corrected. The provision of food gave reassurance to self-doubting mothers, just as its rejection as shit undermined them. Mrs Mothersill, in her squalid kitchen, always provided the worker with coffee made with milk. She expressed amazement that he drank it without fear of contamination. Other women clients pressed expensive and sometimes unwelcomed food on their social worker. Mrs Briggs, when feeling comparatively happy, would make potato cakes for her family, probably feeling that in this way she joined kinship with a long line of godly Irish matrons. For a social worker, conscious of debts and impending eviction, the spectacle of the wife spending money on steak for a husband who never returned from the pub to eat it was irritating in the extreme. It was also sad to realize that a yearning to provide something essentially good lay behind her abortive behaviour.

The importance of food was related partly to the histories of some of these clients who when they were children had been literally hungry as well as starved of love. And in the present, the fact that for a man to operate as a satisfactory attachment figure he had also to provide materially for his wife, meant that emotional relationships were tied up with their economic circumstances. Unemployment was not a large problem and only 18 per cent of the core sample had spent any substantial period out of work during the course of the project. Low or erratic wages were a problem for some, but were not obviously associated with debt. Heavy debts, however, were more often incurred by massive expenditure on food, alcohol, tobacco and household appliances on hire purchase. In the Whitesides' leaking flat, due, and more than ready, for demolition, the deep freeze and the refrigerator competed with the open fire between them; the fire always glowed brightly, even in July, with coal 'nicked' from the yard; and the colour television sat on the freezer, the black and white one on the refrigerator.

The need for comfort and its displacement on to objects is implicit in much that we have been saying about houses and food. The tendency to displace in this way may well have been learnt young and be related to techniques of child-rearing. Some of the families seemed to live by token economies, love being dispensed erratically through the provision of sweets and expensive biscuits interspersed with smacks. When the child became adult, the sweets and biscuits were succeeded by yet more expensive cigarettes and alcohol, sometimes interspersed with battering. One problem with the use of such mother substitutes is that the demand for objects, being essentially a demand for something else, becomes inexhaustible.

> Mrs Mothersill said she was ashamed to go into hospital for her confinement as she had no dressing-gown. Mr Mothersill drew on the Provident and got her one. She attacked him for being extravagant and said he ought to have got nappies instead. He returned the dressing-gown and bought nappies. She attacked him for getting expensive nappies.

We suggest that what Mrs Mothersill really wanted was for someone to be with her and allay her unbearable anxiety. By displacing this on to a need for objects, she obscured her true need and, as she was never satisfied, she further undermined her husband's shaky confidence in his ability to act as an attachment figure.

The difficulty seemed to be that the spouses knew at some level the nature or, at least, the intensity of the anxiety that underlay the demand. Its acuteness undermined their ability to handle the situation. Either they attempted to meet the need in full — an impossible task — or alternatively, they evaded it, made promises they did not keep or refused in a highly sadistic way.

The fact that the spouses attempted to meet the anxiety through the provision of tokens rather than through emotional support is important. Tokens, in fact, often provided the fodder for a diversionary tactic, whose purpose was to obscure the underlying need when this was painful and dangerous to acknowledge. The reader will remember that Mr Flimsby claimed he married his wife for money and sex and Mrs Flimsby that she had been too high on Mandrax to know what she was doing. In this respect, the behaviour of the Flimsbys had much in common with that of other clients, who, at whatever apparent cost to their image, wished to emphasize that they stayed together only out of habit and convenience. The wives could say that they wanted washing machines out of their husbands, not the latter's support; the husbands that they only stayed with their wives for the sake of the children or because they did not wish to leave their house; they argued that their wives only wanted them for a meal ticket, while, in practice, they found it extremely difficult to provide emotional support.

This process, whereby the function of the tokens is to obscure an emotional relationship, shades into another whereby it seemed that the client had given up on human relationships and related to objects in a way that others might be expected to relate to people. Some clients seemed to feel genuinely more upset about losing their house than about losing their spouse. Some clients with a drink problem seemed to love alcohol more than anything or anyone. Other workers with whom they were in touch described these clients as demanding and dependent, but it was very important for the clients themselves to assert that they were independent. It was as if they needed to claim to have absolute control over anything on which they had come to depend.

We believe that the central preoccupation of most of the clients in our core sample was the image of an inadequate mother and a deprived child. Whether conscious of this or not, they behaved as if they were likely to play one or other role in this dyad or act as spectator to it. Anything that could be related to this underlying theme produced defensive denial or over-reaction: a child's cry became quickly unbearable; a mother's momentary anger proved that she was as bad as her own or her husband's mother had been.

This picture of the world was self-reinforcing. Difficult features in a relationship suggested to the clients that it was totally bad. Their previous and current experience of rejection inclined them to interpret the mildest slight as a severe rebuff. Their quickness to see only the black side of things explained why, when sex or economic factors were unsatisfactory, they were used to prove that the marriage was equally bad and based purely on sexual or economic need.

The salience of the black and the absence of the grey meant that the only alternative to their current situation was highly idealized. A vicious circle was created. The more they idealized and envied the lot of other people, the less they felt they had left themselves. And the less feasible their solutions became.

8 Patterns of Attachment

*Is it truly possible to be willingly treated
unjustly or is all suffering of injustice involuntary ...? [Or] is all suffering ... sometimes
voluntary, sometimes involuntary?*

Aristotle

The marriages with which we were concerned lasted longer than
anyone might have expected. Over time they had acquired patterns,
systems of behaviour, in which both partners engaged. In the
theoretical terms we outlined in chapter 4, these marriages
contained the partners, but the containment was used defensively.
Although the actual behaviour of the spouses was often polarized
into the two sides of their mutual ambivalence, the fixity of the
patterns of behaviour and the inability to part permanently
suggested an unconscious agreement between the partners to
maintain the *status quo.*

In this chapter we examine some of the more stereotyped interpersonal strategies our clients used. Each strategy was consistent
with the basic rules:

Cast blame on someone else:
Get your own needs met without making yourself vulnerable:
Beware of relationships between three people.

Each partner reinforced the fundamental ambivalence, repelling as
well as attracting. We have classified four strategies.

Coercing
Delinquent depending
Subversive caregiving
Ailing.

119

These categories of behaviour could be applied to the behaviour of a young child who wished to prevent his parents leaving him with a baby-sitter. He could try to compel them to stay at home by hitting them or throwing a temper tantrum (coercing); he might try to ensure their continued presence by his naughtiness (delinquent depending) or by illness — being sick or announcing a headache (ailing); or he might try to bribe them by being good and laying the table for them, a strategy which later may lead to subversive caregiving. Most parents will have known their three-year-olds try these manoeuvres.

We are concerned with the sophisticated adult version of these techniques and the interactive play between them when two or more are employed at the same time. Each technique could elicit one or more of the other three as a response and it was quite possible for the spouses to employ more than one pattern at a time. We consider these techniques under two headings; coercing and subversive caregiving. Delinquent depending and ailing juxtaposed with both.

COERCING

We defined coercive manoeuvres as the use of power with the apparent aim of controlling the behaviour or proximity of the other person. Often the overt aim was to prevent the partner from leaving, but as these manoeuvres usually produced tension and fear, they tended to result in fission as well as fusion — the couples parting in crises as well as staying together out of fear.

One of the simplest coercive techniques was that of blackmail, of which the most dramatic example was a suicide attempt. In approximately four out of ten of the couples in the core sample one or other was known to have made a suicide gesture and the number would rise to five out of ten if one included couples where there were suicidal threats or where the children made suicidal gestures. This figure is likely to be an underestimate, since it often happened that attempts were not taken seriously and threats were even less remarked. As a method of acquiring help, however, the suicide attempt was powerful, controlling and accusatory.

Mrs Redhead blatantly admits she is punishing everyone when she takes an overdose. 'If I do something big, they'll have to look after me.'

While effective in ensuring attention, the suicide attempt tended to arouse guilt and anger in the attachment figures at whom it was directed. Unlike the other techniques we describe, most of the suicide attempts of which we knew in detail were reactions to specific events, particularly actual or threatened desertions, rather than recurrent patterns of behaviour. Mrs Redhead was an exception in that her suicide attempts were recurrent and consciously aimed at eliciting care and concern which she consciously felt she had never had and which, when offered, she unconsciously rejected.

A much more systematic coercive technique was one we came to call 'imprisoning'. As practised by two male clients, one in the core sample and one not, this involved spasmodically locking their wives in the house, sometimes padlocking their wives' clothes, usually keeping the key to the house, holding all the money, doing the shopping, and trying to isolate their wives from other members of the family. They also objected to almost all contacts between their wives and outsiders and to their wives doing a job. The technique aroused fury and desperation in the women exposed to it, who became effectively deprived of any role on which to build their self-esteem. They then fed their husbands' suspicion and provided justification for their imprisonment by stealing, drinking and periodically deserting.

Yet attempts to break the pattern by arranging for one woman to have the housekeeping money and the other to have a key to the house were sabotaged by the women themselves. The first drank — or, at least, lost in suspicious circumstances — the money destined for food; the second refused the offered key. Each woman displayed considerable anxiety about meeting people outside the house and when they left home, which they periodically did, they proved unable to manage for any extended period of time. Their husbands' imprisoning of them, however much they complained about it, also provided a convenient excuse.

The husbands, apparently so keen on keeping their wives with them, were, in fact, also ambivalent. Both on occasions locked their wives out as well as in. One would throw his wife out of the house telling her not to come back. After she had got to the bottom of the block of flats, he would run after her and pull her back. The other confessed to a wish to see his wife in a genuine prison.

Other wives were imprisoned less obviously by husbands who

objected to their having any contacts, either male or female, outside the house. The objections reinforced the women's agoraphobic tendencies which were, in any case, accentuated by stress. A vicious circle resulted; as tension mounted, so that it became more important for the women to contact outside help, they were less able to leave the house to seek it. Nor did their fear of going out diminish their resentment or dislike of their homes.

> Mrs Redhead said that she had tried to go out, but felt panicked trying to get back home. Either in or out was unacceptable, and I felt her untenable position may have contributed to yet another suicide attempt.

Battering was a common coercive technique. Two out of three of the core sample marriages were known to have involved some degree of violence and this is no doubt an underestimate. Usually, the violence was from men to women, although one woman probably broke her husband's arm and another produced detailed plans for murdering hers. Occasionally, the violence resulted in cracked bones, twisted noses and cuts which needed stitching. Within the course of the project none of the sample was detained in hospital as a result of the violence. The fear was much more about what might happen than about what did. In a few marriages, however, violence was without doubt potentially serious and quite frequently reported.

In discussing violence it is useful to examine why certain men used violence as a technique, why they used it at the time they did and the underlying dynamic it served. Culture and temperament both played a part in the selection of violence as a method of getting their own way. One man claimed a cultural justification for hitting his wife 'when she stepped out of line', contrasting his behaviour with that of others who beat up their wives 'for the fun of it'. Another used family tradition as an explanation, saying that in his family asking was always done with fists; another invoked the concept of temperament, saying that he was subject to sudden attacks of rage in which the world would go blank in front of him and he would lash out. Drink played an important part in marital violence. Although some violent husbands did not drink at all, some were only violent when drunk and others were more seriously violent or more likely to be violent when drunk.

Apparently random attacks were probably more feared than others. For example, Mr Stockdale did not understand why he attacked his wife. The unpredictability and inexplicability of his attacks added to *his* terror as well, no doubt, as to hers. Similar to many clients in the core sample, but more able to consider his behaviour, he helps in our understanding of the others.

Mr Stockdale sought contact with a social worker, previously having refused to see one when his wife applied for help. She was living separately, had just had her first baby and was in continued contact with another social worker.

Despite having asked for the interview, he found it difficult to begin or know what he wanted to discuss, but eventually he talked of his fear of his violence which he felt unwarranted and akin to madness. He went into some detail of his history, especially referring to his horror, guilt and remorse over a murder in which he had been involved as an accessory, and to his harsh, unsympathetic upbringing in a large working-class family where his father, quarrelling violently with his mother, was often drunk. His father died when he was fourteen.

After leaving school he could not settle, wandered from city to city, getting into bad company, and eventually went to Borstal where his crime gave him a reputation for toughness and ruthlessness which he felt compelled to live up to, although at the same time hating it and himself.

His life seemed to contain little kindness and gentleness except from a recent landlord. Mr Stockdale loved his wife and found his violence towards her quite inexplicable.

In subsequent interviews some of the sources of his rage were exposed and were found in his childhood struggles for love within the alternately violent and apathetic environment of his home. His failure to get love had led to a basic depression against which his own violence and anger seemed to be a defence. It was this link between violence and depression which made sense to him and relieved his anxiety that his violent behaviour was inexplicable and a frightening madness which had no meaning.

This enabled him to reassess himself and take a job where he was in charge and responsible for ensuring that others were properly trained. He began to meet his wife regularly, to take her and the baby out, to press for her to take him back and withdraw divorce proceedings.

The link between violence and depression which made sense to Mr Stockdale can be expressed in terms of a defensive reaction to loss, or threat of loss, of an attachment figure. As Bowlby put it, a child separated from his parents displays 'sometimes the protest of hope, sometimes the protest of despair'. Rather than acknowledge his earlier powerlessness as a child and face the sadness of what he felt he had never had or had lost, he could only continue to express his protest through the means he had learnt from his parents.

We do not know from the record what aspect of his wife's behaviour felt rejecting to Mr Stockdale but, in view of our earlier analysis of the difficulty of threesomes, it is, perhaps, not surprising that the break-up of the marriage was precipitated by the expected birth. With his background, Mr Stockdale may have been doubtful about his ability to stand up to the 'pressure' his wife put on him to be a good husband and father. Violence in such cases could be a frantic denial of helplessness or arise from a fear of emasculation — as another violent man put it, 'of being a Boeing with no engine'.

In the core sample pressure to reform or to meet needs was a common precipitant of physical attacks, as when the wife upbraided the husband on his return from the pub or demanded something he felt unable to provide.

In such cases violence was both a method of trying to push away need and a method of asserting a stereotyped status. One man, woken by his wife from a drunken sleep, leapt up shouting, 'I'm not going to be dictated to by you', and attacked her with a chair leg. His words, inexplicable in the immediate circumstances, probably arose from a deep sense of the inadequacy of men and the dominance of women, a dominance which other parts of his behaviour in fact encouraged.

The wives in the core sample who were frequently involved with violence often knew what precipitated their husband's attacks. This did not necessarily mean that they wished to give up some of their own behaviour or their husband. An entry in one record reads:

We have now voiced that Mr Calder will probably never change and she has either to live with it (which will involve misery or change in herself) or separate. She does not favour the latter as Jim has threatened to 'get her' if she resorts to separation.

This was said with a certain degree of triumph. She stresses that he needs her too, so she could not go. She does not accept that she needs him except for the rare times he is a good companion. She does not see that she seems to need a weak husband, so that she can appear the strong one.

A later entry reads:

There followed more descriptions of their rows and then Mrs Calder said 'I know I'll come out on top. If I win I'll stay on top. If he gets nasty, I'll punch him back.'

As with this couple, violence was sometimes sexually tinged and exciting, and may in a peculiar way have been valued for itself. It would be rash, however, to suggest that many women in the core sample actually wanted to be hit. Those who knew the ways in which they provoked their husbands might confess to 'putting on pressure', 'a need for attention' or 'a wish to get even', but they did not enjoy the battering that resulted from these techniques. They willed the means rather than the end. A wife who screamed at her husband, in effect continually calling him useless, made it difficult for him to escape the dilemma between despair and protest. If assertion on the husband's part produced yet more vigorous verbal attacks on the part of the wife, violence was a common result. In this way the behaviour of the wife reinforced the choice outlined by Mr Stockdale — depression, or violence as a defence against that depression.

Once violence had occurred the wife might use it to further her own ends; for example, to blacken the husband before the children, or to increase her control over her husband through the introduction of external agencies.

External agencies are, of course, involved in sanctioning the ending of marriages. Their use in regulating ongoing marital wars is less well documented. However, spouses, in addition to attempting to use social workers, probation officers, marriage guidance counsellors and the like as power to their elbows, may also use legal devices of calling the police, getting injunctions, or invoking various types of matrimonial order short of divorce. They can also, if exceptionally, use medical methods, arranging for a spouse to be put into hospital and thus achieving the separation without the necessity for a divorce. A variant of this is the case of Mr and Mrs Waterhouse.

> This case began with a letter to the social services from a consultant psychiatrist describing a visit he had made to Mr and Mrs Waterhouse (where he had been introduced to Mrs Waterhouse by Mr Waterhouse as an officer of the social security department) and saying that he thought that Mrs Waterhouse should be admitted to hospital under a Section. This was based upon Mr Waterhouse's account of her and an angry, suspicious exchange with Mrs Waterhouse, who caught him talking privately with her husband on the landing. A visit from a social worker and another psychiatrist in response to this letter did not confirm that Mrs Waterhouse was in need of treatment and, indeed, this psychiatrist thought that it was Mr Waterhouse himself who ought to be treated. He made no attempt to propose that Mr Waterhouse should be admitted. However, Mr Waterhouse wrote angrily and lengthily to the social services to complain about this, saying how afraid he was of his wife and how mad she was as any one of a large number of people, named in the letter, would testify. It was possible to see what it was that led the second psychiatrist to believe that Mr Waterhouse was sick.

The irony of this example is that it later emerged that Mr and Mrs Waterhouse were already divorced and there was no actual necessity for him to stay with her. When the worker commented on their difficulty of separating, Mr Waterhouse said, 'I suppose I'm too soft-hearted.' In this example, coercing becomes compulsive caregiving as well.

SUBVERSIVE CAREGIVING

We defined caregiving as subversive when the recipient was kept in an infantile position in order to keep him attached. It undermined his confidence in his ability to act for himself. It is, of course, possible to do this by accident and probably most looking-after carries with it the risk that the person receiving care will simply lie back content to let others do things for him. The undermining inherent in subversive caregiving was revealed by such things as a reluctance to hear the recipient's protestations of competence, a tendency to treat the recipient (child or adult) as much younger than he or she was, and sometimes by behaviour which reinforced the illness from which the recipient was supposed to be suffering, encouraged delinquency or courted dependence.

A number of these features are illustrated by Mr and Mrs Beattie. Mrs Beattie was a middle-aged competent woman, apparently tyrannized by the epileptic attacks and suicidal gestures of Mr Beattie. She complained that she could not have her friends in the house because they upset him and that the burden of his need for her and the anxiety of looking after him was such that a feeling of claustrophobia came over her as she approached her front door on return from work. Yet, when Mr Beattie wanted to talk to the social worker, she prevented him from doing so; she cried when he went into hospital; for some time she tried to prevent him from taking a holiday on his own. The following extract is taken from the report of the first interview.

Mr Beattie produced a brochure of the place to which his firm was going to move and showed it to me. Mrs Beattie told him not to be silly; he was too ill to work there. She continued to speak for him - portraying him as incompetent and bad-tempered. She said the sort of job he could get would be fit only for drug addicts. A better job would be bad for his brain and make him bad-tempered.

At this point Mr Beattie went out into the kitchen and started swearing at Esta. Mrs Beattie went out and told him to shut up. She came back and complained about him to me. Things were hopeless, she said; wherever she went, he would come with her. (This recalled an earlier remark when Mr Beattie said he would 'tag along' and Mrs Beattie had said with a smile of triumph, 'Yes, he will tag along allright.')

Mr Beattie then came in and showed me his patent medicines and shambled out again. Mrs Beattie said he was upset because I was there. She was anxious for me not to see him again.

This example illustrates the burden and anxiety characteristic of subversive caregiving together with the reluctance to acknowledge the efforts at independence displayed by Mr Beattie as, for example, his wish to work. This was combined on other occasions with a genuine concern about Mr Beattie's predicament and interacted with Mr Beattie's ambivalence about whether he wished to be employee or patient. (His offering of the medicine bottles to the social worker demonstrated one side of his own ambivalence.)

The subversive caregiving often covered the denied dependency of the caregiver. By making the most of the ills in the other, they vicariously looked after the feelings of deprivation in themselves. The negative aspects of subversive caregiving were most strongly revealed in the cases in which one spouse was looking after an alcoholic partner and seemed intent on feeding the spouse with drink. Mr Briggs who did this was unable to explain his behaviour except by saying that he had to keep the peace and it was the only way he could keep his wife. Mrs Frizington was essential to her husband because when he was drunk he would sometimes vomit in his sleep; but for her intervention he might have died. Later he came off the drink, but one evening told his wife he was worried about his recent promotion at work. She replied, 'Why don't you take a drink then?', and he began again. In both these cases alcohol was offered as a token in lieu of the ability to offer direct emotional support.

Some clients stuffed food into others and themselves as part of a general need to offer care irrespective of whether this was acceptable to the recipient. In her first interview with a social worker, Mrs Sowerby apologized for being so fat. From the age of nine to fourteen she had cooked for her own large orphaned family. More recently she had spent much time coaxing a severely disturbed child to eat, with excellent results. In one interview, however, she spoke of how deeply offended she had been when she discovered that meals she had proffered to a neighbour had all been put in the dustbin. In her turn, she complained that her husband was imprisoning her, not by coercion, but by care. She explained how she felt:

> 'Go away! You are suffocating me!' She thought this happened because she had been too dependent on him and that this dependence was reciprocated by her husband, who was very worried if she were ever late and very jealous if he ever saw her talking to somebody else. As a result of this she felt very unsure of her own identity and she had to protect this by not telling her husband how she felt. She thought that all this was now much better and she had been able to say to her husband that he was 'killing' her 'with love'.

Subversive caregiving was sometimes countered by delinquent dependence. The behaviour in delinquent dependence was overtly quite independent. The man, for example, went to the pub where he fraternized till late at night, sometimes justifying this behaviour on the grounds of his wife's impossibility or the fact that in his particular employment jobs were only obtained in this way. The male society there usually supported his attitude to his wife. For example:

> I called at the Mothersills and found Mrs Mothersill and the children in a state because there was no food and no money for the weekend. Mr Mothersill was apparently in the pub and I set off thither to remind him of his responsibilities. Mr Mothersill received me with some guilt and hostility and, calling me by my Christian name, introduced me to a West Indian who at once bought me a drink. This friend then went on with his story of how he had returned home at 4.00 a.m. on the previous morning and his girlfriend, suspecting he had been out with a woman, had tried to cut off his thumb. 'You wicked fellow, how could you?', said Mr Mothersill looking at me.

Alongside this bravado were expressions of dependence. Some men claimed they could only get attention from their wives when drunk and one said that he only knew that his wife cared for him because she 'reared up on him' when he had had too much to drink. Another said that when depressed he had taken to drinking and on return to throwing beer cans in the yard; he hoped his wife would 'come after him with the rolling-pin'. (In fact, she assumed he had another woman and reacted accordingly.) Mr Entwhistle, a violent and formidable man, would often return home with a cut hand, allegedly having been hurt in a fight. Mrs Entwhistle believed he cut himself and that this was the only way he could ask for sympathy from her.

In relation to subversive caregiving, delinquent dependence allowed the delinquent to deny his need for his wife for so long as his delinquent behaviour ensured her attempts to enfold him. He could then attack her for her possessiveness which, in fact, his behaviour encouraged. In some cases the wife had obtained vicarious delight from the husband's delinquency, but this delight was usually a thing of the past. Mrs Beattie felt that she had got her 'independent spirit' from Mr Beattie who, before his illness, was supposed to have been quite a 'big time' criminal. Some of the wives appeared to have subsidized their husbands' drinking before marriage and taken pleasure in going about with a 'tearaway'.

Illness and helplessness could also be a counterpart to subversive caregiving. Illness was common in the core sample and contributed to the clients' stresses, as well, no doubt, as arising from them. In some cases, it was also used to further the ill person's end and may have been feigned or exaggerated. Mr Doggart, for example, was able to convince a doctor of his blindness in his bid to keep Mrs Doggart looking after him. She was quite clear that he could see when he wanted to.

When the illness was genuine, as it was with Mr Beattie, it usually aroused ambivalence. On the one hand, the ill person was angered by the disability and wished to deny it. On the other hand he wished to be taken care of. If these spouses could encourage subversive caregiving, it enabled them to deny their need for support and consciously hold in their mind only one side of the ambivalence — their anger at being looked after — while their spouse acted out the other. Mr Beattie said that his wife 'worried too much'. In most people's view she did, but probably he would have been angry if she had not.

INTERACTIVE PATTERNS AND FAMILY STRUCTURE

These interactive patterns repeat the themes of earlier chapters. The first of these is that of blame, particularly in the presentation of the other as a bad attachment figure. The subversive caregiver, the suicidal spouse, the battered wife, the righteous invoker of mental health sections, and the imprisoner of the errant mother could all argue that their partners were incapable of undertaking the responsibilities of looking after them or were wilfully negligent in doing so. The delinquent dependent, battering, imprisoned or sectioned spouses had a harder job in this respect but usually claimed that their partner had driven them into any dereliction of duty.

Secondly, there was the denial of dependence and its projection on to someone else. Mr Waterhouse could claim that he was soft-hearted, looking after his needy spouse. Mrs Waterhouse was adamant that she was not married to Mr Waterhouse and wanted nothing to do with him and yet remained in the flat. The imprisoned spouses claimed that they were kept with their husbands against their will; the subversive caregivers and sometimes the battered wives that they were trapped by their husband's needs; the imprisoning and battering husbands that they were caring for needy spouses and fighting off screaming demands. The delinquent dependent husbands could claim that they had no need of their wives and only wished that they would leave them alone; the battered wives that they stayed only out of fear.

The third theme relates to the undermining of parental roles and the maintenance of the underlying shared fantasy that there could be only one good parent in the family. The subversive caregivers, the suicidal or battered wives, the imprisoners and the invokers of mental health sections could all point to their spouses' uselessness, cruelty or madness and thus attempt to alienate the children from the spouse and more firmly attach them to themselves. In this way the clients tried to deal with their fear of being the odd one out.

These themes were often expressed in two types of family structure which we called 'Caliban and the Virgin' and 'The Woodcutter and the Stepmother'. In the former the wife was the one good parent, in the latter the husband. In some marriages there was a dispute about which structure applied, but the belief that there was room for only one good parent remained.

In part this segmental structure may be a cultural inheritance. The bulk of the core sample came from Irish, Middle-Eastern, West Indian or London working-class backgrounds. In all these cultures, wives are traditionally supposed to draw much of their support from their mothers, and some of our clients looked back to an idealized matrifocal society. Parental rejection, emigration and rehousing had cut our clients' contact with their mothers. The feminine support available was now non-existent or a pale shadow of what it was supposed to have been. To all intents and purposes, they were now on their own with their husbands.

The segmental structure provided a convenient base for the use of the defences of denial, splitting and projection which were employed in the techniques we have described, and it fitted the bleak model of relationships which the clients carried within them.

Finally, the techniques we have described and illustrated in this chapter all reflect the ambivalence of whether to split up or stay together. Coercive techniques expelled as well as imprisoned, and caregiving techniques were usually accompanied by fury at the person to whom care was given. As we have shown, this ambivalence could be disguised by the fact that each could accuse the other of being the dependent one. We suggest that the mutual fantasies in these marriages were mainly centred on the dangers of being alone, the dangers of being attached and the dangers of more than one person being attached to another.

In concluding this part of the book, we wish to emphasize that the behaviour we have described in the last four chapters is not peculiar to our core sample, nor to our whole sample. The germs of it apply to us all. Who can claim that they have not at times traded on their own helplessness, been consumed with distrust, denied their need for attachment, over-controlled in their insecurity, and blamed others for their own inadequacies? Who at times has not been overcome by ambivalence, envy or jealousy? Who has not by a variety of means tried to coerce or manipulate an attachment figure into staying nearby?

The differences between these clients and others is the crudity and lack of flexibility in their use of the various strategies we all use and the degree of separation anxiety which lay behind many of their actions.

We have described some of the fears that bound the core sample clients in their marriages and the attachment difficulties and interpersonal strategies which made family life so difficult for them. We believe that the essence of the model on which most of the core sample operated was an unconscious belief that relationships could only be satisfying if they carried no risk, had no imperfection and no ending; such a relationship would only be possible if they could control the behaviour of another and make them into an illusory figure, ever reliable, ever loving, and never angry or attending to the needs of others when they themselves required help.

In the next part of the book we look at what happened to us and other imperfect social workers who, like all human beings, were prey to some of these fears (particularly at times of tiredness and stress), when the clients tried to control us and get us to fit into their model.

PART THREE

The Clients and
The Workers

There was a longer silence. Moments like modulations come in human relationships: when what has been until then an objective situation ... one it is sufficient merely to classify under some general heading (man with alcoholic problems, woman with unfortunate past, and so on) becomes subjective; becomes unique; becomes by empathy instantaneously shared rather than observed. Such a metamorphosis took place in Charles' mind as he stared at the bowed head of the sinner before him. Like most of us when such moments come — who has not been embraced by a drunk? — he sought for a hasty though diplomatic restoration of the status quo.

He followed her with his eyes. And perhaps he did at last begin to grasp her mystery. Some terrible perversion of human sexual destiny had begun; he was no more than a footsoldier, a pawn in a far vaster battle; and like all battles it was not about love, but about possession and territory. He saw deeper: it was not that she hated men, but that her manoeuvres were simply part of her armoury, mere instruments to a greater end. He saw deeper still: that her supposed present happiness was another lie. In her central being she suffered still, in the same old way; and that was the mystery she was truly and finally afraid he might discover.

John Fowles

133

9 Suckers or Bastards

Who, with herself, or others, from her birth
Finds all her life one warfare upon earth:
Shines, in exposing Knaves, and painting Fools,
Yet is, whate'er she hates and ridicules.

Who breaks with her, provokes Revenge from Hell,
But he's a bolder man who dares be well:

Alexander Pope

'Fuck off,' said Mr Ingledow. I decided to match the deed to the word and left feeling there was little that could be done to help him.

This is a fairly natural reaction to a client's compulsive independence, as is 'Oh, not her again', said on the fourth telephone call from one client in one day in respect of that client's anxious attachment.

These are conscious responses which Winnicott termed the 'objective countertransference' — the worker's love and hate reactions to the actual personality and behaviour of the client.[1]

At other times the behaviour of the worker is an unconscious reaction to the felt, but not understood, behaviour of the client who can convey an emotional message which is discordant with what he has said or done. Thus a worker may leave an interview with a feeling of panic or doom for which there is no apparent justification. Or, with no conscious connection with the interview, the feeling can creep up on him later in the day.

Sometimes the client's effect on the worker seems consciously or unconsciously intended.

[1] Winnicott, D. (1949), 'Hate in the Countertransference' *Internat. J. Psycho-Anal.* 30.

135

And the whole way Mrs Orton deals with every problem is to make sure that nobody knows, or to enlist you as the only person who does, so you are always left in a terrible web of not knowing what to say to whom and, therefore, what you can say and what you can't.

Mrs Orton was a client with teenage children, several of whom were in trouble. The worker had to muster all his strength not to get taken over and manipulated when she tried to treat him as she did them. From a large leather armchair she portrayed herself as a hardworking, virtuous mother, a self-righteous martyr and a controlling virago. In discussing the case in one of the project seminars, the worker referred to his anger at her controlling manoeuvres, his fear of her and, if her defence broke, his apprehension of 'drowning in a well of need' and of 'being trapped beneath her madness'. This is a useful indication of what her husband, lover and children may have felt in relation to her and of the strength of her fear of her own madness.

At other times the client's effect on other people seemed the accidental, rather than the intended, consequence of their way of behaving. 'And is the LEB batty?', asked a worker when the Whitesides' confusion over their electricity debts seemed to affect even the clerks in the London accounting office. Electricity accounts, often difficult to understand at the best of times, became completely nonsensical to the worker when the Whitesides' name was on the top of them. And the worker later discovered that they were trying hard to pay off debts which had not been theirs in the first place. Even the rating office was charging them for a flat in which they had not lived. It was hard to see that this state of affairs was in any sense what the clients wanted, consonant though it was with the chaos of their inner worlds.

In this and the following two chapters we deal with conscious and unconscious, intended and unintended, effects on the caseworkers. The reader will remember our clients' attempts to create a predictable world and how their behaviour invited a predictable response, but not the one they wanted. In terms of our clinical theory, we are not saying that a particular piece of disturbed behaviour must produce a particular response, only that when the behaviour is defensive it tempts the worker to use a defensive response as an avoidance of the underlying pain and anxiety. Social workers have a limit to the amount of pain that they can bear. In many social work situations this factor does not detract from their work; they are not always acting as caseworkers and the efficient and fair delivery of services may be impeded by close personal relationships. However, even when wishing to effect change in behaviour, there are times when, not surprisingly, they join with the clients in defensive manoeuvres. At times they are manipulated by a controlling and demanding client despite their better sense. At times they are caught in a dilemma between what they believe to be a more therapeutic approach and their statutory obligations and other demands upon them. And, at times, the pressure from spoken or unconscious anxiety in the client and in themselves may seduce them into defensive behaviour of a reciprocal nature to that of the client.

The fact that the worker is invited to behave in ways that others in the client's circle have traditionally done has implications for the casework. It means that the worker can confirm the client in his strategies and views of the world. Or, having got caught up in the system and from his experience understood a little more of the power of what he has been subjected to, he can consciously try to alter his part of the transaction and help the client to change his.

The following example illustrates a determined attempt to fit the worker into the client's pre-existing picture of the world, in itself improbably based. When the worker, with his wish to care and his powers of control, entered this world, he was no more likely to be trusted than any other person representing these attributes, and perhaps even less so, because of the social and legislative authority invested in his role.

The case was not one in the sample, but the IMS worker will not forget for a long time the one afternoon when he met Mrs Yates.

She was an Irishwoman, separated from her husband and living in homeless families accommodation. Several offers of permanent accommodation had been made to her which she had declined on various grounds. She was very disgruntled and claimed that she and her children were not being properly treated by the department. She had a very explosive temper which her worker found, to put it mildly, difficult.

My only contact with Mrs Yates was on one rather traumatic Friday when she visited the office. My curiosity was aroused by hearing a woman's voice repeatedly screaming 'fuck off' in a very distressing and disturbing way. I went to see what was happening and discovered Mrs Yates kneeling on the floor of the entrance hall with a child in front of her whose shoe and sock had been removed. Mrs Yates was screaming loudly, refusing all assistance and claiming that a fire-extinguisher which had either fallen off the wall or been knocked by the child might have killed him, although he was obviously unhurt. She continued to refuse all assistance, although she continued to shout obscenities and demand that the police and ambulance be sent for.

The area officer arrived and tried to cope with Mrs Yates, and I joined to try and comfort the child. Nothing could be done to quieten Mrs Yates and, in fact, she became more and more enraged, eventually left the child, and rampaged round the office attempting to pull cupboards over and do other damage. She attempted to smash a telephone and we restrained her and she fell to the floor weeping helplessly. She eventually got up and stood weeping and complaining of the awfulness of her life, and I made one or two comments to her about her fear of her own rage and her wish to kill people, us in particular. She gave some sign of hearing and became calmer, although she still refused any comfort like the offer of a cup of tea. She eventually became calm enough to leave, but did so threatening vengeance on all our heads.

In this incident much has already been revealed about the probable world of Mrs Yates. Her life was not only awful, but also apparently unsafe. She did not see the fire-extinguisher which had fallen or been knocked off the wall as a life-preserver, but rather as the psychological equivalent of a grenade, hung up on purpose by the department to injure its clients. In this transaction, Mrs Yates saw herself as blameless and powerless and the department as harmful and to blame. She faced the dilemma of the helpless and untrusting which we discussed in chapter 6. The alternative view held by the workers, however, was that Mrs Yates was the one who was powerful and dangerous to her children.

This was not the end of the incident. Later in the afternoon Mrs Yates returned and demanded money for the weekend. It had been decided that no supplementation of her social security money would be made on this occasion although it had been in the past. It was known she spent large sums of money on long-distance telephone calls and that this was why she could not make ends meet.

Mrs Yates did not like our refusal and so demanded that we took the two children into care. However, at the same time she became hysterical about what it would mean to them and insisted that any place they might be taken to would be terrible and that they would be ill-treated. She made it impossible for the request to be proceeded with and, while demanding that we took the children from her, clung to them tightly and they to her, so that in order to remove them we would have had to fight her. We refused to do this and insisted that she either hand them over calmly or take them away with her. By this time they were thoroughly distressed, pleading with her to take them away, but she was quite deaf to their pleas.

There then followed a long argument, with her alternately demanding money to see her through the weekend or that we take the children from her. The area officer and I needed each other for support to withstand the fury and obstinacy with which we were confronted. In desperation I asked Mrs Yates why she had to make us behave like such bastards towards her. She screamed that we were bastards and rather wearily I agreed that maybe we were. Almost at once she began to soften and decided to leave with the children. She left us drained and shattered.

The workers spent an anxious weekend. They wondered whether they had done right and they were concerned lest the children had been put at risk. A further offer of permanent housing came through a week later and, to the workers' surprise, was accepted by Mrs Yates without question.

In this example, Mrs Yates displayed a number of psychological characteristics which we have described in part two. Firstly, she showed the social workers her difficulty in acting as an attachment figure to her children, which, together with her homelessness, constituted her ticket of entry to the department. This allowed her to play a role analogous to that of the delinquent dependent, since the more mothering difficulties she displayed the harder it became for the social worker to leave her alone. She also attempted to coerce the social workers by threatening to put her children into care if she did not get what she wanted.

Mrs Yates employed on the social workers the tactics we have already described spouses employing on each other and which, one may guess, she employed on her own spouse when he was around. It is not just that Mrs Yates displayed ambivalence. She also involved the social workers in it, since each time they moved to accept one of her requests, she countermanded it. While displaying her helplessness, she also displayed her distrust in a very controlling way by threatening the social workers with the police and rejecting the help they tried to offer. While her crying betokened a need for emotional support, she claimed vigorously that her needs were for money and refused all sympathy.

In keeping with our previous analysis, Mrs Yates' behaviour invited two possible destructive responses: it would have been easy to batter her back, perhaps even snatching her children from her, thus invalidating her as a mother; alternatively, it would have been easy to give in to her and keep her dependent on the social services by providing her with small sums of money which, in contrast to the offer of a house, would have been quite incommensurate with the realities of her material situation and her underlying emotional needs. How easy it would have been for Mrs Yates to split the workers, one made into the bastard — the withholder; one into the sucker — the giver and giving in. It is unlikely that one worker on his own and without comparable seniority could have resisted this demand, particularly as there were young children involved. It is not surprising that both workers were left drained and exhausted, anxious and presumably doubtful of their efficacy. (It would be interesting to know how far these feelings correspond to those of her husband.)

The potential split reflects institutional as well as personal factors. The workers were struggling to combine two different aspects of their role. On the one hand, they attempted to show concern for Mrs Yates in a way that she could accept. On the other hand, they tried to control her physically at one stage in the afternoon, but primarily through setting limits to her demands. They also considered, but rejected, a direct use of power — that of taking her children away from her by force.

This conflict, which is inherent in the role of the social worker, interacts with the clients' splitting between love and anger described in part two. The effect of this interaction is to make it difficult for the workers to handle consistently their wish to care and their powers of control. The next two chapters are concerned with this dilemma.

10 The Problems of Limits

Johannes: *See Catherine comes! To her, to her,*
Let each his several miseries refer;
She shall decide whose woes are least or worst,
And which, as growler, shall rank last or first.

Edward Lear

Not surprisingly, the disturbed attachment behaviour of our core sample clients, expressing as it did so much need and ambivalence, stimulated conflicting feelings in the social workers. The wish to help and the fear of being overwhelmed were simultaneously aroused.

This chapter is about this ambivalence. It is also, necessarily, about limits, both those imposed by the clients' denial of need and those used by the workers consciously or, more often, unconsciously when the clients' demands were felt to be limitless. We deal with three different sorts of situations; those where the clients avowed need; those where they denied it; and those where they were overtly ambivalent about it.

THE BURDEN OF ANXIOUS ATTACHMENT

'If I came to you whenever I had problems, I'd be with you all day', said Mrs Izatt.

Mrs Parkin called by appointment carrying a hot water bottle. She told me she nearly fainted with pain from her ulcer while coming to see me. I am not sure whether this was meant to show how much she wanted to see me, or how guilty I ought to feel.

Both these examples contain an explicit appeal for help and an implicit complaint that the social work help would not be enough (to be a substitute for a mother in one case and prevent pain from an ulcer in the other). Both approaches were likely to arouse a wish to help, perhaps even to the impossible degree suggested by the complaint. They were also likely to arouse conscious or unconscious anger at being put in an impossible situation.

The problems facing the predeterminedly helpful social worker when confronted with feelings of helplessness are well known and have been discussed in the literature.

> Most caseworkers set out to be helpful and see themselves in a good parental role *vis-à-vis* their client ... but there is a danger, especially for the beginner, to have to *prove* to the client (and in the back of her mind, to herself), that she is helpful. ...[1]

The extent of the pressure to be helpful and the degree to which it is reinforced by the office culture is illustrated by the following example. One of the IMS workers, 'on cover' one day, took a telephone call from a girl who announced she was pregnant and asked what she should do about it as the date of confinement was fairly imminent and no hospital bed had been booked. She mentioned her probation officer and the worker suggested that it would be more appropriate at this stage if she talked to her about her problems. Within the hearing of a trainee she discussed the pros and cons of this and at the end of the conversation advised the girl to get in touch with the officer herself. This produced an angry response in the trainee who felt it was proper and appropriate to telephone the officer on behalf of the client and with great efficiency immediately did so.

The wish to care for and keep the client young may be encouraged by statutory responsibility.

> Miss Skelton had been in the care of the council since the age of fourteen. At fifteen she became pregnant and decided to keep the baby. She rejected the young putative father and chose to live with an older man who was accepted with her into homeless families accommodation. The two sides of this girl's mixed feelings about whether she was child or adult, typical of most adolescents, were spoken for her: the staff at the college she attended thought she was

[1] Salzberger-Wittenberg, I. (1970), *Psycho-Analytic Insight and Relationships* (Routledge & Kegan Paul).

too young to care for the baby; the staff of the day nursery that she should accept her responsibilities as a mother. Unlike social security, the social work division seemed to see her less as a wife than as a child and, although her cohabitee was earning well, continued to furnish her with an allowance of £10 per week. When the couple were housed, the area officer signed the tenancy agreement.

We can imagine Miss Skelton evoking these polarized responses from the different workers. With the social services one who represented the parental role (Miss Skelton was still a child in care), she wanted to be taken out to tea as she had been in the past, but did not want to introduce her cohabitee, with whom there were problems. The worker became uneasy about the role assigned to her and tried to work with Miss Skelton to bring the child and adult aspects of her personality into closer relationship. When she attempted to arrange interviews with her and her cohabitee on their marital problems, she was firmly rejected.

Sometimes the wish to care is expressed by small compulsive actions for which the client is not asking. At one stage in the IMS worker's fitful contact with Mr Flimsby the following incident occurred.

Mr Flimsby called again with the usual string of bewildering demands, leaving me uneasy and unsure. When he announced that he wanted to telephone, I offered him 10p with which to make the call. He was furious.

In this case the worker had been having a struggle to remain in touch with Mr Flimsby and to sustain within himself a feeling that his efforts were in some way helpful.

The referrer of the depressed and very fat Mrs Sowerby, who loved cooking for her husband and neighbours, suggested that she should be introduced to a Sunday luncheon club. Just as Mrs Sowerby could not notice when her neighbours did not want her good food, so too the referrer could not see that food was unlikely to be the answer to her problems or that Sunday was a time Mrs Sowerby normally spent with her husband. We may wonder, however, whether Mrs Sowerby, in complaining of her depression and lack of identity, had unconsciously complained of a feeling of emptiness in herself and asked to be 'filled up' with something. It may have been this to which the referrer responded.

Unconscious subversive caregiving of this nature may have several origins. The worker's need to be helpful is often accentuated by clients like Mr Flimsby and Mrs Sowerby who project their own feelings of helplessness on to the worker. The client tries to get the worker to appreciate the impossibility of his plight by asking him to do something about it. The worker reacts by trying to prove his own competence and, by doing something which invariably fails or is irrelevant, is made to feel inadequate. Both client and worker behave as if a solution were possible to a problem which, as it is stated, is insoluble.

One worker put in a great deal of time, effort and loving care with Mr and Mrs Redhead after they were referred for rent arrears. It emerged that there were severe problems with the two teenage children. As these receded, the problem came back to roost with the parents. The debts increased, the house became increasingly shabby, a sexual problem came to the fore and Mrs Redhead's suicide gestures, after which she sometimes walked to the hospital in her nightdress, became more frequent.

The worker presented the case to the project group after a new crisis when Mrs Redhead had again threatened suicide. He had responded and visited immediately, and then three days later she had actually taken the overdose a few hours before her next and appointed visit. He was 'useless', he reported. The group was at first silent and overwhelmed by the worker's description. Then, in the ensuing discussion, Mrs Redhead's problems took over and those of Mr Redhead got lost. No one had ever loved her, Mrs Redhead had proclaimed, although her mother had, on her deathbed, told her she loved her. Was the worker expected to love her and love her only to have all his efforts rejected? Or did knowing that someone cared mean that person would immediately die? What was his role if not meeting her constant demand for attention? The group members became very angry, but it did not feel as if their anger could be used effectively, as Mr Redhead could not use his. It was tempting for the meeting to go on and on beyond its time-limit, just as Mrs Redhead went on and on, with nothing getting resolved.

The worker left the group feeling that his needs had not been met. The members had become increasingly angry with Mrs Redhead's response to his efforts and yet had offered nothing better to take their place. He felt deprived of his caring role. This was a useful reflection and gave an indication of Mrs Redhead's feelings that if you did not get what you wanted there and then, there was nothing left or nothing worth having. If so overwhelmed by trying to help, was it better to give up completely? The task of the worker and the group was to continue to struggle with their own ambivalence between these two extremes and find some mean which did not collude with the phantasy of 'all or nothing'.

The worker's sense of burden in response to the demand for 'all' can be reinforced by clients' reactions to breaks in contacts. When the worker has become important to the clients, holidays often signalled a crisis. Mr and Mrs Gilcrux were referred by the day nursery after they had been seen too often weaving a drunken course across the road when collecting Beryl, aged four. Within six weeks of the offer of a long-term contract, Mrs Gilcrux was able to curtail her intake of cider, but she was again reported drunk by the nursery staff when the worker was away for a week. She was later able to see the connection and when the summer holiday break (one month) came up she and Mr Gilcrux were better able to prepare themselves for the worker's absence.

The month apparently went quite well, but the worker, unaware of her own ambivalence about getting into the work with them again, delayed in sending the letter confirming the appointment which she had arranged before she went away. Consciously, she knew they had a poor sense of time, that a month was a long break and that they might initially reject her on her return. This knowledge was not enough to stir her into action and she wrote the letter only on the day previous to her intended visit, arriving two hours after the postman.

Some months previously Mr Gilcrux had instituted his 'Children's Day'. On his day off from work he took Beryl and her friends to the library, helped them choose books and then brought them all back to the flat, fed and read to them. On the post-holiday visit the worker heard, even before she reached the doorstep, Mr Gilcrux's drunken, bawling voice. Inside the flat, she learned that Mrs Gilcrux had started a job and was out; Mr Gilcrux was having his 'Children's Day' but was in no fit state to be having it. The worker despatched the other children and made strong tea. Partially sobered up, Mr Gilcrux accused her of not letting him know she was back.

We managed for four weeks which was the time you said and then we thought you weren't back after all. You didn't come and then your letter came on my 'Children's Day'. I hate you. No, I don't, but you don't understand.

Previously Mr and Mrs Gilcrux had asked her if she would be their proxy mother, grandmother and other relatives whom they did not have all rolled into one.

Clients who make these sorts of demands seem to confront the social workers with the alternative of a god-like, ever-loving omnipotence, or a resigned weary impotence. In this situation it is easy to reject the clients whose unceasing demands deprive the workers of the satisfaction of feeling that they have given anything. There is a sense of weariness, burden and sometimes anger as the worker enters yet another graffiti-covered lift or descends to yet another gloomy basement to deal with yet another squabbling family whose lack of change is an indictment of his efforts but whose troubles are such that he cannot leave them alone. At such times it is convenient to have excuses for setting a distance between worker and client or even for getting rid of the latter altogether.

The worker's rejection can take the form of denial of the client's emotional need which, if expressed in the form of material demands, can later be refused as unreasonable. Mrs Yarwood made 'heavy, then farcical, demands' on a social work assistant, trying to use him as 'the great provider'. The assistant, biased towards 'doing' and offering material aid, was, reported his senior, 'pushed to his limits; the team was so furious and fed up with the client that they pressurized him to close the case'.

This way of handling the problem of need goes with the temptation to define the job as that of a functionary. In social services departments there are useful, limited, practical tasks to be done. To provide a telephone is not necessarily to be involved in its user's anger at his disability or his fear of death; to persuade the DHSS to provide a long-distance travel warrant is a task which, once accomplished, can give a solid sense of satisfaction. (Such satisfaction was felt by an IMS worker when, after months of uncertain and exhausting work, he succeeded in despatching his client to the other end of the country.)

Even when work with relationships is being attempted, however, it is still possible to deny the severity of the problem, as in the case of Mr and Mrs Hardknott. The conscious wish to help is overshadowed by the unconscious anxiety. The worker presented the case to the project group in a flat and slow voice quite unlike that which he normally used. He described them as 'babes in the wood' who out of the chaos of their disturbed backgrounds had somehow found each other. He made little of the fact that the hospital consultant had been so disturbed by the baby's bruising that he had wanted a place of safety order or, in lieu of this, had insisted on a signed statement from the social services department that it took responsibility for the baby's return home.

In the course of the discussion the worker was able to bring out a number of features of the case which were, indeed, disturbing. He then had an interview with the couple, in which it emerged that Mrs Hardknott had attempted to commit suicide after discovering that her husband had been unfaithful and this attempt had resulted in an abortion. Mr Hardknott dealt with his wife's depression by refusing to hear anything about it; he spent his evenings listening to his hi-fi through his earphones.

The worker, not normally afraid of getting into the problem, responded by not fixing the next joint interview. Wishing to see the marriage as 'all right', he too 'put on his earphones'.

If the worker is to avoid 'drowning in a well of need' (Mrs Orton), it is useful to be able to persuade himself that he does not matter to the client. Clients on the whole are quite willing to go along with this attempt, since it fits their own wish to deny their attachment to others. The following example of another interview with Mrs Parkin, in severe pain from her ulcer, illustrates the ambivalence of client and worker as they skirt round the question of their attachment to each other and the limits of what the worker can do.

> Towards the end of the interview she yanked a case out, opened it and gave me a purse. She said she had intended to give it to her father but he had died before she could. I thanked her for it and she said, it was 'just a present'. She only had drinking friends and there was nothing much she could talk to them about.

> All this made it difficult to tell her that I had decided to see her fortnightly instead of weekly, but I did tell her. I also said that it must be difficult for her not knowing why I came or how long I would be coming for. She said that she did not see any point in my

coming. What she wanted was to get rid of her pain and I could not help her with that. I said we could discuss that next time.

I left depressed at all this and turned back and knocked at her door and asked her why, if there was no point in my coming, she had given me the present. She said with a smile, 'Psychiatrist go home, You're in the wrong profession'. She missed the next appointment.

We wonder whether the worker's conscious decision that the client was getting more than her ration of interviews was related to an unconscious anxiety about her affection for him.

MUTUAL REJECTION

Obviously it is difficult to form a relationship with clients who exhibit compulsive independence with its accompanying lack of trust.

The situation became too painful for Mr Fell and because his only way of dealing with distress about his wife was to cut himself off from anything that would remind him of her, he refused to see the worker who also saw his wife. He also declined the offer of another worker.

Mr and Mrs Eilbeck warded the worker off as they did everybody else, so that it was difficult to get into a position to help them effectively.

Needless to say, the rejected worker, perhaps relieved because of other demands on his time, is also left feeling a failure when he has not been able to establish contact. 'Would more skill have got me into some much needed work?' These rejecting clients, however, sometimes reappear, as did the 'fucking off' Mr Ingledow and the 'I'll shoot you' Mr Garstang. Rejection invites rejection. The worker may be relieved, at one level, to be in touch again and consciously forget his resentment. Still there, but split off, particularly if the prospective work is likely to be painful and difficult, the resentment will be picked up by a client already over-sensitive to rejection and contribute a further detachment, by now a mutual process. Kept conscious and used in the work, it is much less damaging. A year and a half after the start of the non-work with Mrs Buzzard, she might have been more amenable to help, but this time, the worker had 'had it'. During the course of the eighteen months, she had been reported to the director by another social services department, accused of various misdeeds by a voluntary agency and had resisted being taken off the case on Mrs Buzzard's complaints to the GP and the education welfare. Her concluding handover report sadly concludes:

> I failed to do any therapeutic work with Mr and Mrs Buzzard. The children are now showing symptoms of deprivation and maladjustment. Mrs Buzzard might be mothering the children a bit better if eventually she had been able to accept some care and concern from me. Her behaviour, however, was such as to alienate me and I found it very difficult to get any care across on the few occasions when she did turn up for an interview. It was probably unrealistic to attempt to get through to her given the frequency of visits, but by this time I had not got the heart to put her on to weekly visits with so little chance of success.

Some clients in our sample who were able to engage with the worker initially later often acted out their anger at not being given enough or exactly what they wanted by rejecting the worker. Mr and Mrs Whiteside were overtly pleased to have a worker visiting regularly but after a few months they started missing interviews and were out when she called. The worker was almost relieved to have the additional time and be spared interviews in which she found it extremely difficult to understand what was happening. She suggested that she should make the visits fortnightly rather than weekly. They then cut alternate ones. It could be said that monthly was the working interval which suited the Whitesides but their problems showed no sign of any remission. When the mutual rejection was drawn clearly to her attention in a seminar, the worker was able to discuss this with them, emphasizing her part in the process, and the Whitesides were then able to state their need and ask for a resumption of the weekly visits.

When there have been breaks in the work of the worker's making, the rejection and anger are acted out more vociferously. Before he sobered up, Mr Gilcrux was quite explicit that his drinking bout was directed at the worker. 'You interrupted my 'Children's Day', he bellowed. 'You didn't let me know you were back'. His anger was held in a strong relationship which had existed for some months and the following week he and Mrs Gilcrux were sitting down in the interview and able to discuss the outburst: 'Did I really say all those things to you about hating you?' Sometimes, however, the strength to hold on against repeated rejection after a break has to be that of the worker. The longer the break, the greater the rejection.

Mr and Mrs Underwood, a young West Indian couple with a baby, were both delinquent. The worker was first involved with them when they were in homeless family accommodation. Mr and Mrs Underwood were both charged with offences and sent to prison. The worker remained in touch with them and worked extremely hard on their behalf for Mrs Underwood and the baby to be kept together in Holloway rather than receiving the child into care. On Mrs Underwood's subsequent transfer to a borstal in the north of England contact was maintained by letter. Her release came up before that of Mr Underwood and she asked for the baby to be received into care. It seemed, however, that her concern was more related to herself and who would care for her. She was again accepted as a homeless family and the worker thought it important that she herself should travel north to collect the two of them. The journey provided a good opportunity for the re-establishment of the working relationship.

> This, however, was almost immediately disrupted by Mrs Under-wood's anger after she became settled in the accommodation. The worker had another client in the same building and her attention to this person coupled with her refusal to collude with all Mrs Under-wood's demands led to their mutual anger. Mrs Underwood rejected the worker and demanded to be allocated another.

The worker resisted Mrs Underwood's attempts to reject her and despite her own angry feelings hung on to the contact in a determined way. Eventually, instead of refusing to speak to her, Mrs Underwood telephoned and asked to see her again. This led to some change in her use of the worker and she started to be more reflective about herself and to try to understand what was happening to her. She also resumed a broken contact with the grandmother who had mainly brought her up, and she began to see herself as less lost and hopeless than hitherto.

Clients disposed towards detachment and only starting to risk attachment felt even inadvertent cancellation of an interview by a worker as a 'let-down', which, of course, it is.

Mrs Dockeray was 'restrained and wary' when she showed the worker into an extemely cold but respectable furnished room and sat herself at the opposite end. However she was able to use the interview and express the quandary she was in.

> As for her reactions to me, she responded with a smile to my suggestion that she felt I might look down on her and that she was not worth taking trouble over. I also suggested that she was not sure if I were trustworthy, as she said, 'Nowhere is confidential'.

The following week the worker had influenza and wrote to her explaining why he could not keep the second appointment they had arranged. This letter was answered by one from her declining any further contact.

> I hope you are feeling better. ... Thank you for visiting me. I hope you don't think too bad of me if I cancel the appointment you suggested.

Because of Mrs Dockeray's initial hesitancy, the worker did not expect to see her again, but, with the part of him that wanted to go on working, he wrote and again offered her an appointment; with the part of him that did not believe she would come and did not want to get any further into the problem, he forgot to check with reception. Something in Mrs Dockeray's approach to the receptionist was diffident enough to get her forgotten and the worker was not informed of her arrival. Forgotten clients are not just the fault of an otherwise reliable receptionist. Mrs Dockeray, if less ambivalent about seeing the worker, could have reminded the receptionist of her presence instead of sitting there for forty minutes. When she was eventually discovered, in the twenty minutes left of the worker's available time she showed that she had, in fact, made good use of the previous interview. Another appointment was made, but, not surprisingly, she chose to cancel it and was not seen again.

The examples of independence we have been discussing have, perhaps misleadingly, mainly related to female clients. In practice, husbands were usually more difficult to contact than wives. If they were working and their wives were looking after the children, they were less likely to be at home when the worker called. Culturally, it was also harder for men to acknowledge need. 'I can see a man being like that, but not a woman', said Mr Boothroyd when his worker offered an explanation of Mrs Boothroyd's need and her wish to deny it.

Delinquent dependent men were unwilling to contact the worker voluntarily not only because of their way of handling any relationship as we described in chapter 8, but also, as we discuss in the next chapter, because their wives were often excluding them from the work, casting them in an unfavourable light and making sure that their husbands knew they had done this. As a result, these male clients retreated into pubs, overtime, or even into bathrooms or other places where their mainly female workers found it difficult to follow.

AMBIVALENCE SQUARED

Ambivalence was the hallmark of our core sample clients. Its effect on the workers could be immobilizing or confusing in that it was unclear what the clients wanted; or it could impel the workers into drastic, but in the long run futile, action, as if the only way to overcome the problem were to act before there was time for the other contrary message to be restated. The difficulty was compounded by the fact that ambivalence is rarely, probably never, in the client alone. In the two previous sections of this chapter some examples have already illustrated the ambivalence of the worker in conjunction with that of the client. In this section we are more closely concerned with the interaction of ambivalence on ambivalence and with the ways in which social workers can explain it to themselves.

Mrs Boothroyd was a client who behaved as if the only way out of her intolerable dilemma was to take an irrevocable step before she had time to think of the consequences.

> She rang the social services in desperation. She complained of her leaking house, her cohabitee, her over-active child, her dog, her neighbours and certain other family troubles. She was seen once and offered a further appointment which she then failed to keep. She was offered another appointment, came in, decided on further action (not involving the social services), but said she would be in touch again. A chance meeting in the street prompted her to come in with her suitcase demanding to be accepted as 'homeless' or to have her

child taken into care. Both demands were refused. She left home with her child, returned home, and then left home without her child. She was found by the worker in a pub and finally returned home. A housing offer was obtained. She and her cohabitee both reacted violently to this news and she was arrested for being drunk and disorderly. She moved into the new accommodation with her child and Mr Boothroyd remained behind. Later he moved in, and then out again.

This brief record states the facts, but not the effect on the worker. Mr and Mrs Boothroyd were as ambivalent in their reactions to him as they were to each other. Appointments were arranged and broken, demanded at short notice and broken, and kept but allegedly forgotten ('Mrs Boothroyd put her head out of the window and said, "Oh Christ, not you"; thus encouraged I went in.'). He was continually presented with practical problems to which he would suggest solutions, all of which inevitably were found to be useless. As continually, he was accused of trying to maintain the marriage and of failing to understand that 'things were hopeless'; there was, therefore, no reason for any discussion; when things were 'good', there was again no reason for him to 'upset the applecart'.

The worker's plan, which he put to the Boothroyds, was that they should try to acquire a rehousing offer and that in the meantime they should work together to see if they would wish to move together into the new house. He never, however, managed to obtain any agreement from them to discuss their marital problems. Feeling useless, he was relieved when Mrs Boothroyd apparently made good contact with a female social worker while he was on holiday. He suggested to this worker that they share the case and that he would work with Mr Boothroyd, who was slightly more disposed to keep appointments. This change was made abruptly with scant courtesy or respect for the previous contact, and reflected his lack of confidence in what he had been doing. The worker confused had also become the worker inconsistent. In this way he justified Mrs Boothroyd's distrust; but, to his surprise, she then endowed him with a variety of virtues and refused to have contact with the new worker.

On looking at how the clients' ambivalence activated that of the workers, it may be useful to consider three consecutive extracts from the diary of one of the IMS workers illustrating this theme.

In the afternoon I went with a senior worker, Jane, to see two geriatric clients. As we walked along she told me about them. The wife was an alcoholic and the husband was senile. The psychiatrist had wanted to place them both in the psychiatric hospital. Jane had resisted this, but as they had alienated the home help, she had found herself visiting almost every day. On this day she had previously visited in the morning and learnt that they had apparently lost the £30 pension she had cashed for them the previous day. The wife had accused Jane of stealing the money and punched her on the nose.

We rang the door bell several times before a client from the next-door flat appeared. This young girl expressed annoyance that she had twice been to the home help office to ask for something to be done for this couple; she has also called the police. She thought the wife could not look after her husband and, when she herself had gone in, she found the mattress covered with shit. She did not think the old woman would agree to going into a home and she sympathised with Jane for having an impossible job.

Eventually the old woman let us in. She was apparently naked except for her dressing-gown and some red garment which had fallen round her ankles. She was all over Jane and said what a lovely girl she was. Jane said she would go and get the pension and the old woman expressed alarm that she was leaving. All that mattered, she said, was that Jane came back. During this time the old man hummed something from the bedroom. Jane went and came back and the old woman was again touchingly affectionate to her.

On our way back Jane said she did not know if it was worse when the old lady was fond of her or when she was aggressive. Jane did not know if she could stand the pressure much longer and thought she would have to section the old lady.

In the event the psychiatrist made a domiciliary visit the next week and was berated by the old woman ('two slips of girls prying into my business'). The day after that the two clients were compulsorily admitted to a psychiatric hospital and removed from their home in an operation involving the police, ambulancemen, two social workers and spectators. The ambulancemen were friendly, telling a number of half-truths to get the couple into the ambulance.

The ambulancemen had an easier job than Jane, who was caught between the community's wish to have no untidy deaths, other demands on her time, and her relationships with the couple.

I decided that, given the pressure of my caseload, I could not go on seeing two cases as frequently as I had been doing. The first of these two, an old woman, Mrs Yellowly, turned up unexpectedly in the home help office when I happened to be there. As she had come a long way and was tired, I offered her a cup of coffee. Her pleasure at seeing me made me feel guilty at the thought that I had decided to cut down my work with her and rather than sit with her while she drank the coffee, as I could have done, I kept popping in and out on various errands, 'acting busy'.

Our final extract refers to a worker's departure, a time at which these difficulties are often most acute.

At lunch Sheila was describing leaving her cases, including a six-year-old boy in care whom she had visited since he was a baby. His sister, also in care, had recently returned to live with their mother. He had asked Sheila when he could see her again. She had replied, 'Never'. He repeated the word 'never' as if failing to take this in and had clung to her without crying. Sheila was upset when she told us this incident. The drastic nature of the break and the manner of its communication reminded me of my behaviour and that of Jane.

In these cases the workers had involved themselves in a relationship with their clients and were extracting themselves from some or all of the demands that then ensued. This process was painful for them.

More commonly the pain was evaded through avoidance of the relationship which is its precondition. Leaving, for example, is not always as traumatic as in the case described. Cases who have not been seen for some time may be closed without a visit. (The vague and indefinite nature of the contact with them makes it hard to know how to close the case anyway. It would be as if one's GP suddenly announced that he was closing one's case or that he had come to visit to cushion the emotional shock of his going.) Clients who react to the news of the worker's impending departure by becoming elusive can be sent letters regretting that they were not there on the final visit but giving them the name of a new worker. Other clients provide more than enough by way of material crises to keep the worker occupied. Leaving is a sad experience, but it is also a busy one — a hectic matter of writing up records, arranging handover visits, attending the leaving party and looking for accommodation near the new place of work. Busyness provides an evasive technique peculiarly adapted to the social worker's situation at this and other times.

And in long-term work excuses for evading the importance of the relationship were equally numerous. As we described in chapter 3, there were more often than not practical reasons for the contact between social workers and their priority clients who invariably had multiple problems. Valid questions about rehousing or supplementary benefits, for example, needed to be discussed, but at the same time could provide a means to avoid discussing anything less tangible. The marriages of these clients were often in their eyes held together by practical convenience and they put pressure on the workers to establish a relationship with an economic basis. They threw up more than enough by way of diverse concrete problems to keep their transactions with the workers on a practical footing.

It was tempting to adopt a supportive-suppressive approach to these clients, telling them not to worry — advice that was usually so out of keeping with their situation that in itself it tended to create a barrier. The number of times social workers were heard to tell their clients over the telephone 'not to worry' made a major impact on the IMS workers at the beginning of the project. Such advice may in the short run be reassuring for both worker and client, but in the long run, if the clients' problems are to be faced, anxiety is surely inevitable.

11 The Problem of Control

Catherine — Proceed to growl, in silence I'll attend,
And hear your foolish growlings to the end;
And when they're done, I shall correctly judge
Which of your griefs are real or only fudge.

Edward Lear

Social workers are in a position of power. Individually or collectively, directly and indirectly, they can influence other people's personal lives for good or ill. In this chapter we are concerned with powers of control.

Some powers of control are vested in the worker directly by the legislation. Other powers are vested in the council or the social services committee or the courts. The social workers are agents for these bodies. Acting on behalf of the department, they can initiate investigations — for example, in situations of suspected non-accidental injury to a child; as a result of these investigations, people can be taken to court. With court orders, the social workers can remove children from their parents; they can return children to their parents; they can recommend that the committee takes over parental rights and duties and they are the people who then exercise them. For childless couples, and again as agents, they can offer babies for adoption; they can refuse to place a child or a second child. For the old and disabled, they can recommend the issue of aids, telephones, television licences and arrange for adaptations to property; and they can refuse to support applications for these things which might make a considerable difference to a person's life. They can advocate admissions to old people's homes. They can influence the cost to the clients of some of these services. Their presence and signature may be legally required when a person in the community is compulsorily admitted to a psychiatric hospital; in

157

certain circumstances, they can override a doctor by refusing to sign.

As far as the department in which we worked was concerned, the workers exercised most of these powers only after consultation with a senior member of staff. The exact powers of control were, however, sometimes difficult to determine even within the department. They are held in a changing world, not only of new legislation, but also of public and professional opinion which influences how they are exercised. Different courts and different committees can impose varying procedures.

Outside the department, these powers are, in general terms, known to the public, but, understandably, the knowledge is even less accurate. Sometimes social workers are attributed far greater powers of control than they actually hold. The actual possession of some powers, however, and the fantasied possession of many others, produces strong external pressures on the social workers to act as agents of control.

At the time the project began, the official enquiry into the case of Maria Colwell had emphasized the expectation that social workers carry out tough and unpleasant tasks. The report on that case and a later report on a similar one were circulated and discussed, and generated anxiety and anger. In the mental health field, the occasional refusal to commit a person to hospital under a compulsory order could bring sharp reactions from doctors. One worker was told that the client on whom he had refused to sign an order would commit suicide and that the doctor would shout out the worker's name in the coroner's court. Another was told by a doctor that by her action she had committed professional suicide.

Keenly aware of these expectations and anxious to respond professionally to them, workers would at times be heard discussing their legal powers in terms, for example, of the advantages and disadvantages of the various methods of gaining a legal stake in a child's future. More often than legalities, however, the words 'caring'. 'need' and 'resources' were used in the area offices and reflected the ethos of a profession concerned to see itself as compassionate. Overall, the social workers preferred to see themselves as people who gave rather than as people who controlled or withheld.

Faced with this conflict between their own definition of their role and the expectation of others, the workers were uneasy about the

authoritative aspects of their jobs. One of the workers interviewed
in the survey voiced this conflict in respect of one of her cases:

> What my role is? It's not a word I like to use, but I'd say it was
> controlling the situation.

A record of a conversation over lunch ran:

> Margery had been concerned with a possible reception into care
> which had taken until 9.30 the previous evening. Margery said that
> when she had to use her authority her casework skills went out of the
> window. She was not sure whether she was supporting a mother in
> hospital or wielding the big stick and telling the mother that she was
> not looking after her children properly.

The clients were likely to be even more uneasy than the workers
about this authority since they had often previously had
unfortunate experiences with those (including their parents) who
had powers over them. With their feelings of helplessness, their
own threats of separation, their obsession with blame and alliances
and their need to control, they were likely to be preoccupied with
questions of power and wary of those who might remove them to a
psychiatric hospital or take their children away. They were unlikely
to be relaxed with an official intimately concerned with fault and
adjudication.

It does not take much imagination to see how they might view the
official power nor would they have to be excessively paranoid to
perceive the worker's offer of help in the following terms:

> Would you like to be visited by a woman who may be younger than
> yourself, who will assess the adequacy of your care for your child
> and your general family relationships? It is her job to try and alter
> your family relationships 'for the better'. She can remove your
> children if she thinks fit, but she might not remove them if you think
> fit. She may visit your home as often as she will and, if she wishes,
> without appointment. Friends and neighbours may come to know of
> her visits. You are to understand that even if you get fond of her and
> start to trust her, she may leave on a month's notice and at her
> discretion, without discussing with you whether there is time to finish
> what you started working on together and without informing you in
> advance.

This is a stark view of a client/worker relationship and one that seldom emerged in totality. Mrs Flimsby, for example, at first made it very clear that she was afraid of the worker's power to form an alliance with her husband and remove her to hospital, but later in the contact she emphasized her helplessness and asked for simple advice on how to look after her child. We might ask, however, whether Mr Flimsby's demand on the worker to control his wife defended against his own fear of being controlled. Certainly many of our core sample clients sought to neutralize the worker's power or to get her on their side. Sometimes, in their ability to split the good and the bad, they overtly welcomed the worker's offer of help and denied her power.

In so far as these techniques of denial fitted in with the ambivalence of the workers, who were often observed to exercise their power with a distinctly velvet glove, the client/worker relationship was kept good and the anger directed elsewhere. This denial, however, suggested that our stark picture had some reality and was related to the underlying fear of the clients and the guilt of the workers. In this chapter we examine the ambivalence surrounding the issue of power in terms of the worker's uneasy use of it and the clients' counter-strategies.

COMPULSORY POWERS

Social workers in the area in which we did our survey seldom invoked their compulsory powers. Of the seventeen workers interviewed, only five had ever applied for a place of safety order (one of them had done so twice). They had more experience of compulsory admissions under the Mental Health Act, and in the three months prior to the survey one worker had been involved in six of these and six other workers in ten between them. Situations like that in which the barred doors of a schizophrenic were broken down by the police were rare, made news in the area office, and could be preceded by research in the public library to determine what the exact powers of the social worker were.

The actual, as opposed to the potential, use of statutory powers was even rarer in the context of the ongoing relationship between worker and client. As far as we could see, the majority of compulsory admissions to psychiatric hospitals took place on duty days, and involved clients previously unknown to the workers. In the core sample only four clients were detained in a psychiatric hospital under an order, and in only four cases were children compulsorily removed under place of safety orders. In one case this happened twice.

The lack of ease with which statutory power was exercised was symbolized in the written records. For example, the account of the work with Mrs Flimsby was full and sensitive until she was compulsorily admitted to a psychiatric hospital. The relevant entry read:

> Section 25 completed on Mrs Flimsby.

And this was despite the fact that the first fear Mrs Flimsby had expressed was that of being forced into a psychiatric hospital by a conspiracy of social workers.

In the record of Mrs Ruddick for the ninth day of the month there was a forty-two-line account of an important interview followed by six lines about telephone conversations with the staff of a psychiatric hospital to which she was shortly admitted. The record continued:

> 27th: Phone call from St Kraepelin's. Mrs Ruddick is now on a section 30 which the hospital would like converted to section 25.

> 28th: Section 25 completed on Mrs Ruddick.

> 30th: Visited Mrs Ruddick in St Kraepelin's. She was in a side ward without much ventilation and was in nightclothes although allowed up ... On getting up she was unsteady. However, her mental state was good and there was certainly nothing psychotic about her. She was fed up with St Kraepelin's where the staff treated her as a child. She had told me in the past that she would defy anyone who made her do things and there seemed to be a battle of wills going on. She was bruised from the many injections and she had twice 'escaped' as far as the tube station ... She was worried because the staff would provide no air letters to let her write to her family ...

Again the administration of the order was dismissed in one line. Moreover, the emphasis in the report of the 30th was on the battle of wills between Mrs Ruddick and the hospital rather than on that between Mrs Ruddick and the social worker who had, in fact, helped to put her there. A number of other workers, including an IMS one, later saw Mrs Ruddick, but none of them picked up the crucial significance to Mrs Ruddick of the social worker's authority although, with hindsight, it was clear in much that she was reported to have said.

The ambivalence about the use of compulsory powers was not only in the social workers. The legal department was sometimes instrumental in dissuading a worker from taking a case forward if there were any doubt as to proof and outcome. Magistrates were equally concerned about proof and could be seen to be troubled by the excruciatingly difficult decisions they at times had to make. Of the four instances in which an application was made for a care order on a child whose parents were in our core sample, only two were instituted. In the other two, the case was not proven to the magistrates' satisfaction.

In one of these cases, the worker thought she had misjudged her timing, but that her action had been

a landmark in the client/worker relationship, with each acknowledging openly the authority behind the action.

The worker refused to sidestep the issue and later again applied for an order, this time successfully:

The situation finally escalated into a melodramatic breakdown when the children were on holiday from school. Following the discovery of a dead cat in the garage, supposedly killed by one of the children, Mrs Greenhalgh became hysterical and was admitted to St Kraepelin's on a compulsory order. A place of safety order was taken on the children, who seemed relieved to be removed from the situation. Unfortunately, the psychiatrist failed, as had everyone in the past, to recognize Mrs Greenhalgh's desperation, and she was discharged after seventy-two hours. After displaying considerable anger with the worker when she was informed of forthcoming court proceedings for a care order on the children, Mrs Greenhalgh was able to say that having the children taken away had come as a relief, as she could cope no longer.

The client's ambivalent feelings about control were sometimes met by ambivalent and extreme responses from the worker. After one of Mrs Redhead's suicide gestures, the psychiatrist argued that she should either be compulsorily admitted to hospital or sent home without any support at all. When two professionals were involved, one sometimes represented one extreme of the client's mixed attitude, while the second stood for the other. When continuing to discuss the case of Mrs Redhead with the psychiatrist, the social worker argued that a compulsory admission would do no good and the psychiatrist that the social worker's efforts had done little better in the past. We have already encountered this split between the ineffective sucker and powerful bastard in the two previous chapters.

In the following example, with which we end this section, the same worker plays both roles, but has difficulty in balancing one against the other. The benign sucker suddenly becomes the powerful bastard. The worker's guilt about his sudden, powerful action may have been one of the determining factors in his subsequent behaviour. He first met Miss Nanson when her baby was a few months old.

> They were homeless and the department provided temporary accommodation and day care provision for the baby. Miss Nanson evidently did not find this arrangement satisfactory, for soon after this she failed to collect her from the day nursery. The baby was then received into care under section 1 of the Children Act 1948 and was not discharged until six months later when her mother reappeared.

It is interesting to observe that on this occasion the abandonment of the child was dealt with by a fairly informal procedure as if the mother had requested that her daughter be received into care. Two further brief receptions into care were both under section 1 and there appears to have been no suggestion of a resort to the use of compulsory powers, although the baby seems to have been regularly deserted and on one occasion was in the hands of the police.

In spite of Miss Nanson's erratic behaviour, the efforts of the worker were directed towards maintaining the relationship between mother and child and working towards their permanent settlement together. His observation of mother and child together when she visited the baby at the residential nursery led him to believe that the bond was strong and important. His hopes for them may have become invested in the possible marriage of Miss Nanson to Mr

Gibson, whom he had come to like. When this seemed to be coming to nothing the baby was returned to her mother, again in homeless families accommodation. Two weeks later the worker found Miss Nanson stupefied after taking Mandrax and wine. He took her to hospital and the baby back to the residential nursery.

> Although by this time the baby knew me quite well, she was very distressed at my taking her from her mother. I was carrying her and she screamed in anger and distress for some fifteen minutes and hit and kicked me in her panic at the separation. I decided that for the baby's immediate protection a place of safety order was necessary and I applied for and was granted one at 8.30 p.m. that evening.

Unless the feelings of the worker can be understood and taken into account as an important element in the decision-making process, it is difficult to understand why this occasion differed in substance from any of the previous ones when the child was admitted to care on a voluntary basis. It was as if at any one time the worker could only be in touch with one side of his own and his client's ambivalence. In the first year of the work he could not give enough recognition to the rejecting behaviour of the mother. In the last instance, when the child (by now at the peak age of attachment) displayed strong attachment behaviour, he probably could not bear the baby's cry and the whole account in the case file reads as if the baby's panic got into him.

After a care order had been made the worker saw Miss Nanson twice, once when she was pregnant again and in danger of miscarrying. She then disappeared for a month, but on her return told the worker that

> it distressed her very much to leave the baby in the nursery and she became depressed each time when reminded of her failure to make a home for the child.

The worker faced what he obviously found a distressing choice: maintaining the separation or ending it, thereby denying the reality of the mother's rejecting behaviour. He evaded the choice and placed the child with foster-parents, as they wanted to believe, with a view to adoption; as the mother wanted to believe, for fostering only. He made no objection when the foster-parents gave the child a new Christian name, but he introduced a second worker to Miss Nanson and Mr Gibson, who was now back in the picture, on the grounds that work with this liaison (and marriage as it became) would enable her to give a home to the child. He gave different versions of the fostering/prospective adoption to his senior and the child care advisor. He then left.

In a series of intensely painful interviews the second worker sorted things out to the extent that the mother consented to the proposed adoption. Despite his efforts, he then lost contact with her.

This story naturally inclines the reader to blame the first worker and give credit to the second, but it is a story with no heroes. Later, an unconfirmed rumour reached the second worker that Mrs Gibson, separated from Mr Gibson, had committed suicide. The rumour may have been true. If the pain of separation was so intense for Mrs Gibson, it is not surprising that the first worker could not face it either.

Such behaviour was fortunately not typical of the work that was done with our core sample, but we have included it because of the light it may cast on the interaction between other clients and other workers. We believe that the possibility of using compulsory powers to remove somebody from his home influenced the clients and the workers to a much greater degree than the rarity of its occurrence would suggest. The clients were unlikely to know the figures regarding the use of compulsory powers, or the complexity of the law, or the provisos, safeguards and rights of appeal which protected them and which often deterred the worker from taking precipitate action. But the clients did read of cases which made headline news and they had their own ideas and unconscious fantasies of the power and authority of the State. Workers who denied the authority they carried, to the clients and themselves, were probably more likely to abuse their clients by the suddenness with which they brought it into action.

THE CLIENTS' USE OF POWER

The worker's use of compulsory powers can determine many major consequences, including a labelling of at least one member of the family as mad, bad or inadequate; a drastic change in the family's situation; and often, although not always, the appearance of an alliance between the social worker and one or more members of a family against the other or others.

The fear of such consequences may arise in the client when no compulsory powers are likely to be invoked. After all, the worker's visits may still be seen as casting blame, threatening change, or altering the balance of power in the family through the formation of a new alliance.

Mr and Mrs Pooley came to the attention of the department under the Disabled Persons Act and a marital problem was noted by the referrer. They had never got on well together. Mr Pooley had Parkinson's disease and Mrs Pooley looked after him nobly, if gruffly. The worker visited occasionally and, as he thought, in a supportive role. Both Mr and Mrs Pooley talked at length about some of their problems, but when the worker tried to clarify his role with Mrs Pooley, she said that:

> he came to see if she were mistreating her husband and that he wrote his report in a black book. She criticized him for making his visits by appointment and said that realistic visits of inspection should be made unheralded.

Another client was not drawing supplementary benefit to which she was entitled and refused to do so because of an unfortunate experience with social security in the past. Only as the worker was leaving did he learn that he had offended her, when she said,

> Funny job yours — visiting the poor.

Blaxter noted similar misperceptions of social workers by their clients:

> The great majority of people misunderstood the social work department's function. Whereas the social workers saw themselves as helping agents, the potential clients saw them as arbitrating and inspecting officials almost exclusively concerned with financial aid, decreeing whether this electricity bill might be dealt with, or allocating charges for this house adaptation.[1]

Obviously, however, the advent of a social worker was more likely to be felt as stigmatizing by those who would commonly be defined as having failed in some way or who had failed in their own

[1] Blaxter, M. (1976), *The Meaning of Disability* (Heinemann).

The Problem of Control   167

eyes. Mr and Mrs Briggs disputed whose fault it was that the social worker called and Mrs Mothersill maintained that in her case it was only because of the 'pressure' she was under.

Faced with such a threatening or stigmatizing situation, clients took counter-measures that seemed appropriate to them. The simplest and most effective of these measures was to refuse contact with the social worker or arrange to be out when he called. If contact was not broken completely, they could try to ensure that the assumptions on which the contact took place were favourable, that their power in the transaction was enhanced or that of the social worker reduced, or that the social worker's alliances with members of the family were favourable to themselves.

Our long-term clients, like most clients at the intake stage, were offering a definition of their problem which was central to what they wanted the worker to do and how they wished to be seen. It was important to them that the worker accepted their definition. The client who asked for her husband's name to be removed from a tenancy agreement and her own substituted did so on the grounds that he was unreliable and irresponsible and she was the responsible mother. Clients who wanted their spouse compulsorily admitted to a psychiatric hospital defined him as mad. Wives asked for homeless families accommodation because they were battered, thus proffering not only a justification for their request, but also a definition of what was going on which was acceptable to *them*, but not necessarily to their spouse and not always to the worker.

Faced with a conflict of definition, some clients applied coercion, often involving other people for help in this. Female clients persuaded female workers in children's homes that the social worker had been hoodwinked by a plausible husband. Doctors, health visitors and social workers were set at odds. In the course of the first year of the project, the IMS workers, carrying between them a caseload numerically no greater than that of the other workers in the department, were the subject of eight complaints to various officials ranging from the CID to the director of the department. One of these complaints had nothing to do with a client, and another by a doctor arose from a refusal to carry out a mental health section. The other complaints, although often administered by professionals, had their origins in the clients.

Other clients, equally afraid of what might happen, rendered the worker helpless by demanding the impossible (often rehousing) immediately. Others spread despair by announcing that there was nothing that could be done. Others gave both messages and demanded contradictory things simultaneously or in quick succession. Such a client was Mr Quinn.

We called by appointment and were met by a genial Mr Quinn. However, it quickly became apparent that he thought we were some-one else (the CID, I think) and that he and his wife believed that we were coming next week. As it turned out this was the first of many confusions.

Mr Quinn made a number of highly conflicting statements, the effect of which was to leave us more than confused. Thus:

He called her 'darling', but said he used the word metaphorically.
He said he had no feeling for his wife, but repeated with satisfac-tion the doctor's question to Mrs Quinn, 'If your husband does not care for you, why does he visit you?'
He wished to be master in his own house, but he also wished to be 'dominated'.
He could not leave his home because of his job, but he was thinking of leaving his job and therefore his home.
He thought his wife should 'find' herself, but complained about her independent actions.
He felt his wife had broken the marriage, but he was the failure.
He appeared angry and obsessed with violence, but said he was not violent at all.
He said he did 'mysterious things' and that he was completely honest and open with his wife.
He said he was 'everything' to his wife and that she paid more attention to other people than to him.

That list could be called 'putting up a smokescreen'. Indicative as it is of a client unsure of his own identity and of what he thinks and feels, it also serves to keep the other person helpless, useless and not knowing how to respond. Faced with such conflicting statements, the workers had difficulty in knowing what was being asked of them, and remained powerless.

A different but analogous situation occurs when the workers are split by the contradictory messages given at different times. Mrs Fell, separated from her husband, was pregnant. Whether she kept the baby or not, she faced an inevitable change — to that of the active mother or to that of the bereaved mother.

> As the birth of the baby approached, she showed increasing signs of panic. While she seemed in some respects not to want to keep the baby, she nevertheless showed considerable fluctuations in her attitude, oscillating between a wish to keep it herself, a wish for it to be adopted immediately, and a wish to delay the decision by having the baby fostered while she finally made up her mind.

> However, she managed to involve the hospital staff, medical social workers and others in this problem and got them to act out the various aspects of it in relation to her social services department worker. She made various of the other workers into the harsh, punitive ones who wanted to rob her of the baby and to make her give it up for adoption. By contrast, her social services worker was seen as siding with her wish to keep the baby.

This tactic was intended, consciously or unconsciously, to put responsibility on to the workers. By dividing them into those who would not let her keep the baby and those who would, she could avoid keeping the conflict alive within, and making the decision for, herself. One set of workers could then be blamed for the decision she could say she 'was forced to make'.

The client's perception of the workers' power plays a part in this strategy; and the workers' feelings and bias about mothers keeping or not keeping babies can determine on which side of the power struggle the client places them.

Issues concerned with family alliances were equally crucial for clients. Some acted as 'gatekeepers' and laid down the terms on which the social worker was to be allowed contact with the family. Mr Pennington was one of these. (The problems of this family were many, but they did not come into the core sample as Mr and Mrs Pennington did not acknowledge the marital problem the project group believed that they had.) Three of his four boys had committed a string of offences and were on supervision orders. They seldom appeared for office interviews, but, on one occasion when one appeared, Mr Pennington had paid him to come. Family interviews in the house were equally unsuccessful. 'Now talk to Mr Ogden', said Mr Pennington and strode out of the room. 'No, that's not right', he interrupted, as he strode back into the room.

'Now talk to the man, as I told you to'. On another occasion when Mr Pennington was out, the oldest boy, not on an order, announced from an adjoining room what he felt about control by playing at full blast a record of one of Hitler's speeches made during his rise to power in the 1930s. Eventually the family opted out with a completeness that amazed the worker, considering the organization required to get six people either out of the house or hidden every Wednesday evening at the appointed time, particularly Mrs Pennington, who was disabled.

It proved impossible with this family to set up a working alliance and make a contract which was acceptable both to Mr Pennington and the worker. Mr Pennington wished to be seen as a powerful father, but at the same time he experienced himself as powerless; three of his children were getting into more and more serious trouble. His oldest son probably experienced a similar conflict in his identification with his hero, Hitler. The advent of the competent male social worker threatened Mr Pennington's fragile masculinity and the precarious balance of power in the family. Mrs Pennington was never accessible enough for us to learn where she fitted into the picture. The implications of not getting into the work in its turn put another pressure on the worker to exercise further power in taking the boys back to court.

This family, like many we have described, formed within the family strong alliances which excluded other members. One of the characteristics of the alliances between Mr Pennington and different boys was the rapidity with which they changed. When a bad boy became good, one of the good boys became bad.

Alliances were central to the difficulty of setting up a contract to work with both partners of the marriage. The partner who exhibited anxious attachment behaviour was often as instrumental as his more evasive and detached partner in keeping the latter away from the worker. Two things often occurred. Firstly, one of the clients would strive for a good relationship with the worker and want to define the basis for contact as the badness of the other spouse. Secondly, as one client became attached, often anxiously so, to the worker, he became afraid that his partner would seduce the worker away from him. This attempt at pairing and fear of seduction by the partner often followed a sex basis, women clients trying to pair with women workers and vice versa.

Mrs Vasalli was referred by a psychiatrist who had diagnosed her depression as related to a marital problem. She defined the basis of contact as the badness and dependence of her husband who, not surprisingly, chose to avoid the worker.

> Mr Vasalli was present in the house when the visit took place, but the worker found it impossible to involve him in the discussion. It seemed as if Mrs Vasalli did not want him to join in and he made no attempt to do so himself. He walked in and out of the room without making any acknowledgement of the worker's presence. Mrs Vasalli complained about his dependence upon her, his lack of interest in the children, his incapacity as a provider and his inability to be in touch with her. The last point was graphically illustrated in the interview. The worker felt quite paralysed by this behaviour, wanting to invite Mr Vasalli to comment on what was being said about him, but feeling unable to do so and suffering acute embarrassment at the predicament she was in.

The need to isolate the other spouse and to use the worker as a vehicle for arousing jealousy became paramount as the attachment to the worker grew; it was sometimes complicated by the client's or worker's actual sexual attraction.

The following report describes what had been arranged to be two joint interviews:

> On the first of these two occasions, Mr Garlick, although available, remained outside the house for quite a long time. He eventually joined in the discussion with Mrs Garlick, but clearly disliked being involved, especially as she made an attack on him for not letting her know about what he was doing. She seemed to relate this to her depression. He denied any fault. She tried to shift the blame on to him and he could only let himself be seen as blameless. By the end of the session he conceded the field to her and indicated that he wanted no further contact. It was not clear whether he wanted the social worker to stop seeing his wife.

> On the second visit, the worker found him alone because Mrs Garlick had obtained a part-time job. His hostility had disappeared and was replaced by a seductive quality which made the worker most uneasy and which she was unable to confront directly. The interview was full of sexual innuendo, particularly about a woman for whom he had done a job and who had suggested that payment should be by sex rather than money. It seemed to be aimed at her and an attempt to have an exclusive relationship. By the end of the session, needless to

say, Mr Garlick was quite keen for the worker to return, but she was uncomfortable and reluctant.

The reader may remember the Calders and that Mrs Calder disliked not being the centre of attention when Mr Calder helped James with his fractions. She always made a very determined effort to keep the worker for herself. At one interview, tea was sent to Mr Calder upstairs and his presence in the house was not mentioned. Jealousy was the theme of that particular interview which Mrs Calder insisted on having for herself. At last she mentioned her husband: 'He thinks highly of you ... Oh, I see you're blushing'.

In another interview Mr and Mrs Calder again enacted their difficulty in sharing the worker, although this time Mr Calder was slightly less isolated and did succeed in getting himself into the room; but when Mrs Calder sat down in front of the worker, he could only sit behind her, and with his back to her and a raised paper in front of his face.

Mr Cabassi provides another example of this theme. He had to go abroad for a month and sent regular postcards to the worker as if afraid that his wife would capture her for herself and that he would be forgotten if he did not keep reminding her of his existence. One of the rows between Mr and Mrs Cabassi provides a particularly good example of jealous and controlling manoeuvres in relation to a worker.

The row started because Mr Cabassi was late home from work. Mrs Cabassi was frantic and said she was going to telephone me. Mr Cabassi said it was far too late to do that and, in trying to stop her, got hold of her by the hair. Mrs Cabassi screamed and this brought the children out of their bedroom. One was told to telephone the police, who then arrived and told Mr Cabassi to leave the house. After wandering round the streets until six o'clock in the morning, he managed to get Mrs Cabassi to let him in, but she remained upstairs locked in one room with the children.

I was told this story the next day by Mr Cabassi, who arrived an hour early for what was supposed to be a joint interview. He was in such a state that I thought I had better see him. He tried to bind me to secrecy, saying that his wife would kill him if she knew he had told me what had happened.

Our final example, which covers many of the points we have been discussing, relates to the Beatties. This couple were referred to in chapter 8 when Mrs Beattie's behaviour was given as an example of subversive caregiving. We now give the interview in more detail, using it to illustrate the clients' fear of change and their need for alliances and to have their own version of affairs accepted. It also illustrates the tactics clients can use on these occasions.

> On calling at the house by appointment I was let in by Mr Beattie, a large shambling man who seemed heavily doped and who was apparently uncertain if he knew who I was or liked me if he did. He showed me to the sitting-room where Mrs Beattie received me in a friendly enough way. Mrs Beattie, however, began by saying that there was nothing I or anyone else could do.

Mrs Beattie's first move states what she feels to be the hopelessness of the situation and gives no opening to the worker, who was temporarily neutralized. Nevertheless, she proceeds to complain about a practical matter on which, because it has occurred in the past, the social worker is powerless to act.

> The social security had forced Mr Beattie to go to Aldershot to get his money and once there blithely told him that they had made a mistake. They had not even given him his fare. He might have had a heart attack down there and she would have had to go down to Aldershot hospital to visit him. I said something (I forget what) which made Mrs Beattie angry with me. I said she seemed to think I was on the side of social security, but I did understand that the worry she had been caused was worse for her than the incompetence. This mollified her a bit and I said to Mr Beattie that his wife seemed to worry a lot about him. He said she worried too much.

Thus far Mrs Beattie has succeeded in defining her needs and troubles as arising solely from her husband. Mr Beattie now tries to present himself in a different light, but Mrs Beattie does not let him get away with this.

> Mr Beattie then produced a brochure of the place to which his firm was going to move and showed it to me. Mrs Beattie told him not to be silly; he was too ill to work there. There then followed what I felt to be a disastrous piece of the interview in which Mrs Beattie continually spoke for her husband, portraying him as incompetent

and bad-tempered. She said that the sort of job he could get would
be fit only for drug addicts.

Mr Beattie then presents his pathetic side to the worker, who
continues in a conflict of definitions with Mrs Beattie before
conceding the field.

> In the course of this it emerged that Mr Beattie was in very severe
> pain, allegedly nervous in origin, for which he was buying private
> medicines. I made some fruitless attempts to find out what sort of
> job he wanted (a light, rather obsessional one seemed what was
> required, but Mrs Beattie said that this would be bad for his brain
> and make him bad-tempered). We also fruitlessly discussed housing.
> Finally I more or less gave up trying to bring Mr Beattie into the
> picture and started a rather depressed conversation with Mrs Beattie
> about their daughter, Esta, who had got a job.

Mr Beattie now reacts to the worker's failure and to his interest
in the daughter, his rival for his wife's affections. (Esta had already
replaced him in the marital bed and he was, not surprisingly,
extremely jealous of her.) And Mrs Beattie restates, as if it needs
restating, the hopelessness of the situation.

> At this point Mr Beattie got up, went out into the kitchen and started
> swearing at Esta. Mrs Beattie went out and told him to shut up. She
> then came back and complained about him to me. She said that
> things were hopeless and that, wherever she went, he would come
> with her. (This recalled an earlier remark when Mr Beattie said he
> would tag along and Mrs Beattie said with a smile of triumph, 'Yes,
> he will tag along all right'.)

Mr Beattie, however, makes another attempt to get the male
worker to ally himself with him, only to be met by a response to
him and his wife together.

> Mr Beattie then came in and showed me his patent medicines. I said
> something about how he and his wife had a basinful. Evidently this
> was the wrong thing to have said and Mr Beattie shambled out again.

The final part of the interview illustrates the triumph of Mrs
Beattie's definition, her alliance with the worker achieved at her
husband's cost, and her belief that an agent of change can cause
only upset.

Mrs Beattie then said Mr Beattie was upset because I was there. (I didn't agree. I thought he was upset because of the way we'd all treated him.) Esta came in and there was some desultory and depressed conversation and Mrs Beattie suggested I came back in three weeks' time. They were anxious for me not to see Mr Beattie and upset him. I left, saying that I would write to him.

There is an aftermath. The worker's report concludes:

This interview made a major impression on me. That night I had a dream in which I was a doctor dispensing medicines to Mr and Mrs Beattie. The medicines consisted of a barrel of gunpowder and a lit fuse.

There may be numerous interpretations of this dream, but the following ingredients were certainly in it: the anxiety about the circumstances; the wish to help; the destructive and powerful nature of any intervention; and the fear of the process of change.

The fear that any change would be destructive and is, therefore, to be avoided, and the implication that something different is bound to be worse than the wretchedness already known, is an important factor in building up the despair both in the client and in the worker. The latter has to carry his own despair when the client renders him useless; but he can also introject the client's projected despair and carry a 'double dose'.[2] This is apparent when the worker is left feeling more defeated and dejected than usual after contact with a particular client and only later learns that the client felt better.

Many of the examples given in this part of the book have left their own messages of despair. We will not repeat them all, but just remind the reader of Mrs Buzzard's worker who did not have the heart to put her back on the weekly interviews, and of the ruined and anxious weekend experienced by the two workers after their interchange with Mrs Yates — two bastards filled up with despair.

In Part 4 we outline what we believe are the most important factors in any therapeutic endeavour with clients as vulnerable, untrusting and despairing as those we have described.

---

[2] Guthrie, L., and Mattinson, J. (1971), *Brief Casework with a Marital Problem* (Institute of Marital Studies).

PART FOUR

The Clients, The Workers and The Work

The resultant blend of positive and negative, of trust and fear, of hope and doubt, of attraction and repulsion, is characteristic of the initial relationship. It is the νεῖκος καὶ φιλια *(hate and love) of the elements, which the alchemist likened to the primeval chaos. The activated unconscious appears as a flurry of unleashed opposites and calls forth the attempt to reconcile them, so that, in the words of the alchemist, the great panacea, the* medicina catholica, *may be born.*

The doctor knows — or at least he should know — that he did not choose this career by chance; and the psychotherapist should clearly understand that psychic infections, however superfluous they seem to him, are in fact the predestined concomitants of his work, and thus fully in accord with the instinctive disposition of his own life. This realisation also gives him the right attitude to his patient. The patient then means something to him personally, and this provides the most favourable basis for treatment.

C.G. Jung

12 Getting Engaged

*I labour for peace, but when I speak
unto them thereof; they make them
ready to battle.*

                    Psalm 120

Social services departments were set up to provide a variety of services. Clients and workers of these departments approach each other for many reasons.

Some clients may want practical services. Others may want help with their emotional problems, although seldom overtly. Others may want both, and the two may or may not be connected. Many of them may have mixed feelings about asking for either of these types of help and their requests, as we have already illustrated, may be ambiguous. Some are referred and want nothing to do with any social worker.

The social workers may have to assess the need for practical services and they may have to check up on situations serious enough to warrant a child or an adult being removed from his home. They may want to offer a therapeutic service for the emotional misery in which they find some of their clients. Or they may discover that some of their clients, to their own detriment, cannot use the practical service offered because of their emotional problems. Whether they like it or not, the workers are sometimes faced with clients like Mrs Yates, who initially was not able to accept a reasonable housing offer for herself and her children.

In this part of the book we concentrate on our attempts to work with the emotional problems of our married clients — what we call the therapeutic endeavour. We are not implying that this is the only proper aim of social work. Often, indeed usually, with families such as those in our core sample, the social workers needed to combine several purposes — therapeutic, practical and monitoring.

179

The combination of these purposes inevitably affected the therapeutic one.

Coming from a clinical situation in the IMS, we started work with these families with a strong belief that a therapy concerned to promote emotional growth and change needs to be grounded in a strong personal relationship between worker and client. We also believe that what happens in that relationship is a primary agent which enables the client to change his behaviour with other people. This carries a belief in the value of the caseworker's own personality — his ability to use his own emotions in a real way and, at a 'gut level', to know about pain, suffering and troubled feelings. This needs to be combined with his understanding of deprived and pathological behaviour and processes of interaction. When the project was nearing its end, we believe we were more effective with some of our clients. By that time our understanding of their main emotional and interactive problems, as we have analysed them in this book, was becoming clearer. At the same time, we were less anxious and, therefore, increasingly able to use this understanding in our own individual ways. Thus Mrs Buzzard, one of the first clients on our joint caseload, received a less effective service than those who came on to the caseload a year later. In the first few months of the contact the worker failed to relate to her despair, uncertainty as a mother and terror of being on her own.

These chapters show the development in our thinking and the use we made of it as well as the problems we experienced in working with such deprived people. By attempting to clarify our practice in this way, we hope that other practitioners can test their own experience against ours.

In chapter 3 we described the difficulties the local authority workers encountered in doing marital work in a social services department. Neither clients nor referrers expected them to do it and both put much more emphasis on other tasks they wished the workers to perform. We found that the variety of roles we could choose to play, or which clients could choose to demand, necessitated an ongoing negotiation about the purpose, length and nature of our contact with the clients and the reasons for which we left them. In this chapter we deal with the initial and probably most crucial phase of negotiations. In the next we deal with the ongoing work and final parting.

THE NEGOTIATOR

Only after we started work in the social services department did we realize how much of the initial work with the clients in the IMS is done by the organization. It has decided that the work is to be about marriage. It says both partners must attend and that contact must be regular; clients must attend for interviews once a week. The only negotiation done by individual workers is relatively minor in terms of interview times, length of contact, and fee to be paid. Clients who do apply within this publicized framework accord the worker the right to work with their marital problems. If clients or workers do not like these terms and feel they cannot work with them, they leave.

Because of the range of the clientele, the types of problems and the scope of their statutory obligations, social services departments cannot define their terms of work to the same extent. If anyone is going to state the terms to an individual client, it has to be the worker himself.

Because the clients were often defining the problem in limited and concrete terms and attempting to control the worker within their own set way of relating to people, there was often a wide gulf between their and the workers' intentions. We found this gulf needed negotiating from the beginning, and the more explicit this could be the more comfortable we (definitely) and the clients (probably) were. If an explicit negotiation was not attempted fairly quickly, the opportunity seemed to get lost. Inexplicit and hidden negotiations continuing throughout the contact failed to set a base from which more tightly defined therapeutic transactions could develop.

These clients were often 'all over the place', consumed with anxiety, often desperate in their frustration and from the results of their more destructive activities. We are not wanting to suggest that they could all be quickly or easily marshalled into a regular and organized working situation or that a firm offer made by the worker of what he was prepared to do or not do was necessarily heard or believed with any sense of conviction.

The continued negotiation of an agreed definition of the problem was often part of the ongoing work and we return to this in the next chapter. It appeared, however, that many of the clients were reassured and responded better in the initial stages if the base from which the worker negotiated and acted was firm and secure in intention. At the very least, it gave them a chance to say 'No, that is not what we want', either in words or actions. It offered a model of respecting their autonomy and ability to make a choice.

> After a number of calls which entailed much fruitless knocking, some discussion with Mr and Mrs Mothersill over the milk bottles on the doorstep, and a half-veiled threat from Mr Mothersill, I was finally allowed into their dark basement flat. The first impression was of enormous clutter, but surprisingly the place contained only one chair. I sat down on this and said I had come to discuss whether they would like me to come once a week to talk over their marital problems.

So far the worker has demonstrated a confident and rather rude persistence, pursuing the Mothersills, despite their manifest reluctance to have much to do with him, and then sitting on their only chair. He also defined for himself a role (a discusser of marital problems), offered a context within which to perform the role (weekly visits) and asked the Mothersills if they would accept this. Their reaction was disconcerting.

> In response, they began to shout at each other at the tops of their voices. I could not understand what they were shouting about, so I repeated my question. They continued to shout, and again I repeated my question, and again they went on shouting, the noise they were making getting, if anything, even louder. Eventually I shouted above the din that what they seemed to be asking me was whether I could *stand* coming once a week to discuss their marital problems. At once they fell quiet, and Mr Mothersill then said that 'in a manner of speaking' that seemed to be what they were asking.

By their response the Mothersills had implicitly confirmed that they had marital problems (no one in the room could have doubted it) and raised a very real question as to whether these were not so entrenched and desperate that they were beyond the worker's capacity to endure or skill to handle. The worker's next response related to this implicit question and also, perhaps, to the Mothersills' previous experience that social workers were 'birds of passage'. He responded definitely and confidently, temporarily making even more noise than the Mothersills.

In this way he defined for himself a more precise role than just a discusser of marital problems. His sitting on the only chair may indicate the exhaustion he felt, his determination to establish the entry he had finally gained, or a confidence that he had something to offer and time within which to do so. Certainly, he offered himself as a person who *stands* things and, by coming once a week, stands them on a regular basis. By 'stand' we do not mean withstand, although at times the clients need to be withstood. Rather, we mean 'bearing with', 'staying with', 'sticking with', the clients, their problems, and their fear, rage, despair, anxiety and, above all, their ambivalence.

We came to attribute importance to this 'stand' on a regular basis and to interpret it in the light of Bowlby's attachment theory. We were, in effect, offering ourselves as an attachment figure. We came to believe that such a role was a prerequisite for emotional change. Although it was not enough to achieve such change, it was a necessary starting-point. In our initial offer we tried to convey our willingness to stick with the emotional problem.

NEGOTIATIONS: CONTAINMENT

This offer to see the couple at regular intervals implicitly ruled out the idea that the only purpose was to deal with practical problems. Even the core sample clients had weeks when there was nothing practical to be done.

The regularity and willingness for regularity also offered containment. The willingness offered an emotional containment stemming from the authority of our belief that we had something in ourselves to offer. The regularity offered a practical containment and set a firm scene, which had three advantages. Firstly, in terms of time and place, it provided a firm boundary round the work, giving both clients and workers a security which enabled them to dare to get close, and experience and work with disturbing feelings together. Secondly, it met the need of these particular clients to have things expressed in very concrete terms, including the comings and goings of the workers. And, thirdly, because of the range of social work practice, these clients had had no consistent model and did not know what to expect. They had often had several workers in the past, some of whom had approached the problems only at a practical level, some of whom had offered something less tangible, sometimes defined, sometimes not defined. 'Oh, but you won't be here then', said one client on a winter's day, when the worker proposed a plan for the next summer.

The offer to visit regularly — once a week or once a fortnight — was a start and obviously offered many of our clients some relief. Either explicitly or implicitly, however, it raised a number of issues. Obvious as the existence of a marital problem usually was, the worker needed, from his point of view, to assess the particular problem, its severity and the resistance to working on it. At the same time, and from the clients' point of view, he needed to relate to the crisis for which they were referred. Some of us found we could not use the phrase 'marital problems'. It was too vague for these clients, not their language and, in their eyes, not related directly enough to the actual issue they presented. We found our need to assess the situation and make a further definition of our role was, quite appropriately, more acceptable if it were seen to connect with the anxiety of the immediate situation in which we first met them. Sometimes the degree of confusion in the clients affected our diagnostic ability and made further definition of our role impossible. Sometimes, however, we were able to negotiate an assessment period.

Mrs Levens referred herself by refusing to go home from a hospital appointment because of her husband's perpetual drunkenness and violence. She declared herself and the children homeless. The intake worker placed them in homeless families accommodation (a hotel) and the case was transferred to an IMS worker whose first contact the next day was with Mr Levens, who, in his deserted state, was threatening suicide. This first interview centred on his collapse and despair, and his view of the marital situation, but was interrupted by a telephone call from Mrs Levens to her husband to say she and all the children were ill. Mr Levens asked the worker to speak to her. The worker sympathized with Mrs Levens on being ill in a hotel and arranged to see her the following week. In concluding the interview with Mr Levens, the first offer she made, which he accepted, was

I have seen you today. I will see Mrs Levens next Thursday. Then I will see you both together the following Thursday. Then I will tell you what I can offer you in the way of help (like we have been talking today) and then you can tell me if you want to accept it.

And then, in a very practical way, she said that if Mr Levens really wanted his family back, he had better take the opportunity the illness presented him with, hail a taxi, collect them and then nurse them back to health and strength.

A second offer was made the following week. Mrs Levens had allowed Mr Levens to bring her and the children home. The joint interview immediately followed the single one with her.

> From what you have told me separately and together, I can see that your marriage is 'as dead as a dodo' when Mr Levens is sober and too lively when he's drunk. I am able to see you once a week for three months to see if you can get your marriage more lively when sober, so you don't have to get drunk so often. If you want to accept this offer, at the end of three months we will see where you are getting; if you are getting anywhere, we can continue the meetings.

As with the Mothersills, the worker made it clear that her interest was in an emotional issue — the marriage. An advantage of her limited offer was that it dealt in a straightforward way with the clients' fear that the worker will somehow take them over. The handling of this fear seemed to be a key part of the early negotiations. Our later experience, however, suggested that the offer made to Mr and Mrs Levens was too short and did not give them enough security. The work continued with them for eighteen months and they might well have responded more quickly if the initial offer had been for a year.

A more appropriate limited offer was made to a couple who were not in the core sample. The difference lay in the priority accorded the case by the department (and hence in the possibility of leaving them alone), the couple's capacity to manage, and the limited nature of the focus which was chosen. Mr and Mrs Westgarth were a sophisticated couple living in a luxury flat.

> Both of them had many difficulties, but did not worry. It was obvious that when one of them got near to worrying the other switched off completely and started talking about foreign stamps or a holiday in the south of France which they could not afford.

> The workers could do nothing about their actual difficulties — for example, his age, the age gap between them, his decreasing earning capacity, their finding the alternative accommodation they wanted;

but they would be able to visit weekly for ten weeks to try and help them to handle these worries in a more mutually helpful way.

The short-term offer underlined the wish to tackle a problem which might be resolved rather than those which could not be.

Although in these examples we have stressed the need to be straightforward in the initial negotiations with clients, this principle is limited by the need to take account of what the client is in a position to hear. Often there was a large gulf between the worker's initial assessment and her explicit offer. The reader may remember Mr and Mrs Gilcrux, who were referred by the day nursery for weaving too drunken a course across the road too often when collecting Beryl. The worker found a very frightened couple who were afraid of what she might do, and Mr Gilcrux tried to define the problems only in terms of his wife's difficulties.

The worker made an offer at the end of the first interview, after the family had expressed some acceptance of her. Beryl had climbed on her lap and asked to be read a story. Mrs Gilcrux had chosen the story, 'The Tale of Mrs Tittlemouse', and Mr Gilcrux looked for the book. All three had listened attentively.

Things are very hard for you and you seem so frustrated with each other. I can see you every week and we will work on this and see if we can 'de-frustrate'. You seem very worried that I will remove Beryl, but I can see with my own eyes that there is not much wrong with her at present. I shall be coming to see you, not Beryl. But, if I ever get worried about the way you are looking after her, I will tell you. I don't expect you to believe me now, because you don't know me. You'll have to find that out.

Again the worker emphasized her concern with an emotional issue — frustration. At the same time she tried to relate to their immediate fears — that she would not stick with them, that she was more interested in the child than in them, and that she would use her power to remove the child. Despite the seeming complexity of this offer, she was straightforward on each of these issues.

Back at the office, however, she expressed her understanding differently. The report ended:

The mothering this couple demand, need and refuse to give each other has got off balance and is causing enormous frustration to them in terms of complete lack of satisfaction and inability to manage their lives adequately. There seems to be gross emotional immaturity and a complete lack of masculinity around apart from Mrs Gilcrux's drive to be both mother and father to Beryl. Both Mr and Mrs Gilcrux related more strongly to Beryl than to each other.

Initial goal: to limit the work to help them get the mothering into better balance; too ambitious to think in more heterosexual terms.

It is unlikely that Mr and Mrs Gilcrux would have accepted this definition of their problem, even if they could have understood it. Obviously it is not enough for workers simply to say that they wish to work with emotional issues. They have to demonstrate a competence to do so. This is probably partly conveyed by the confidence with which the worker makes an offer, but also by some demonstration either in words or action of an ability to recognize and accept some basic aspect of the clients' emotional needs. Thus in contrast to the first interview with Mrs Buzzard, the Mothersills' worker related to the desperation of the situation ('Can I stand this?') and the Levens' worker to the emptiness from which Mr Levens took refuge in alcohol ('Your marriage is as dead as a dodo when you're sober'). With some of our core sample clients, actions seemed to speak louder than words. The Gilcruxes' worker simply acted out her understanding of their need for mothering and comfort by reading 'Mrs Tittlemouse'. Rather than make any interpretation about the mothering being off balance, she temporarily mothered all the family out of her feelings towards them at that moment. As we see it, what was important in her response was her genuineness and the warmth in the demonstration of a relatively accurate understanding.

Reading the story of 'Mrs Tittlemouse' was important in an emotional sense, but not in a practical one. Sometimes, however, a couple's immediate situation was so unfortunate that it seemed impossible not to do anything practical. This could make a longer-term therapeutic task more difficult by diluting the message that the worker was also concerned with emotional issues and by appearing to make the worker, rather than the clients, responsible for the outcome. The following example illustrates the worker tackling the practical problems and, nevertheless, enabling the couple to stand on their own feet. He was not, however, able to work with the underlying emotional issues.

Mr and Mrs Scattergood, lavatory attendants, were evicted, but managed to get themselves into hospital when found sitting among their possessions on the pavement, singing, but 'dead drunk'. Discharged to very unsatisfactory temporary hostel accommodation, they felt too insecure to resume their jobs. Mr Scattergood's disabled leg circumscribed their walking distance and their income from benefit was not sufficient for them to make much use of public transport or to find the deposit or down payment of the exorbitant rents in the area in which they had worked.

I was left with the impression of a disabled pair having nobody else in the world but each other, clinging together helplessly in adversity and not daring to allow any angry feeling to enter their relationship with each other. I felt that it was important to try and mobilize their own capacity to help themselves which I suspected might be around, despite the appearance to the contrary.

In order to do this I found that I needed to be quite active myself in making suggestions to them about how they should go about the business of finding more suitable accommodation and trying to ensure that they did it. I also set about attempting to raise some money from charity in order to get in a position to help them with any payment of a deposit or rent in advance. The effect of both being active myself and endeavouring to mobilize them into progressive activity was quite dramatic. They quite soon agreed to meet me at the office instead of visiting them in the rather miserable circumstances of their room, where they appeared to be so trapped and helpless.

The difference between their appearance in that room and their appearance at my door was quite stark. In place of the helpless puppets, activated by the puppet-master, there appeared two well-dressed, confident-looking people.

The practical problem of getting them out of their insecure, inadequate temporary accommodation was relatively easy to resolve and they were soon settled and attempting to make plans to re-establish themselves.

As this began to happen and Mr Scattergood's health improved, so Mrs Scattergood became more depressed and more complaining. This confirmed a fantasy I had about them fostered by an image of them as lavatory attendants, occupying adjacent lavatories, coming in and out alternately like the two figures on a barometer.

While I had been engaging on the practical effort with them I was also trying to listen and respond to the cares about their marriage. As his health improved I tended to concentrate my attention on Mrs Scattergood, who became more depressed and angry. I explained to them both that I was continuing my contact because of my concern for Mrs Scattergood, but making sure that I saw him every third week.

In this case a contract to work with the marriage was never made explicit.

Their inner wretchedness which their appearance and behaviour so often expressed was also etched in the legitimate wretchedness of their situation. A working problem, however, was that the dire straits in which they found themselves were very readily discernible, while their inner distress and its causes could only be uncovered slowly. It also seemed a problem that in working from the social services department I may have been seen by them as being primarily concerned with the environment rather than their inner distress, so that without very explicit linking of the one with the other it was difficult to obtain more than fleeting access to their enduring pain.

The negotiation of a therapeutic as opposed to a purely practical role was often more difficult when the case was transferred and the new worker wanted to work in a different way from the previous one. The Whitesides were transferred, had numerous problems but not an overt marital one; it was only the outside world that was bad and made life so impossible for them. They welcomed the first offer, however, which was simply, as with many cases,

I can come and see you every week at this time, if you want me to.

As already pointed out, the offer implied a purpose beyond their continual material propping-up to which the Whitesides had been exposed. The implications of this were spelt out again. On the first visit the Whitesides had asked for a clothing grant and the worker had said that she could not arrange any grants until she knew them better. On the fourth visit Mr Whiteside asked when the worker was going to give them the grant.

'I'm not recommending you for a grant; you had one in ...'

'But that was for winter clothes and now they want summer clothes'.

'You'll have to buy them out of your own money'. The Whitesides were dismayed.

'Obviously you don't like it when I say "no". Perhaps you have difficulty in saying "no" to the children. I haven't heard you say it.'

Mr Whiteside looked puzzled and then said, 'No, you've got it wrong. When we've got it, we give it; when we ain't, we don't.'

'You've read the papers and know as well as I do that money is short; the Council ain't and I don't'.

Mr Whiteside also defined the meaning of the contact in negative terms. The next week he solemnly announced he had passed his HGV test (at his third attempt) and solemnly thanked the worker. She disclaimed any responsibility and congratulated him. Again he thanked her, so she asked him what he was thanking her for.

'We had all that talk about it, but you didn't wish me luck'.
'Why's luck so awful?'
'Why? Luck's always bad'.

The use of the concept of luck is revealing. The idea that all depends on luck and the idea of helplessness go together — unpleasantly so, if, as with Mr Whiteside, your luck is only bad. Mr Whiteside was therefore relating to the core of the worker's endeavour — her wish to get the Whitesides to a point where they were not at the mercy of luck and officials and could manage on their own.

The worker did not like the relationship to be defined only on the negative terms of what she did not do. Three months later, when weekly visits had been re-established after a mutual period of rejection, she was still not clear where she should focus the work, and asked them to define the purpose of her visits.

'Why do you still want me to come every week?' 'I can't explain', said Mrs Whiteside. After much thought she added, 'You sits'.

Three months later, when asked again, she got a little further:

'I still can't explain, but you sits and you listens; that's all I can say'.

Five months later she herself reopened the subject.

'I've got it now why you have to go on coming. You sits, you listens,
and when you do that, then I don't think I'm as silly as I used to'.

NEGOTIATIONS: LIMITS

In the negotiations we offered ourselves as an attachment figure
whom the clients could depend on to be at the office or on their
doorstep at regular intervals. We offered the same day, the same
time and the same length of available time. This regularity is usual
in clinical practice and we took this way of working with us from
our clinic to our new setting. When going on holiday we gave
several weeks' or even months' notice. We did not offer locums,
and although some clients were given the name of another worker
they could contact, they rarely did this. During the period of
heightened attachment we sent them postcards to let them know we
had not forgotten them, and to remind them of our return.

Despite the degree of our clients' disturbance we did not offer
unlimited access, either by inviting the clients to 'drop in' at the
office or by giving them any expectation that we would see them if
they did so. In doing this we adopted a role that differed from that
of the traditional attachment figure. Initially, at least, a mother
comes more or less when she is called by her toddler. There were,
however, several reasons why we kept our contact with clients
within a clear schedule.

Firstly, we assumed any therapeutic work is concerned with very
painful and ambivalent feelings about the problem, the request for
help and the possibility of change. We believe that clients and
workers feel safer and, therefore, more responsive to each other if
interviews take place on a regular basis and have a set allocation of
time. The attempt to achieve such regularity also has diagnostic
value. It is not possible to work with the problem of the client's
disorganization, unreliability or inability to wait, if the worker does
not provide a framework against which this can be experienced, or
if he himself is behaving in a similarly disorganized manner. Nor is
it possible for the worker to experience his idiosyncratic response to
a particular client (which is of diagnostic importance) if his own
behaviour is perpetually idiosyncratic. His own confusion, muddle,
or forgetting an interview does not help him to understand what the
client does to people if that is typical of the way he normally works.

Our second reason for scheduling our appointments related to our part-time status in the department. This made it important for us to contain our clients. We did not want the full-time workers on 'cover' duties burdened by our cases during the half of the week when we were not there. We therefore told our clients that we were part-time and which days we were actually in the borough.

Having begun in this way we came to believe that our clients were not suffering by our practice of making appointments and that regular and reliable contact was of more benefit to them than unlimited access. Although the Thistlethwaite family was one of the more disturbed families (attempted murder, family violence, school refusal of a twelve-year-old, inability to work of a twenty-year-old) on the worker's caseload, the situation was contained on fortnightly visits and showed some change and improvement on this amount of contact. The IMS worker, used to working on a weekly basis and comfortable with this timing, does not know why she offered this family fortnightly contact when she did have time to see them weekly. Perhaps she made an unconscious compromise between Mrs Thistlethwaite's expressed need of her and Mr Thistlethwaite's fear of her.

One reason for providing limited access was to demonstrate to the client that although the worker had other calls on his time and could not visit on demand, this did not mean that he was unreliable. By working in this way a worker can avoid a 'switchback' effect whereby he vainly tries to meet the client's demands and then reverses his strategy as these pass his threshold of tolerance. Such behaviour can only reinforce the client's belief that support is a matter of all or nothing. In contrast, a worker who arrives regularly and on time challenges a client's assumption that a person who has left them does not care and will not return. Such workers provide a means whereby the client can build up trust that a promise can be kept.

A further reason for providing limited access was the hope that it would foster the clients' ability to help themselves and to distinguish between real and unreal crises. Unlimited access can easily lead the worker into subversive caregiving, and thus encourage the clients in the belief that they are helpless, or that the help they need can only be met outside their own circle. In work with married couples it is important not to fall into an illusion that the worker can meet a need normally met by a spouse. It is not possible to get into the work with these clients without being sensitive to their infantile needs, wishes and fears. At the same time it does not help them to forget that they are adults, are married and in the last resort responsible for their own actions.

Obviously, limited access did not mean that we were not prepared to make additional visits in times of crises as, for example, when the worker visited Mr and Mrs Jafferji two days running, when the baby was collected from hospital. In fact, some of us preferred to do our own crisis work and asked for urgent messages to be telephoned through to us at the IMS on the days that we were not in the borough. On five occasions during the two years we felt it necessary to visit on our non-borough days. Two of us, once we had established the major boundaries and knew our clients, ignored the night and weekend duty system, giving our home telephone numbers to some of our clients when it appeared that they might not be able to hold their anxiety until the appointed visit, even if, as an exception, it had been put forward. We preferred to deal with any such crises, believing that it was the specific attachment figure that was important and who would be more likely to hold the panic. The two numbers were used four times during the two years. They were offered explicitly with goodwill and trust that the clients would not abuse them unnecessarily. As some said, knowing where they could contact the worker, enabled them not to have to ring.

As expected, however, the assurance of this regularity kept down the panic crises. In fact two of our additional weekend visits related to celebrations, although one of these was requested in case something went wrong. Mr Gilcrux's long-lost son was arriving for the weekend. It was as important to him to show off his son as it was to have some support available if the reunion went wrong. (But the worker did not produce the gift she had bought for the celebration until she was sure they were celebrating.) On another Saturday, the worker attended the wedding of Mr and Mrs Thistlethwaite, who had been cohabiting for seventeen years, because, as they said, 'it is all your fault, making us respectable'.

NEGOTIATIONS: MARITAL WORK

As marital caseworkers, we were obviously concerned to work with both partners, believing that the marital relationship can be an important element in many family problems. Because of our core sample clients' difficulties with third parties, we did at times have to be quite opportunistic.

On a transfer visit the new worker said she would come and visit once a fortnight on a certain day at a certain time, but on that visit met only Mrs Thistlethwaite. Mr Thistlethwaite, heavily disabled by a paralysis, would not see the workers. On the next visit he was still kept hidden or hiding himself from the new worker, who then asked if she could meet him. The request was refused but by this time used to raising her voice above the rows of some of her clients, she lifted it once again so that it could be heard in the bedroom. A fortnight later the door to the bedroom was open, but she was again informed that Mr Thistlethwaite did not want to see her. However, in this interview, Jasper, the twenty-year-old son, who in previous interviews had refused to acknowledge the worker's presence, deigned to talk to her. After one of her shouted comments which referred to his identification with his father's paralysis, there was a contradictory bellow from the bedroom.

'I think we're in the wrong room', said the worker, upon which Jasper flung himself into the bedroom, quickly followed by the worker dragging Mrs Thistlethwaite behind her. All three landed on the bed on Mr Thistlethwaite's paralysed form. At the end of what was a highly charged interview the worker said, 'We'll go on talking about these things next time'. But the next interview did not have to take place on the bed. Mr Thistlethwaite was up and ready in his wheelchair.

Mrs Thistlethwaite, however, was not sure that she wanted these family interviews and had been used to seeing the previous worker, sometimes several times a week, on her own. Before the next fortnightly visit she called at the office with another problem. The worker was not there to see her, but sent a note to say she had got the message and would be visiting, *as arranged and promised,* to discuss it.

As seen in the above example, and as discussed in chapters 3 and 10, it was often difficult to negotiate a contract which genuinely involved both parties. Even when contact had been established on this basis, it was easily lost.

The Gilcruxes' worker made her initial engagement with both of them, but was then overcome by her curiosity about certain features of Mrs Gilcrux's behaviour and offered her some single interviews. This gave Mr Gilcrux the opportunity to opt out before he had become firmly attached and reinforced his view that the problem was all in Mrs Gilcrux. She quickly came off the drink and started to function very much better. The soberer she became, the drunker Mr Gilcrux got and the marital situation deteriorated even further. Met in the street, he looked a woebegone, 'down and out' sight when he thanked the worker for what she was doing for Mrs Gilcrux, but he still refused to join his wife at the next interview.

Concerned about what she had done, the worker then refused to discuss any of their joint financial problems with Mrs Gilcrux on her own. There was stalemate until the worker commented on Mrs Gilcrux's enjoyment of having the interviews on her own and the feeling of having the worker just for herself. Mrs Gilcrux sheepishly agreed and the worker wondered why she could not share her with her husband. Mrs Gilcrux had no idea, but again nodded when the worker suggested she might feel that she would lose out and perhaps feared that the worker might like Mr Gilcrux better than herself.

The next week they both arrived for the interview, Mrs Gilcrux looking resplendent in a smart coat, the gawky pony-tail into which she had previously dragged her hair from the temples replaced by a short hairstyle shaped round her face. 'Look at my wife', said Mr Gilcrux; and the worker agreed how nice she looked, admiring both the coat and the hairstyle. Mrs Gilcrux was noticed. In single work, attention could have been focused on her growing attachment to the worker, perhaps dressing up for her, perhaps identifying with her. In marital work the emphasis needs to be more on the interaction between the husband and wife and in this instance the focus could have been directed towards the two of them sharing the worker. But the worker was too anxious about Mr Gilcrux, could not wait for this to emerge and commented that, although it was nice for Mr Gilcrux to have his wife looking so good, this was perhaps also difficult for him when he was not feeling so good himself. Mr Gilcrux said he felt pretty awful and drew attention to his face, which was one mass of blotches. The suggestion that they should have a joint discussion about how they were going to manage their finances and debts and then that Mr Gilcrux should remain for a single interview was accepted. Only by the skin of her teeth had the worker got the work back into the marriage, their joint problems and their interaction in which they were so undermining of each other. The work then continued in a mixture of joint and single interviews.

LIMITED ATTACHMENT

In this chapter, we have recorded our response to a dilemma. On the one hand the worker needs to offer herself as an attachment figure to clients who are in extremes of despair and anxiety. On the other hand, for practical and other reasons, the worker is unable to offer anything like the attachment experience the clients probably want and certainly never had. Clients given too brief or limited an offer for attachment are lost or at least fail to engage with the worker. Clients given too much are in danger of exhausting the worker and failing to learn that they themselves can resolve situations and that even limited attachment relationships can be helpful.

The characteristics of our offer were that we tried to keep a tight boundary around our work and avoid unlimited access. We challenged the clients' emphasis on 'material tokens' by offering a contract concerned with emotional problems and, again contrary to what the clients often wanted, we tried to involve both spouses from the beginning. Our refusal or inability to meet many of the clients' practical or emotional demands evoked their anger and became an important part of the work with them.

In this way we could be said to be 'challenging', although we hope not 'attacking', in trying to work with what we saw as the emotional problems underlying the families' difficulties. But we did this within a firmly offered framework and then within an increasingly familiar and strong relationship, which, like all close relationships, contained conflict and negative as well as positive feelings on both sides. We do not think we could have looked at some issues with the clients until we had become familiar and were experienced as relatively safe and caring, even if we did not always do what they wanted or even took a court order. To anticipate the next chapter, one worker does not think she could have banged her clients' heads together in fury and desperation if they had not known of her affection for them.

13   Wading Upstream

And we are here as on a darkling plain
Swept with confused alarms of struggles and flight.
                                          Matthew Arnold

We cannot neatly divide the subjects of this chapter from the last —
the beginning of the work from its continuance. In the ongoing
work we tried to engage with both partners in a contained and
regular way. We offered them a relationship with ourselves which
could then be used in modifying their relationship with each other
and with other people. And we continued to negotiate the gulf
between their and our expectations.

As for the outcome, it must already be clear that we cannot write
about 'cure'. We can write only about what we found to be possible
with some of our clients. In these terms, we believe we helped some
of them to become less destructive towards themselves, each other
and their children. Such changes did not necessarily mean that our
clients stayed together. Our core sample clients were unable either
to leave each other or to live less miserably together. For us, a
positive outcome was an easing of this dilemma. This could mean a
continued togetherness with less misery and less threat of
separation. Or it could mean an ability to remain separated and to
tolerate and manage being on their own. We had successes and
failures among those who stayed together and those who parted.
For example, we considered the work with the Briggs a failure and
with the Mothersills a success even though both couples stayed
together.

Our assessment, in more particular terms, related to changes in
behaviour connected with characteristics originally defining our

197

core sample and the more specific features of behaviour we
described in chapters 6 to 8. We were concerned not only with a
lessening of the ambivalence of the marital bond, but also with our
clients' ability to form more supportive links with either relatives or
neighbours; to maintain a better standard of child care; to manage
their own affairs and problems; to be less obsessed with blaming
others; to handle three-person situations more comfortably; and to
seek what they wanted in terms of care, affection and attention in
less counterproductive ways. With those who eventually separated,
we hoped they would not have to repeat exactly the same pattern
with another partner. With those cases in which a child was in
trouble of one sort or another — for example, an adolescent unable
to free himself from parental clutches — we were concerned with
what happened to other members of the family. We did not think
the outcome was good if one child benefited at the expense of
another member of the family.

At the end of the project, when we left the couples with whom we
had worked on a sustained basis over a period of months or years,
we could not say that any of them showed distinct changes in all
these areas. Changes, however, there were. The Whitesides, for
example (not coming within the definition of the core sample, but
one of the more disturbed couples on the caseload) spent more time
out of bed during the daytime than in. Mr Whiteside could
maintain much longer periods of work. Mrs Whiteside did not have
to accompany him on the lorry and was, in fact, able to take, for
erratic periods of time, various jobs to help pay off the debts and
even to get herself promoted to chief cashier. The children were
healthier and functioning more in accordance with their age. All
the family had ceased to 'go septic' at regular intervals. The outside
world became less of an enemy to them and even a judge in court
could be experienced as behaving sympathetically towards them
over their debts. They became able to quarrel and get irritable with
each other. Sadly, Mrs Whiteside did not know whether she was
still in love with her husband. Moreover, their debts were still large;
and their transactions with their relatives, friends and enemies,
whom, in reaction to stress, they imported into their flat in large
numbers, continued to amaze the worker.

Sometimes the outcome was better for one partner than for the
other. Mrs Arncrow left her husband and took the two children
with her. She had great difficulty in managing on her own in

homeless families accommodation and returned to the marital home when her worker was on holiday. Six months later she left again and this time the circumstances of the accommodation were kinder and more supportive than the previous ones. Even so, she became very depressed and barely able to manage the children. Fortnightly visits were increased to weekly ones. Eventually she was able to stir herself and prepare for a move to self-contained accommodation which she did not want to make. When established in this, she started to make it into a home and ceased to agitate for nursery places for the children. After the worker left, Mrs Arncrow got herself involved as an accessory in a shoplifting offence, but was not charged.

The work with Mr Arncrow, however, did not, apparently, have a good outcome. During the period of his telephone threats to kill the worker for 'abducting' his wife, there was one interview with seemingly little effect. After further threats, he failed to maintain any direct contact. Finally the threats lost momentum and then ceased. It is not known what happened to him.

It is of course, questionable whether the changes in the behaviour of Mr and Mrs Whiteside and Mrs Arncrow were connected with the efforts of the workers. In the light of our theory of casework, we believe that they were if two conditions applied: if the clients' problems of relating came up in their relationship with us in such a way that we could then work with them; and if these same problems were then lessened in relation to other people. Thus, if we worked with the clients' fear of being attached and their difficulties in managing mixed feelings as they were shown towards us, and they then became better able to be attached to their partner, we thought this outcome owed something to our efforts. Since our theory of casework is implicit in our interpretation of the material, the interpretation cannot be used to test the theory. Nevertheless, by looking at our cases in this way, we can examine the plausibility of the theory and illustrate the processes to be expected if it is true.

Despite the different courses the work could take, towards either more satisfying togetherness or sustained separation, there were certain recurring themes with which we worked. These were, necessarily, related to the particular features of behaviour we analysed in Part 2 and, we believe, to outcome. We have called them 'The Three Ss'. They are concerned with *Surviving, Splitting* and *Separating*.

SURVIVING

At the beginning of the work with a family there is a comparatively safe distance between worker and client. Previous experience can be brought to bear on the problems of another couple. Unknown clients may promise an interest, while many of those known over previous months and years seem to provide only intractable problems from which any attempt to escape is welcome. There is the intellectual attempt to understand the clients' interaction before the worker is dragged into the muddle, confusion and despair. There is often a wish to reach out with warmth, encouragement and hope to distressed people — another case with which to do better than the last.

With clients like those in our core sample, this excitement can quickly diminish to a feeling which one of our local authority colleagues described as that of 'wading upstream'. Experienced workers do not even feel the initial excitement, volunteering for such cases out of a sense of duty rather than for the sake of professional challenge. Hard-pressed seniors trade 'heavy cases' between groups, trying to keep the load of their team at a tolerable level. There is a sense of a stage army of such clients travelling from group to group, accumulating voluminous files as monuments to the heroic, if transient, efforts of the social workers thrown in their path.

Experience may bring disillusionment to clients no less than to workers. Initially a new worker can offer hope — 'At last, the Messiah'. With core sample clients holding this type of fantasy there is often, when the worker has offered to commit herself to the awfulness, an immediate improvement — a honeymoon period.

For example, the Mothersills' worker was initially taken aback by their violence and the dangerous nature of much that seemed to go on between them. Nevertheless, he felt he should stick to his promise and he descended weekly to their appalling flat. To his surprise, they were always there to meet him and, even more to his surprise, started to find their life somewhat better. They bought their eldest child a desk, and visited a jumble sale where they acquired two smart red chairs which Mr Mothersill carried to their home. They had their first Christmas tree in seven years of married life, and after Christmas a quite uncharacteristic peace descended on their joint interviews with the worker.

The worker was by now uncertain of what he should be doing and inclined to get out while the 'going was good'. He cut his weekly visits to two-weekly ones. The Mothersills responded by a return to their old pattern of rows. At first the worker refused to reinstate the weekly visits. At the point when he had decided that they were essential, there was a melodramatic incident involving the police and the night-duty social worker. The police forcibly removed the two children and the work which had begun so promisingly was now in a shambles and back to 'square one'.

We suggest that if the marriage were to endure and be in any way helpful to the partners, it was necessary for the worker and the clients to experience not only the honeymoon, but also a stint of uphill work. The return to 'square one' varied according to whether the clients separated or remained together. With clients who had separated, the children could become as blamed as the spouse had been. Or there could be a return to the spouse. For those who remained together, it could be a further flurry of alarms and acting-out, to which separation seemed the only solution.

Whichever way the course went, work with this kind of client holds little excitement except that of an offensive and escapist nature. Every ounce of the worker's resourcefulness is required in sticking with the clients and their emotional problems and in trying to use his feelings creatively rather than reproduce the reactions the clients generally get from other people. In doing this, the worker's essential task is, we believe, to survive, acknowledging the awfulness of the clients' situation, but retaining a sense that change is possible. In this way, the worker differs from the clients, who have little certainty that anyone will stick with them or that they themselves can ever emerge from their distress.

Initially, or after the return to 'square one', much time was often spent in trying to keep in contact with the clients and help them pick up the pieces after the various crises.

> I was coping like they were. I was trying to stop the whole thing from falling apart.

The survival of these crises, unpleasant though it was, could seem less difficult than the survival of the underlying despair. The maintenance of regular interviews often cut down the crises, but what does the worker do then?

Mr and Mrs Levens' despair came to the fore in the second joint interview after the negotiation with them to work on getting their marriage 'more lively when sober'.

In the first and preceding regular interview, 'they fairly quickly went into a row about Mr Levens' behaviour, Mrs Levens making all the accusations'. The worker commented on their having to show her what the rows were like. There ensued a working interview about Mrs Levens' attempts to take over Mr Levens, her prophesying his actions and his fulfilling the prophecy. Mr Levens' increasing attempts to say what he felt were made even more difficult for him by Mrs Levens' interruptions and her telling him what his feelings were. The worker felt relatively satisfied and had more idea of how they behaved together; Mr Levens was encouraged enough to proffer his work times for the next month so the next four interviews could be scheduled to fit with his shifts.

The next week they

> came in looking rather pleased with themselves and said that things had been much better. He had not been drunk and they had been talking. They then lapsed into dull apathy and seemed to have nothing to say.

The worker's comment that the previous week they had had to show her what the rows were about and that this week they 'had to show me what the dullness was like' was appropriate as far as it went, but did not go far enough. What they were offering for work was their hopelessness and despair and the worker failed to relate strongly enough to this and to hold on to it. She was almost relieved when they went into another row with Mrs Levens becoming more belligerent and talking to Mr Levens as if he were a naughty child. If not exactly entering into the row herself, the worker expressed Mr Levens' feelings for him and said to Mrs Levens that if 'you spoke to me the way you speak to Mr Levens, I would be tempted to hit you too'.

The next week they had another crisis. According to Mrs Levens, Mr Levens had been 'completely drunk'; according to Mr Levens, 'slightly the worse for wear'. They had, however, handled the crisis differently and emerged the other side without violence. The following week the apathy and the despair were again offered.

During this period of the work we sometimes, to echo the words of Mrs Whiteside, 'just sat', particularly when the clients' previous experience had been one of being taken over. We tried to help them find new responses of their own, both at a feeling and a practical level.

> 'I'm not going to answer all those questions', one client rather rudely said to a new health visitor who called on her. 'Even my social worker doesn't ask questions like that, but now we tell her. You'd better learn that you won't get it out of me like that'.

Sometimes we 'just sat' because we could not understand what lay beneath their constant complaint or what they were trying to tell us. Looking back on the working reports, we see there were weeks of dull apathy broken by arguments or strife. Sometimes in desperation we entered the discussion, profitlessly offering advice or admonition. These had little effect. The interpretations which apparently enabled them to relinquish or change their behaviour towards each other were few, remain etched on our minds and related to their relationship with us. Those that seemed to have the most effect were often those in which we could include reference to our own behaviour in relation to them, when previously we had got drawn into their interactive strategy and then only belatedly become aware of what we were doing.

We believe the treatment for despair, as opposed to depression, is to feel it, to know about it, acknowledge it, live with it and survive it without offering false comfort or seeking to escape into exciting and tension-relieving activity with the clients. Unlike depression, which is tinged with self-blame and remorse, despair is often offered in a circular tale of woe which gives little entry to the worker to get in touch with the internal 'corpses in the graveyard'.

> Mr Bootle has been out of work for the past two years because, as he says, there is some conspiracy against him which prevents his getting a job.

> Mrs Bootle was not looking so well and the usual complaints were made about various persecuting people who upset her, particularly her husband's mother.

> We went over the usual ground of his difficulty about work and his feeling of being excluded, having, as he put it, 'the bone pointed at him'.

The worker is often first aware of the underlying despair of his most active clients when he emerges from an interview feeling bowed down and even angry that he has been made into the most hopeless and ineffective of all social workers. Anything that he has struggled to say has appeared irrelevant or has been apparently unheard. He is dependent on his own feelings and reactions when he fails to get in touch with the denied feelings, probably of grief and yearning, of his clients. Once they give up the anger and before they can get in touch with these feelings, they seem to experience only emptiness. It is difficult to illustrate the 'staying with the emptiness' of the clients when they start to give up the fantasy of the ideal and some of the rage against their partner. How do you describe emptiness and nothing happening?

> Visited.

> The same old ground. Couldn't do anything about it.

> All they could say was that they didn't love each other. Then they started on the old complaints.

This is a time in the work when the worker can easily give up, particularly if he has not committed himself either explicitly or implicitly to the clients for a definite period. (Despair-avoiding techniques of a subversively caregiving order have been exhausted.) It is a time when even experienced workers, who have learnt with other clients that it can be survived with therapeutic effect, need their supervisors or working group to restore their belief that their own survival is what will strengthen their clients.

It is a painful time, but the worker's failure to be driven away ('destroyed', as it probably feels to the clients) by the slow and 'empty' interviews is apparently what makes the clients feel safer and, therefore, stronger, so that they can make some efforts for themselves of a less crisis-ridden nature. The worker may be the last person to hear about these, but 'throwaway' lines may show that the clients are making some more positive and hopeful moves in their lives.

> The kitchen has now been redecorated, but more important they have shifted the children out of their bedroom.

There was some anxiety that she might be pregnant. I was a bit surprised, but they shyly admitted to having had intercourse on one occasion about a fortnight ago.

Mrs Bootle showed me a ring her husband had given her for her birthday and told of the trouble he had gone to to ensure that the children gave her a present. In the face of this, their usual wrangle seemed rather hollow. He still has a lot of paranoid ideas, but again they are held with slightly diminished force.

Many of the clients in our core sample could not face the despair and offer it as directly to the worker as did Mr and Mrs Levens, who had been able to accept a regular working structure. However, the despair often came to the fore when a couple had been rehoused, particularly if they had come to the attention of the social work division through homelessness and problems thrown up in temporary accommodation. The unsatisfactory nature of the accommodation in some of the hotels which were used and rows with hotel managers provide ample opportunity for both clients and workers to avoid the marital problems which had sometimes been a major factor in the couple's having become homeless in the first place. When the accommodation problem was partially or wholly solved by the provision of adequate self-contained quarters, the despair came home to roost. Couples were sometimes found

> sitting pathetically and uncertainly in an under-furnished room as far away as possible from the uncurtained expanse of plate glass in a modern flat.

Sometimes they were

> surrounded by chaos and odd little photographs and the guitar, bits of disco equipment, all of which did not work, and the motor bike out front which also attempted not quite to work; a sort of Steptoe and Son atmosphere.

Clients were at last faced with themselves. No longer could their problems be attributed solely to the bricks and mortar, or mice in the hotel.

Some of us delayed in supporting an application for rehousing until we felt the couple were more ready to face themselves. Even so, we soon found it necessary, with clients who were visited less than once a week, to increase the visiting after a move to long-desired accommodation. They almost invariably regressed, getting themselves into difficult situations similar to those they had presented at the start of the work. The difficulties were, however, probably less protracted, if the clients knew that we continued to be concerned and understood both the practical and symbolic difficulties of moving house.

Sometimes they were more able to be depressed.

She realized now this was something in her, not the flat, not Sid.

And a similar realization could come after a separation had not brought the relief it promised.

Mrs Arncrow started to get depressed and this mainly centred on Eileen, the elder of the two children. The more depressed and with-drawn Mrs Arncrow became, the more the child regressed and the more demanding she became. It seemed that Eileen expressed the baby part of Mrs Arncrow for her — the part that did not want to manage and just wanted to be looked after and comforted. Presumably it was this attribute of her personality which had been attracted by the much older Mr Arncrow and his 'easy' money. She could not comfort the child. She responded to my comments in this vein and of her wanting me to care for her. She then got a bad bout of 'flu and her depression deepened. But the hotel proprietors kindly looked after her and the children. I increased the visits.

As they started to get more in touch with themselves and their feelings, they were able to bring out some very painful memories and it was more often at this stage of the work that we learnt of the more significant factors of loss and hardship in their childhood.

At this point Mr Bootle burst into tears. It had taken him much of the hour to get to this point. Mrs Bootle listened attentively and made cups of tea.

Those with previously bland faces looked more careworn, sadder and darker under the eyes. But in the interviews they became more thoughtful and self-examining. Some of the oldest hurts between couples, which they had attempted to suppress but which were still festering, were dragged out by one or other of them, not just as an accusation, but in an attempt to explain why they felt so badly.

> When she was pregnant, he had a stand-up prostitute, got infected and then infected her and the baby. This was only discovered when the baby was born. Mother and baby were separated in hospital and she felt herself ill-treated by the nurses. She felt terrible coming home without the baby.

Depression also had to be survived in terms of being lived with and shared. It is painful for the subject and for the sharer.

> After the interview I was powerfully depressed. Mr Bootle was so unhappy as he acknowledged the misery of the situation, the sorrow of his own upbringing, the inadequacies of their marriage and of his life. It was difficult to believe that through this he could come to some more constructive adjustment, and yet it was clear that without reaching his present depression, there was no hope of change for the better.

In contrast to despair, depression involves a greater range of emotion and an ability on the part of the individual to feel guilt and accept some responsibility for his own actions. This leaves the worker emotionally and intellectually freer. The real sadness has to be borne, and yet paradoxically allows the worker much more entry into the tale of shame and misery. It suddenly becomes much easier to see connections and make interpretive comments which previously defied expression. By this time the clients were usually less fearful of getting taken over by the worker, could listen more readily and allow themselves to be influenced.

> Mr Gilcrux tentatively began to work and his feelings started, as he said, to 'flower'. He emerged as a strongly feeling person. And I felt increasingly free to chance my arm, as he was able to tick me off if I got it wrong.

Of course many of the clients were never able to do this and, with those that were, there was no suddenly acquired ability, but much going backwards and forwards to and from the old accusatory despair.

> Somehow we got back again on to Mr Bootle's paranoid system which I found difficult to shift this week. It was as if he had

hardened up on it once more and was determined to have things his way.

Then a few weeks later,

> At the end of the session he made a very moving comment about the children and how he and his wife had not done very well by them in the first part of their lives. Only recently had he been able to understand what their needs were and how they could be met. He talked of his guilty feelings of having harmed them.

And throughout this period of work the same old themes were coming up again and again in the spiral, but with much less heat in them.

> We looked again at the way they both play the threat of abandonment and threaten each other with what they most fear themselves.

> The competition for my attention, however, seemed to be being played less wholeheartedly than it was and there does seem to be an easier feeling between them.

At this stage of the work the gulf between the clients' and the worker's definition of the problem was narrower. The ongoing negotiations between clients and worker and the clients' changing definition of what the work could be about indicated the overall progress.

Mr and Mrs Gilcrux and their worker had four main definitions during the two years. The reader may remember the first, stated by the worker and only dubiously agreed by them.

> 'I will try and help you to "de-frustrate".'

The second definition was attempted by them and corrected by the worker.

> 'You are our family'.
> 'I'm only a proxy'.

The third was suggested by Mr Gilcrux, agreed by the worker and doubtfully so by Mrs Gilcrux.

> 'I know what we're doing. Sweeping out from under the carpet'. (A very depressed phase.)

The fourth negotiation was confidently opened by Mr and Mrs Gilcrux, their base agreed before the worker arrived for the interview. This time she agreed their definition.

'I don't expect you know what we mean, but we've decided you're helping us to grasp the thistle. We say that in Scotland. You can't hold it like that; you have to hold it like this'.

SPLITTING

The model of casework we have been presenting has an analogy to the situation of a child who hurts himself, cries, runs to his mother, is held, and then returns to his play. (It was not only Mr and Mrs Gilcrux who seemed to obtain comfort from their child's sitting on the worker's lap while being read the story of Mrs Tittlemouse. Children of other very deprived couples often seemed to act out the unconscious wishes of the parents when they crawled over the worker. One of us retains a vivid picture of herself regularly peering round and over a tangle of three small bodies, one usually round the back of her neck, another on her lap, a third swinging on her leg, as she tried to listen to the latest tale of woe and relate to the despair beneath it. With other clients, the seating could be an important issue: 'Come and sit on the sofa', and then a surreptitious sidling closer.) What is important in this model is the comfort and confidence which the helpful adult conveys to the child and which enables him to carry on. The difficulty with our core sample clients was in standing by people who were engaging in frantic activity or were deeply despairing or depressed.

This model was important, but not, in itself, enough. Our clients, despite their emotional deprivation, were adults and far less helpless than they often imagined themselves to be. Because of their deprivation they tended to idealize the 'good mother' they felt they had never had. By idealizing and putting all the good into another, they left themselves even emptier than before.

We could very easily get 'hoist with our own petard'. We needed to relate through the misery and awfulness to the underlying need. However, the more successful we were, the more likely we were to get idealized and, therefore, to reinforce the defensive strategy of splitting — in this case between the ideal and the 'impossible'. The more we were idealized, the more denigrating one or both partners became of the other. Idealization of the worker also resulted in a failure of the clients to learn that even the imperfect have their uses. It prohibited what could be a more useful (un-idealized) relationship with the worker being extended to other people.

This idealization was often covert, and such was the strength of the unconscious wish that sometimes we unknowingly responded without picking up quickly enough what was happening. (We think our failure in this respect could be a contributory factor in prolonging a honeymoon period and intensifying a 'back to square one' phase in the work. In the latter the worker fell from grace, often by going on holiday, and, in the estimation of one or both partners, joined the already denigrated spouse or spouses.)

After a year of somewhat harrowing work, the Mothersills' situation was once more in some sort of shape. The children were back home, marital violence had long been in abeyance, and Mrs Mothersill, pregnant with a third child, was hopeful that the pregnancy might be survived more easily than the previous two. Mr Mothersill was making efforts to support her. The worker, however, was due to go on holiday.

> At the last interview before Christmas, the Mothersills started a more than usually fruitless quarrel. Unable to understand any rational reason for it, I shouted at Mrs Mothersill that I didn't understand why she was shouting at Mr Mothersill. After all, it was I, not he, who was deserting her, and he, not I, who was sticking by her over Christmas. At once they fell quiet. Then Mr Mothersill said, 'You have to forgive us. We're very anxious people'.

In this transaction the worker exposed a defensive ploy which Mrs Mothersill often used. When she was angry with the worker, she attacked Mr Mothersill. This was not only unfair, but did nothing to improve the marriage. It did, however, maintain the official picture of the ideal worker, more educated, and apparently more in command of his own affairs and able to help other people with theirs. At the same time this official picture emphasized the apparent helplessness and irresponsibility of the Mothersills and provided an excuse for it. Why should they try when the worker, felt by them to be a superior person, was taking care of them anyway?

This incident made a powerful impression on the worker, who

had previously failed to pick up what was happening. Intellectually he had already understood something of it, but emotionally he had not felt his own part in it. Now he had crudely shattered an illusion. He went home depressed and anxious, thinking of the Mothersills all alone in a frightening world. This interview, however, was a turning-point in the work with the Mothersills, who became, among other things, less anxious to please him, just as he became less anxious to protect them.

Some clients were more explicit in their idealization. After the worker had succeeded in getting Mr Gilcrux back into the work and there had been several joint interviews, Mrs Gilcrux reopened the negotiation of what the work was about. She said she wanted the worker to be 'mother, grandmother, uncle and aunt, all rolled into one'. 'You have to be *our* family', added Mr Gilcrux.

> 'No, I can't be that', said the worker. 'It's a nice idea, and I can see why you want me to be your family. But I can only be a proxy aunt, and only for a period. I can only work with you till December 1975. We can keep on having weekly meetings this year, and next year they will have to be fortnightly and then monthly before I leave you. Then you will manage on your own. You are your family'.

Within the hope we offered of a reliable attachment figure from whom they could dare to be more exploratory, we had to be, in Winnicott's terms, 'good enough'. [1] It was important not to attempt to be superhuman or let the clients imagine that we might be. It is too easy to be the ever-loving, ever-empathic, ever-ready, ever-listening, 'Yes, I will' worker. Such a worker, however, usually gets more and more furious with the apparently unceasing demands of the clients and ends up by giving a double message of lack of boundary and reality of response on the one hand, and of underlying fury on the other. More therapeutic, we found, was to say 'No' when this seemed appropriate, and to face facts which, at times, included the awfulness of the clients' behaviour, and then say, 'I'll come again next week'.

By saying 'No' and sometimes letting our anger show, we invited theirs. At the same time we offered a feasible model for their

---

[1]   Winnicott, D.W. (1965), *The Family and Individual Development* (Tavistock).

behaviour — no one can be understanding all the time — and emphasized our belief that the clients had a part to play in resolving their own difficulties, and were able to play it.

Mrs Cabassi reached one of her peaks of hysterical anxiety about 'the man who would not provide' when, following a period of Mr Cabassi being unemployed, they were threatened with eviction. She provoked him into beating her up and then summoned him for assault. Despite the threat of eviction, and to the worker's fury, she refused to use any of her own earnings to pay off the arrears or even for any household expenses. In one interview,

> she bewailed the threat of eviction. I asked her why she expected me to have sleepless nights while she did nothing but blame her husband. She looked rather taken aback and then said, 'because you care about us, I suppose'.

Subsequently she still refused to help pay off the arrears, but she did start contributing to the household expenditure. In later interviews the worker was quite explicit that she would take no steps to prevent their eviction if they deliberately left rent unpaid and said that she expected them to maintain basic necessities, such as a roof over their heads, if she was to continue to work with them on their marriage. They then negotiated with the housing department how the arrears were to be paid and at the next interview Mrs Cabassi reported, although with one of her most secretive smiles,

> 'We've had no more fights since you told us off'.

An important distinction regarding the refusal of material and monetary and influential benefits has to be made. If a worker considers that his aim is to provide an efficient material service, there is no point in refusing to provide anything that can be acquired or to use his influence to help the clients obtain their desired ends. There is, however, point in refusing if he is attempting, through the medium of a personal relationship, to reduce the felt helplessness and emptiness of the clients and is trying to get their anger as well as their affection on to himself. In these two situations, with their opposing aims, the criteria used on whether to provide or not to provide are quite different.

We refused to meet a lot of the clients' material requests,

particularly when these seemed to be part of their efforts to keep the relationship on an economic and token basis and we were trying to help them to become more self-sufficient. However, we did, of course, encourage them to exercise their welfare rights, and, at times, supported their applications for supplementary benefits 'special needs' grants, drew section 1 monies and applied to charities for private grants for them. But we did this as sparingly as possible, although on one occasion an IMS worker asked for one of the biggest loans on record.

We usually helped our most helpless clients write letters to courts, to landlords, to service boards and to the DHSS by helping with the spelling, and by offering ideas and even phrases, but we refused to write the actual letters. Mrs Whiteside was no writer nor speller, but developed a useful turn of phrase. Her worker got her to dictate what she wanted to say (usually asking for further time to pay), toning down only the most noxious expressions, and then Mr Whiteside copied out the draft.

One worker was put in a difficult situation after refusing to write the required letter and telling her clients they must do it themselves. They had designed a competition and she was to be judge, she was told the following week, when she was offered both versions.

Sometimes we said we could send a supporting letter and sometimes we gave a copy of this to the clients. This served four purposes: it helped to meet *our* distrust of the filing system of large bureaucratic bodies; it associated our letter with the clients' request (when urging them to go down to the DHSS themselves, we suggested they took the copy with them); it also ensured they knew we did what we said; and it was obvious confirmation of our support which they could read and hold in their hands.

It became clearer after a time that the clients could use this type of model and we were able to leave them to do more and more of their own negotiating with officials they had previously seen as unapproachable enemies from whom no beneficence could be obtained. After Mrs Thistlethwaite appeared to have been treated very badly by a public body, she reminded her worker that, in fact, they had treated her well on the previous contact. 'I must say that for them', she said.

Mr and Mrs Whiteside made their first negotiatory bid with a GPO telephone manager by telephone in the worker's presence and with her 'egging' them on. They were given time to pay. At the end of the call Mr Whiteside told the manager that when all their debts were paid, others as well as this one, he and his wife would take the manager and social worker out for a meal. The worker unfortunately could not hear the reply.

At a later date, rent arrears mounted on a new flat and the worker was informed of a notice to quit. She made an extra visit. 'I can see from the look on your face that you've heard', said Mrs Whiteside. 'But you can take it off, because I did it myself. Sit down, go on, sit down, so I can tell you about it. When I got the notice I dashed out to the box to ring you. But then I remembered what you'd say. So I rang Mr Brown [housing officer] and he came to see us. We fixed up what we're going to pay off each week'.

After getting in credit, the Whitesides later acquired fresh debts (perhaps connected with their knowing of the worker's leaving them) and again the worker received a copy of the notice to quit. This time she did not make an additional visit, but on the regular, by now monthly, one, she was told that Mr Brown had told Mrs Whiteside he remembered her negotiating with him before and she was 'quite a negotiator'.

Although we were parsimonious on state and charity monies, we did offer tokens of our affection and goodwill and for this dipped into our own pockets. For example, having refused the Whitesides a clothing grant one week, the next week the worker gave Mr Whiteside a pound so that he could buy his hard-earned HGV licence and hold the actual prize in his hand. This was not strictly necessary; pay day was three days hence and he had the certificate of competence to show his boss and his friends. Mr Whiteside hinted broadly how awful it was not being able to believe that he had passed until he could go and buy the licence. The worker said she had heard the hint and she would prefer him to ask outright because he did now know that she could say 'no' if she felt she had to; but to mark this great occasion she would love to give him the pound. The following week he returned it, although it had been offered as a gift, not a loan.

Such gestures and small tokens could be interpreted in a variety of ways, and, in particular, as guilt money for being very tough on much bigger issues and for the plight of others. One worker queried what she called her 'Octavia Hill tendencies'. Sometimes she gave her couples small Christmas, birthday or holiday presents, and made it clear they were from her personally. The emphasis was on personal attachment. These small tokens, which represented the worker's sentiment, furthered the feeling of worth in the client and could not be construed as filling the gaps of economic mismanagement. This seemed an appropriate use of tokens, as long as the effect was closely watched and seen to further, rather than reduce, the clients' personal esteem.

And we, of course, accepted their small presents.

The therapeutic task was balanced on a very fine line. We had to give them enough support to enable them to undertake the task themselves without taking them over if there was a reasonable possibility of their managing on their own. Our refusal to take over some tasks kept evident our un-ideal nature and our support modified their anger about the refusal.

The outright 'No', which we at times gave, invited their anger on to ourselves. When refusing to obtain grants or to undertake activities for them, we made it clear that this was our decision and not that of another division of the department. Our aim was to get the opposing feelings on to ourselves and not split between us and other workers in either the same or different departments. We had to be known by our clients as persons who could say 'Yes' and 'No', who were caring and affectionate, but at the same time able to take their anger and not reject or let ourselves be rejected or destroyed by it. We also had to show that there were others apart from ourselves who could be trusted.

At times, of course, we failed. There was one occasion when an IMS worker was horrified because a member of the homeless families unit counteracted her plan and did it by speaking directly over the telephone to Mrs Arncrow in a way which, it seemed to the worker, had raised Mrs Arncrow's anxiety unnecessarily. The worker's fury was on behalf of her client and on behalf of herself, for having been overridden on what she considered was appropriate and commonsensical practice, and only having learnt of this from the client.

As she took the telephone and bellowed at the homeless families unit what she thought of it and its methods and policies, Mrs Arncrow, all ears, was certainly supported and knew she had her worker behind her. Such a division of good and bad, however, could well have accentuated her view of an all-good social worker and all-bad homeless families unit. She was not in the office the next day to hear the apology or the resolution. Only afterwards was the worker aware, still amazed at her own aggression and rudeness, that her spluttering rage partly represented that of Mrs Arncrow. She had lost her control in a manner remarkably similar to that of Mr Arncrow. Her subsequent insistence on what appeared to Mrs Arncrow to be an unwarranted move may, however, have been more healing in that it balanced and counteracted the previous fishwife display.

In other cases it was important to demonstrate an ability to share with ministers, GPs, schoolteachers and education welfare officers. One such case in the project group was referred by the police when they had picked up Gloria, aged fourteen. Supporting information indicated she was severely disturbed, more often out of than in the special school she was supposed to attend. The worker, in collecting information, found that her mother, Mrs Steggles, had called in numerous would-be helpers including the wife of the GP. One of the major problems of the worker was her relationships with these helpers, who fell into two distinct categories. There were those who talked in terms of 'colluding with the mother', if Gloria was removed from home; and there were those who talked in terms of 'amputating her from that dreadful woman'. It was difficult to know whether Gloria, by now completely refusing to go to school, should be in day or residential care pending a consultation at an adolescent psychiatric unit. It was difficult for the worker not to get completely seduced by either of the parents' contradictory messages which indicated their extreme ambivalence of wanting to get rid, and not being able to let go, of the girl.

The local authority worker was able to relate to both messages in the single (with the mother) and family interviews. At first by herself and subsequently sharing the task with the staff and patients at the day centre, she collected Gloria in the mornings. When she went on holiday, Gloria's attendance dropped off and her behaviour deteriorated. She reverted to a 'wild, depressed and confused animal', setting fire to the contents of drawers and exhibiting her faeces round the house. But, on the worker's return, when a vacancy in the adolescent unit came up, Mr Steggles was able to take her there with the worker, although 'in rather a detached manner'. He and his wife then visited her together at weekends. After a joint visit by this social worker and the one at the adolescent unit, Mr and Mrs Steggles were able to transfer satisfactorily to the latter.

One of the factors which enabled this to happen, we believe, was not only the verbal therapeutic work done with the mother in single interviews and the whole family in joint ones, but the model of co-operation offered by the social worker and staff and patients at the day centre. With the social worker, who was the attachment figure, the day centre staff refused to enact the split and the family's fantasy that nothing could be shared. In turns they collected Gloria in the mornings, cared for her during the day, and shared the caring with the parents by returning her home in the evening.

By the time of the referral Gloria was a patient in her own right, but she also drew attention to the disturbed relationships in the family including those between Mr and Mrs Steggles. All were helped to the adolescent unit.

The more readily the worker shares and works with others, the better the model he gives his clients and the better their chances of learning to share.

As we have already illustrated in previous chapters, one of the major difficulties of many of these couples was in sharing the worker. Nevertheless the worker's refusal to go along with the idea that she 'belonged' to only one partner could be therapeutic. Mrs Redhead often managed to get the worker's attention focused only on her after her repeated suicide attempts. He always responded with sympathy, although everyone else became increasingly irritated by her. Because the problem seemed so intractable, a co-worker was introduced at a joint interview. Plans were made to continue with these, but were rudely shattered by another suicide attempt three days later. Mrs Redhead was admitted to a psychiatric hospital on a compulsory order. The second worker persuaded the first worker not to follow his usual sympathetic pattern of visiting Mrs Redhead in hospital. She suggested he maintained the contact by letter, replying to one from Mrs Redhead asking for a visit. He wrote saying that the regular interviews with the two workers were continuing as planned, Mrs Redhead was missed and the workers looked forward to her getting home as soon as possible.

Neither Mr nor Mrs Redhead were sure they wanted this, particularly when a housing offer of a transfer to a better flat came up. This was frightening and deprived them both of their proclaimed reason for Mrs Redhead's depression. Much of Mr Redhead thought he had better 'throw in the sponge'. He could not manage a move on his own, he said. He did not want Mrs Redhead to do any heavy work over the move, but, if he changed flats, he wanted her to be there. Much of Mrs Redhead wanted to remain a dependant patient in hospital, but part of her objected to this and to the drugs she was given. The workers could concentrate only on Mr Redhead's ambivalent feelings, but they learnt from him that Mrs Redhead was now hiding, rather than swallowing, her pills. Eventually the two of them together persuaded the doctor to release Mrs Redhead. She arrived home three days before the move. There were no further suicide attempts and the whole situation between Mr and Mrs Redhead took a sudden turn for the better.

In this piece of work the therapeutic refusal was effective. It must, however, be seen in the context of the care she had previously received from the first worker over a period of nearly two years and the promise that he would continue to see her in the joint interviews in her own home. Without this, the refusal would probably have felt totally rejecting and heartless and would have been quite meaningless.

SEPARATION

The theme of separation was important for a variety of reasons; because threats of separation were a defining characteristic of our core sample clients; because a number of them did separate from each other; because, even if they did not, one of the aims of the work was to loosen the stranglehold they kept on each other; and because we ourselves finally separated from them.

In some respects, separation from a social worker who has become an attachment figure raises the same issues as those we discussed in our last section. The person who is left is likely to feel anger at the person leaving and has to take more responsibility for himself. In addition, however, there are feelings of sadness and loss. Examples of a number of separation themes occurred in the Frizington family, where the teenage son's suicide attempt had brought him to the attention of the psychiatric services. It transpired that he had been on drugs. The father was drinking excessively. The daughter was continually failing her examinations even though she was of university material. In addition, the wife, the one person not alleged to be on drugs, alcoholic or highly neurotic, was said to exercise a subversive role in relation to the three other members of the family.

Although the Frizington family were a core sample family, contact with them was relatively brief, over a period of months, and the outcome, although limited, was satisfactory. Mr Frizington stopped drinking, although he later returned to it in a more moderate way. The daughter and the son were able to become more separate; the daughter got herself to university; the son, who had been prevented by a number of phobias from going out on his own, was able to go on holiday and later to return to his studies.

These changes were, like those in many of our clients, necessarily achieved by the family's own efforts. However, the worker also played his part by sticking with them over a particularly fraught period and by refusing some of their overt and implicit requests. The following extract is a typical account of a home visit.

> Saw Mr and Mrs Frizington. Mr Frizington very drunk. He said to show me I could not stop him drinking. Very bad week for them with lots of rows. A bitter confrontation in front of me. Mr Frizington said he had been depressed for the past seven years and his wife had always treated him like a baby, giving him £1 a day pocket money. He had no will to stop drinking unless the situation improved. Mrs Frizington blames everything on his drinking.

The worker said there was nothing *he* could do to stop Mr Frizington drinking. He did, however, suggest that Mr Frizington should seek medical advice about his physical state and the implications of continued drinking. He then refused to agree to the family's request to get the son into hospital and to the daughter's request to continue a brief series of individual interviews beyond the time which had originally been agreed between her and himself. She did not like this, although she said that her previous experience with adults had always been that they took her over and that she felt a failure in relation to them. The worker felt that his refusal to take over could also have been an important element in the outcome.

Another factor may have been the worker's ability to understand something of the background reason for Mrs Frizington's subversive caregiving. When Mr Frizington had gone into hospital, Mrs Frizington, who had previously refused any interviews on her own, welcomed the worker. He learnt that for complicated reasons she had placed the two children in a day nursery when they were young. She had always felt that this was a great loss to herself and probably for the children as well. She had become pregnant for a third time and had planned for things to be different with this baby. The pregnancy, however, ended in a miscarriage. In a very sad interview, Mrs Frizington described the layette she had bought for this expected baby and the terrible loss she had felt after the miscarriage. It did not then seem so surprising to the worker that she had to continue to baby her husband and the children.

In this instance the worker did not relate Mrs Frizington's feelings of loss about the baby to the approaching loss of himself. In other cases, however, the loss of the worker became a major issue. Mrs Calder was outwardly concerned when her worker told her that she was leaving to have a baby. Mrs Calder offered the worker tomato soup, because she had had a craving for this when she herself had been pregnant with one of the children. When the worker was leaving this interview, Mrs Calder made an exaggerated fuss that she must be careful not to fall down the front-door steps. Her expression, however, belied this verbal concern and intimated that she would like to push the worker down the steps. One hand came forward to push her, the other to support and save her.

Needless to say, many of our clients tried to prevent us from leaving:

'But who shall we have to talk to?'
'Each other'.
'But we like you coming'.
'Yes, and I've liked coming too. I shall miss you, just as you say you'll miss me. But you can't have a social worker all your life'.
'I don't mind'.
'Well, you're not having one. I think you two can manage on your own'.

In this example, the pain of parting was faced consciously. With other cases, matters were less clear-cut. The second year of working with the Mothersills included a long desultory phase marked by a complicated three-handed game between the worker, the Mothersills and the housing department in which no side was quite sure of the cards or motives of the others. Matters only began to be resolved when the worker announced that in a few months he thought the Mothersills could manage on their own. Mr Mothersill, who spasmodically was capable of magnificent action, delivered a letter to Downing Street and received a reply and an offer of rehousing in the same week. Mrs Mothersill, faced with the trauma of rehousing and the worker's departure, experienced such an acute attack of anxiety that her GP referred her to a psychiatrist. The worker relented and offered to see them over the move.

The move was fraught and soon the rent arrears mounted alarmingly. However, Mrs Mothersill was able to ask her husband for support and he was able to respond. The marriage became softer. Violence was quite a thing of the past. When the time came for the worker and the Mothersills to part, Mrs Mothersill again became extremely anxious and her anxiety focused on the loss of her teeth. The dentist could not understand why the extraction of two teeth should provoke such an extreme reaction. In the final interview, the worker suggested that perhaps her anxiety was related to his own departure and that for her this must be rather like losing a relative. This remark stopped the fractious quarrel which the Mothersills were managing to whip up. The interview became calmer and Mr Mothersill said that the worker had been like a baby-walker, and that now they would have to walk on their own.

As we stated in the introduction to the previous chapter, the worker's belief in the couple's ability to manage together was an important element in strengthening their self-image. And as important in the final strengthening process was the worker's ability, like that of any parent figure when a son or daughter is leaving home or getting married, to renunciate and bear his own feeling of loss. (By this stage of the work we were often devoted to, although still at times exasperated by, our families and felt a proprietary interest in their future.)

The worker's announcement that he would be separating from the couples in three or six months' time, accompanying, as it often did, a widening of the space between interviews, sometimes set them bargaining.

> 'No, don't say it. I've just got used to your coming fortnightly. I'm not having monthlies.'
> 'We can have fortnightlies till Christmas, but next year I leave you, remember. But we can have three months of monthlies'.
> 'You can't. Let's have a year of monthlies? Come on ...? Well, nine months, then?'

'What about six — a compromise between my three and your nine?'
'I don't like it ... OK. Done'.

Sometimes, at a less conscious level, and even if the time limit had been set right at the beginning of the work, versions of the original problem reappeared. It was important to recognize this as an attempt to keep the worker and to remember the ferocity of the earlier enactments so that these later manifestations could be seen in perspective. Debts would start to mount again or there would be a renewed display of helplessness.

'Would you do something for me?'
'I don't expect so, but tell me'.
......
'You know you're much better at those sort of things than I am'.
'But I might lose my temper. If I go up there, they'll have it coming'.
'No. I think it's me you're really cross with for leaving you. Why don't you go together. You're the two who are sticking together'.

The clients' attempts to make sure that the worker knew they were not cured sometimes made the work appear to go backwards.

The room was looking reasonably tidy and Mr Bootle said he had to show Mrs Bootle how to take the bag off the hoover because she had not done it for ten years. I made some comments about emptying the mess of their marriage, which made Mr Bootle laugh. But the rest of the session seemed very much like a bag-emptying process with almost everything being emptied on my head.

Last visits were sad. We left these clients still with many emotional problems.

14 Mr and Mrs Ingledow and Mr and Mrs Cabassi

This book, no doubt, tells of griefs and needs; still it
is not a book of a man despairing, but of a man believing.

Of course, I neither can nor intend to tell my readers
how they ought to understand my tale. May everyone find
in it what strikes a chord in him and is of some use to
him!

Herman Hesse

This chapter illustrates the previous two chapters with a straight, but abbreviated, account of the work done with two couples, Mr and Mrs Ingledow and Mr and Mrs Cabassi. In neither case was the marital problem the explicit reason for the referral, but in both it was soon apparent.

The work we describe shows considerable variation in style and content and reflects the personalities of the two different workers as well as the way the clients defined their problems. Mr and Mrs Ingledow's worker never felt able to offer them a contract of marital work. In contrast, Mr and Mrs Cabassi were offered six interviews to explore whether they wanted to work on their marital problems, which they then decided to do. The work with them was much more verbal than with Mr and Mrs Ingledow, who more often enacted their problems in front of the worker. At times Mr and Mrs Ingledow were not in a fit state to find words nor hear or understand those of the worker. Yet it was the worker's attempt to understand for which Mr Ingledow thanked him at the end. Mrs Ingledow, however, could only express her feelings about finally losing the worker through her actions and could not answer his goodbye.

Despite these differences, the workers in both cases tried to understand the interaction between the partners and to take account of it in their work. They were also concerned with the interaction between themselves and the partners.

We are making no further analysis. We leave the two accounts to speak for themselves.

MR AND MRS INGLEDOW

Mr Ingledow was admitted to hospital after a suicide attempt. A fortnight later he was discharged and referred to the social services department. The referral noted that he was an alcoholic and that he had had previous contact with the corresponding department of another borough.

Although the referral was in one sense quite straightforward, there was little pressure behind it and it left the intaking team with a lack of enthusiasm and an uncertainty how to react. An IMS worker, conveniently available, was asked to do an assessment. The distaste which was conveyed to him, although not explicitly, became his own and was then confirmed by the worker in the other borough whom he telephoned. A year previously she had admitted Mr and Mrs Ingledow's adult mentally handicapped daughter, Helen, to a residential home on her request because she could not bear the violent rows between her parents. This social worker had obviously been frightened by Mr Ingledow's violence and was not eager for further contact.

The IMS worker's first assessment after the referral was 'unpromising'. With even less enthusiasm he wrote and offered Mr Ingledow an appointment at his home.

> On the day of the appointment, but several hours early, Mr Ingledow arrived at the office drunk and abusive. It was not clear why he had come or what he wanted; but whatever it was, he wanted it at once and proposed to shoot the receptionist if he did not get it.

> He declined to wait for or meet any 'fucking social worker'. Eventually removed from the office, he left a disturbed and apprehensive receptionist.

The worker continued with his plan to call:

The door was opened by a bleary, drunken, elderly [he was, in fact, only fifty-nine] Irishman who agreed rather incoherently that he was Mr Ingledow. I followed him into a room which he occupied with his wife. It was clean and neat and served for all their living functions. He launched into an incoherent story about the DHSS which I failed to understand because of his drunken querulousness. He made several attempts to telephone its central office from a public telephone on the landing. He had difficulty in getting through, ran out of coins, asked me to lend him some which I refused, and then asked me to ring on his behalf. I again declined, but said I would like to try and understand what the situation was so that I could offer some appropriate help. At the end of a long stream of abuse he told me to 'fuck off' and I decided to match the deed to the word and left, feeling that there was little that I could do to help him. Even before he invited me to leave, I felt quite useless following him to and from the telephone.

No doubt, the referrer and the previous worker had felt equally useless. By now fully dissuaded from engaging any further, the worker reported back to the senior who had conveyed the initial 'warding-off' message — *'just* do an assessment' — and he suggested abandoning the case. The senior, however, less immediately affected, made the obvious suggestion that an attempt should be made to see Mrs Ingledow.

The attempt was fruitless, but the next week the worker learnt that Mr Ingledow had again been to the office and asked for help to get to the psychiatric hospital where he had been advised to go by his GP. He had been given a DHSS travel warrant. The worker made a further attempt to see Mrs Ingledow, but

was taken aback when the door was answered by Mr Ingledow. He told me he had gone to the hospital but, when he arrived there, he realized it was a 'mental home', so he left at once.

He was not drunk on this occasion and his friendly welcome was in marked contrast to his previous reception of me. In a beguiling, but sometimes inconsequential, sometimes incoherent manner, rambling from one subject to another, he reminisced about his earlier life and past triumphs. From this account it was clear that he had always been a heavy drinker, but this had not affected his capacity to work until recently. His last job had been as chauffeur to a wealthy family, Mrs

Ingledow being the housekeeper. He had had to give this up when he started to suffer from 'blackouts' (?) which made driving dangerous. Since then he had not worked and felt depressed at being unable to do anything beyond sitting in one room, a lot of the time too frightened to go out for fear of falling down in a faint. From underneath the blustering aggression emerged a frightened disabled man.

In the second interview Mr Ingledow

talked of his 'brain damage' which, he said, various tests had established. He talked of a medical professor in whom he had great confidence who had told him there was nothing that could be done for this condition. In gratitude, Mr Ingledow had donated his body along with those of his wife and daughter to the hospital. He showed me the thank-you letter, which expressed doubt whether he could donate the bodies of other people. He recounted how the previous evening he had watched a television programme about brains and the remarkable things which had been done with electrode transplants in the brain of a cat. He wondered whether it might be possible to do the same for human beings. I felt very strongly that he was struggling with the difficulty, perhaps through excessive drinking, of having done irreparable damage to himself and trying to deal with the consequences of this and yet, at the same time, hoping that after all there might be some miracle cure.

The alternation of despair and hope throughout this interview was very clear. I simply responded by agreeing that he was in a situation which was difficult to endure. I did not think I should flinch from the pain he was feeling nor offer any kind of false hope, but I found myself struggling with my own wish that he might be put right and a growing certainty that he could not.

He agreed to weekly interviews.

This engagement was made with Mr Ingledow and the early phase of the work was concerned mainly with his feelings about himself. But Mrs Ingledow soon joined the interviews, saying more by her actions than her words. They spoke of no marital problem, but it soon became clear that the underlying despair and helplessness was as much in her as in him and its expression shifted from one to the other. They started to care for each other. In one interview, Mrs Ingledow cuddled and spoke tenderly to her husband while he cried for himself and his damage. In another, she lay curled up in bed asleep with some unspecified complaint; when she stirred uneasily, he went over to look at her and gently resettled the bedclothes. They had numerous problems and the worker frequently found himself wrestling with the need to avoid unnecessary activity which would make him feel better and them probably worse. He continued to feel impotent and useless, and embarrassed when they, apparently valuing his constancy, pressed gifts upon him.

Their marital problem became overt when they were given notice to quit their room. In the grip of anxiety about how they would find somewhere else to live, their alternating pattern of helplessness and dependency on each other was intensified, but coupled with angry outbursts against each other. The angry recriminations centred on their daughter. Was her condition a consequence of his drunkenness and violence towards Mrs Ingledow when she was pregnant, or was it the result of Mrs Ingledow's neglect in not noticing for many months that the baby was not developing normally? They threw the guilt at each other. Some work on their owning their own guilt was started, but was interrupted by the landlord taking legal action to evict them. Mrs Ingledow became increasingly helpless and bedridden. As she became more agoraphobic and unable to leave the house, numerous physical complaints remaining unspecified and undiagnosed, Mr Ingledow 'coped with considerable aplomb'. He did the shopping, and when pursuing the worker's suggestions about how to find alternative accommodation and delay the legal proceedings, dressed stylishly for various appointments, outwardly in control.

They experienced the worker's short Christmas holiday as abandonment and he had difficulty in making contact with them on his return. When he did so, he found

> Mr Ingledow in a very distressed condition, Mrs Ingledow faint and ill, although neither of them had been to the doctor. This was one of the few occasions when they were down together.

The worker made an additional visit on the following day and, although they were less depressed, he was alarmed by their physical weakness. He went out and bought bread and milk. Following this demonstration of concern, they made a rapid recovery and thereafter frequently referred to the occasion when he shopped for them.

Shortly after this they were offered a service tenancy in another borough and moved with great delight to their new address, but Mrs Ingledow, still feeling ill and helpless, was unable to carry out her part of the service and Mr Ingledow's attempts to substitute for her came to grief as a result of his drinking. A violent struggle with the landlord ensued which resulted in a charge of assault. The proceedings were protracted when Mr Ingledow denied guilt and elected to go for trial by jury. Mrs Ingledow again became agoraphobic and in the increasing tension between them provoked (as she later admitted) Mr Ingledow into striking her. She telephoned the police, who arrested him and remanded him in custody for a week. This left Mrs Ingledow helplessly alone, the last thing she wanted.

A housing agency, which had become involved through the struggle with the landlord, moved Mrs Ingledow into a block of flats inhabited by squatters.

I found her alone in a dark, dingy flat with their few bits of furniture and belongings piled together. The walls were bespattered with dried blood from a recent stabbing; some of the window-panes were shattered; there was no light bulb and no means of cooking, but an electric fire was connected to a damaged plug. Mrs Ingledow, terrified by this turn of events, huddled on the bed and clung to me helplessly, begging me not to leave her alone, to get her husband out of prison and to make everything all right. All these requests seemed impossible to fulfil, but I succeeded in finding the voluntary worker of the action group on the site, got her to stay with Mrs Ingledow and mobilized the other squatters to look after her. I left feeling more anxious and helpless than I usually did about the Ingledows and having promised to visit the following day. By then Mrs Ingledow did not want to pursue her charge against Mr Ingledow and admitted that it had been her who had threatened him with a weapon. He was released on bail.

When I visited the next day he was in bed, tousled, bleary and drunk. He attempted to greet me in what had become his courteous way, but quickly relapsed into a drunken monologue, complaining that he hated the squat and that Mrs Ingledow should not have allowed herself to be moved. He did not think he could keep the condition of his bail, as he had not the strength to walk daily to the police station to report. This tale was punctuated with swigs of vodka from a cup periodically refilled from a bottle under the bed. He was going to ask the police to put him back in prison; he was better off there. Mrs Ingledow, also taking swigs from the vodka cup (the first indication she had given of drinking) alternately complained about being left and attempted to comfort him as he got drunker and drunker. With his continued reiteration of asking the police to reimprison him, she became more and more distressed. Suddenly, while standing by the bed, she fell in a dead faint on the floor. Mr Ingledow leapt off the bed, exclaiming that she had nothing on under the fur coat she was wearing. Between us we lifted her on to the bed and covered her with blankets. She came round and moaned that he was not to hit her and that he must not leave her. He agreed at once and now tried to comfort her. When she seemed better, I left, shaken by this scene, but also amazed at the way she had managed to turn the tables and stop him from getting himself arrested.

I could only hope that living through this bleak experience with them and surviving with them when they were at their worst and most despairing would help. I increased the regular visits to twice a week, but within a few weeks they had turned their sordid quarters into a pleasant, clean and comfortable flat. On one visit when back on the weekly schedule, I thought I had come to the wrong flat, as the front door, newly painted, was a different colour. Inside Mr Ingledow had decorated throughout with wallpaper remnants and job lots of paint obtained cheaply from a local store. Despite his disability, he had bought and mended furniture. The bloodstains were gone and the windows mended. Mrs Ingledow helped Mr Ingledow alter the kitchen to make it more usable and the next week she began to demonstrate her skills as a cook. From then on I was regaled with large slices of fruit cake and huge helpings of apple pie. If I could not eat it all while I was there, she wrapped it up for my lunch the next day and often added bunches of flowers cut from the profusion of shrubs round the block. Her agoraphobia disappeared.

Mr and Mrs Ingledow's life continued to go smoothly for some time and the worker again became concerned with their mixed feelings about their daughter, Helen, with whom they had had little contact over the last year. Mrs Ingledow had heard that hydrocephalic people died before their twentieth birthday; Helen's was approaching.

I took up with her her growing fear that Helen might soon die. This seemed to have some effect and her fear diminished a little.

Soon after this both Mr and Mrs Ingledow began to feel they would like Helen to spend a holiday with them and made the arrangements with the home.

> The first week of the holiday went well with much gratification all round, with Helen starting to say that she did not wish to return. But by the next week the problem in this family was demonstrated with Mrs Ingledow and Helen forming a tight pair, Mr Ingledow getting more and more excluded. He first expressed his feelings in terms of the danger to Helen when living in their current flat surrounded by 'sex-crazed addicts'.

When this failed to produce the desired effect, he reacted more strongly:

> On my first visit I failed to gain an entrance. Nobody appeared to be at home, and with a sinking feeling I noted that one of the panes of glass on the front door was broken.

> On my next visit, Mrs Ingledow opened the door and looked in control of herself, but Mr Ingledow was sitting in an armchair with a cut down his forehead and obviously drunk. Incoherently he complained that Mrs Ingledow had struck him with a hammer. She denied this and said he had attempted to hit her, but had walked into the door as he did so. The quarrel related to Helen and Mr Ingledow continued to shout obscenities about her, accusing Mrs Ingledow of all sorts of dark sexual misdeeds in the past. As he became more and more drunk, swigging neat whiskey from a cup, he threatened to commit suicide.

> The next day he attempted to do so and was taken to hospital. He was in no danger and two days later he was back. By this time Helen had agreed to return to the home. I had a sharp exchange with the matron, who obviously regarded the whole episode as my fault.

> During the acting out of this trauma I found it impossible to take up the difficulties of the triangular situation for them. Their newly-established strength as a pair seemed threatened by the existence of a third who was actually damaged and about whom they had such mixed feelings, particularly as she could not take her turn in being the strong one who could ever take care of them. Mrs Ingledow could demonstrate her own strength and reliability in relation to her

daughter, but Mr Ingledow, actually left out and particularly
sensitive to exclusion, competed for the attention he wanted for
himself by trying to get himself more damaged than his competitor.

Another turn of events subsequently made it difficult for the
worker to take up this problem of 'threesomes'. On his next visit

> I was met by a jubilant Mr Ingledow who told me that they had
> received a housing offer from the Greater London Council. He was
> mildly and euphorically drunk. Making it clear that he regarded me
> as *his* worker, he despatched Mrs Ingledow off to a neighbour,
> saying he wanted to talk to me alone. He poured out his life history.
> I could not get a word in and I was not clear why he wanted to tell me
> all this, but throughout the saga he conveyed gratitude not just for
> the rehousing but because he felt that I had been able to understand
> him in some important ways. This made a difference to him, he said.
> It seemed that my practical efforts had had much less significance.

Much of the remaining work with Mr and Mrs Ingledow was
occupied with the move, the same interaction between them taking
place — one helpless and dependent, the other active and effective.
Unlike when they moved into the service tenancy, this time it was
Mrs Ingledow who was the competent one, while Mr Ingledow
lapsed into complete incompetence. On the day of the move he sat
helplessly in the lavatory waiting for Mrs Ingledow to arrive with
the removal van which, as it later turned out, he had failed to
engage. She, however, rallied some help from the other squatters,
who found her a man with a vehicle; and she did this with no sign
of the helplessness she had demonstrated a few months earlier when
she was first alone in the squat.

Once installed in the new flat Mr Ingledow regained his
competence and once more set about the decorating. By now they
were in yet another borough and even further away from the
worker's base. He felt he had to withdraw and began to discuss this
with them. They could not bear knowing about what this meant to
them and sharply told him that now they had a permanent home
they could manage quite well. They only wanted to invite him to
call when they had made it 'homely'.

> After a few weeks the invitation arrived. The flat was looking good
> and Mr Ingledow showed me all the work he had done. They started
> a row and I felt very inadequate in dealing with this on a last visit. It

seemed as if they wanted to make sure I knew they still had their difficulties. Mrs Ingledow retreated to the bedroom and later I said goodbye to her through the blanket which covered her lifeless form from head to toe.

A year later the worker received a Christmas card from Mr and Mrs Ingledow saying that 'all is well'.

MR AND MRS CABASSI

Mr and Mrs Cabassi, an Asian and a Scandinavian, applied for help to the children's department (as it then was) for accommodation for their two children, aged four and two, after they had been evicted from a flat on which they had failed to pay the mortgage and rates for eighteen months. They were living separately, one child with each parent, sometimes staying overnight with friends, sometimes sleeping on railway stations. The child care officer thought Mrs Cabassi was 'depressed' (as well she might have been) and received the children into care.

The situation quickly became stable and remained so for five years, the children staying in a long-term children's home, the parents living in separate bed-sitting rooms, visiting the children independently, but occasionally seeing each other and continuing to have intercourse. The first change in this state of affairs occurred after the original worker had left the department and another had taken over. It was notable that despite their partial separation neither Mr nor Mrs Cabassi had formed any long-standing relationship with another partner. After several months of 'yo-yo-ing' back and forth to north and south London, Mr Cabassi refusing joint interviews, Mrs Cabassi complaining that her husband was financially unreliable and she would not consider living with him unless he bought her a house, the worker eventually succeeded in seeing them together in Mr Cabassi's bed-sitting room.

It was a long and difficult interview with both Mr and Mrs Cabassi attempting to prove to the worker that everything which had gone wrong was the fault of the other; each was accusing and accused of being unreliable and violent, of drinking too much and of having extramarital affairs. The worker commented on the one hand on their lack of trust and on the other on their inability to part. She asked them if they would like to explore the possibility of help for their marriage with her and another worker who was more experienced than she was in working with marital problems.

This next interview, quite readily agreed to, was tense for both Mr and Mrs Cabassi, and for the IMS worker and the local authority worker who, despite her persistence with this couple, was unsure of herself in relation to her new and older co-worker. Mr Cabassi did his best to make a good impression with the latter and Mrs Cabassi firmly contradicted everything he said. As she became more and more anxious that he might be the preferred one, she became more aggressive, dragging 'her' known worker into siding with her. At the end of the interview the two workers were punch-drunk with the cut and thrust into which they had been drawn; but Mr and Mrs Cabassi accepted the offer of a further six interviews to explore whether they could face working on their marital problems. To make it easier for them they were offered an evening time for the appointments; but it was emphasized that it was *their* problem and that *they* would have to make the effort, so they were firmly told that they would have to come to the office.

Having picked up the anxiety related to the depth of the conflict and to what confronting the marital problem might mean, the workers had little expectation that they could hold them; but, as it turned out, their practical difficulties of listening for them and peering out of the window week by week in an office kept locked at that time, with no receptionist or porter, were offset by the couple's always arriving punctually, sometimes separately and barely on speaking terms, sometimes together and running up the path hand in hand.

The joint interviews continued beyond the six and were only terminated when the local authority worker left the department. This coincided with Mrs Cabassi's annual visit to her mother and Mr Cabassi's absence on a foreign business trip.

The interviews were exhausting and frequently, after seeing the couple out of the building, the two workers flopped back in their chairs, unable either to move and get themselves home or purposefully to try to understand what had happened in the preceding hour.

It emerged that Mr Cabassi, the eldest son of a prosperous middle-class family, had had his career first determined by his mother, who had persuaded his father to send him to the States to get the 'right' education to fulfil her powerful ambitions for him.

He had been unsuccessful and it was more than a year before he could go home and 'confess' to his mother that he had dropped out of university. She had then married him off to his first wife, whose equally powerful demands he could fulfil no better. He escaped to England, married the present Mrs Cabassi and still found that he could not meet her insistent demands and wishes.

Mrs Cabassi's father, who was said to have been 'hopeless with money, wine, women and song', had deserted her mother when she was four years old. Cared for by an aunt, while her mother worked to keep them, her childhood had been bleak and impoverished. She had missed her father and many times had asked her mother to remarry him, but many years later, when he was dying and sent for her, she shocked Mr Cabassi by her refusal.

The workers described the self-defeating spiral of interaction between the pair:

> Mr Cabassi's masculinity was very fragile and, in spite of his protests, he expected his wife to dominate and bully him. He tried to placate her with extravagant and impossible promises of things he would do and buy, only to be verbally torn to shreds when he could not fulfil them. The more Mrs Cabassi asked of him, the more she ensured her own disappointment and kept alive her strongly-held belief that all men were totally unreliable.

Most of the verbal abuse was hurled by Mrs Cabassi and, when at her most despairing, she cruelly accused him of a sexual inadequacy which was belied by their continuing to have intercourse at weekends and their agreement at other times that their sexual relationship was satisfying to them both. Other than pulling furiously on a cigarette, he would usually remain urbane in manner, but sometimes he described what he perceived as his wife's 'Pandora's box of horrors' which she opened when she had had a drink.

Gradually they were able to increase the time they spent together, but Mrs Cabassi still maintained that she could not consider a more regular relationship until Mr Cabassi provided her with a fully furnished house, although she knew full well that he could not raise the deposit. When she began to modify her demands, however, Mr Cabassi flared up and manufactured an explosive row. She was the one who was accused, and the workers were then able to show them how terrified they both were of closeness and, therefore, the risk of being let down, and how each could always rely on the other to re-create the distance by a fresh onslaught of accusation. In the rest of that interview they were then able to share with each other their fear of not being 'good enough' parents to the children.

Much of what went on between them also got enacted with the workers. As they began to get on better, able to share more and slightly less distrusting of each other, they started to exclude the workers with what the IMS worker called their 'secretive, Etruscan smiles'.

When the local authority worker left, the children were given a new worker and it was assumed that she would be integrated into the work with the parents. Mr and Mrs Cabassi, however, refused to let this happen, saying,

> We're used to you and you know how awful we can be, but we don't want anyone else to know.

With some misgivings, the IMS worker agreed to continue to see them as a threesome, but made it clear that she and the children's worker would be in touch over anything of mutual concern to the whole family.

Three months later, in November, Mr and Mrs Cabassi announced that they now felt ready to resume living together. The worker thought this was premature, as their suspicion and paranoia could still flare up when either of them felt threatened by the activity of the other. Expecting there to be considerable delay before they could get themselves housed and insisting that they continued to work with her during this time, she agreed to back their application for a council house, asking them to agree her report. Both of them were serious when they read her account of their personalities and difficulties, but agreed it was 'fair'. Mr Cabassi was the more visibly moved when faced in writing with the fact that the children would remain in care until they were eighteen if they could not be rehabilitated with their parents.

At the first interview after Christmas, when the children had spent a week with their parents,

> Mrs Cabassi arrived for the interview alone, saying she had not seen Mr Cabassi since the New Year, when they had had a violent row. A few minutes later Mr Cabassi, looking white and nervous, arrived. He gave his account of the row, which seemed to have arisen after his

younger brother had visited and mentioned a former girlfriend of Mr Cabassi who had been enquiring after him. Mrs Cabassi had immediately telephoned her mother to say she was leaving Mr Cabassi and returning permanently to her own country with the children. After this row the eldest child had said she never wanted to see her father again; Mr Cabassi had asked her if that was what she really felt and she had become very distressed and said she did not know what she wanted.

I was furious with them for misusing the children in their manoeuvres and told them so. Mr Cabassi looked ashamed and Mrs Cabassi started to cry.

I then wondered whether I had not allowed them enough room to explore whether they really wanted to part and whether they had suddenly got frightened by their application for a house. I put this to them and told them that the possibility of their parting did not mean that they had to stop working with me.

They then settled down to try and sort out what had gone wrong and were then more open with each other than they had ever previously been about their fears of themselves and each other and of the prospect of living together again as a family.

I gave them three weeks' warning of my impending absence on a course and offered them my home telephone number in case of another flare-up like this while I was away. They were pleased and said their not being able to get in touch after Christmas had felt terrible.

Unfortunately the offer of a council house came through with unaccustomed speed and before the worker thought Mr and Mrs Cabassi were ready to accept it. They, however, decided to take the risk and accepted the offer.

The IMS worker and the children's worker decided that the former should attend the next regular review meeting with the children's home staff, a six-monthly event which she had previously not attended.

I gave an outline of my work with the parents and reported the housing offer. There was general agreement that Mr and Mrs Cabassi should be persuaded not to have the children home until the summer, but the length and frequency of their visits during the intervening

period should be increased to allow children and staff to adjust to the
parting and children and parents to the rehabilitation.

The child care advisor expressed pleasure at the prospect of reuniting
this family — one of the more hopeful cases he had dealt with — but
I was very aware of the strongly feminine atmosphere in the home
and the sceptical comments about Mr Cabassi and the doubt that any
part of the problem could belong to his wife. I was anxious about the
opportunities this gave Mrs Cabassi to reinforce her belief that all the
difficulties were in her husband.

A few days later one of the home staff telephoned the children's
worker to say she felt I had been 'completely taken in' by Mr
Cabassi.

The worker continued to struggle with Mr and Mrs Cabassi's
collusive interaction of the demanding, insatiable woman and the
unreliable, unsatisfying man which was now focused on the
problems of moving into a new house.

Mrs Cabassi refused to leave her bedsitting-room until the house was
completely redecorated and carpeted. Mr Cabassi was willing to
move in alone as soon as he could get bed and bedding, but he had by
now got a better job which entailed his going abroad more often and
on his next trip he might not get back for the children's Easter
holiday. Mrs Cabassi was gratified by his increased status and salary
and furious about his pending absence. He was equally furious that
he could buy a new cooker for £80, but Mrs Cabassi said she would
not move in unless he bought her one costing £175. Nevertheless, he
got most of the painting done, carpets laid, telephone, cooker and
essential furniture installed before he left.

The worker's anxiety was high; still apprehensive about the 'too
early' offer of housing, one client abroad and the other becoming
more elusive and pleading pressure of moving house as an excuse
for missing some interviews; but she was surprised by the number
of postcards she received from Mr Cabassi, ensuring that she did
not forget him.

Mr Cabassi had got himself a job which enabled him and his wife
to maintain in a different form the partial separation they had set
up seven years previously. No doubt Mr Cabassi escaped
thankfully at times, and Mrs Cabassi oscillated between pride in his
new achievements and anger at his continuing to leave her, but was

gratified by being able to join him abroad for a holiday.

Unfortunately, just before the children broke up from school and were due home on a permanent basis, an internal political upheaval in the country in which he was working cut Mr Cabassi off from any communication; he could get neither message nor money back to England. Mrs Cabassi, who had given up her job, could see this only as proof of her basic feeling that all men were thoroughly unreliable.

> She was furious that there was no money for the promised holiday to her mother, nor even for the rent. Any concern for Mr Cabassi's safety was transferred to the youngest child, who was almost hysterical that his father was stuck in such a 'dangerous place'.

Mr Cabassi got home in the autumn and was put off work and on half-pay until business could be resumed in that country. The Cabassi family were under one roof all day and every day.

For a few weeks everything apparently went fairly smoothly, but suspiciously so. The children settled in at their new school, worked steadily and were well liked. At home they appeared happy, but almost too conforming and well-behaved. All they could say to their worker about life with their parents was 'nice'. Mr and Mrs Cabassi presented a similar tranquil picture and the worker could not believe that such a dramatic change could have occurred.

Eventually Mr and Mrs Cabassi admitted they were terrified that, if they now confessed to any difficulties, the children would be 'whipped away'. Only when this had been fully aired over three interviews were they able to ask the children's worker to continue to call and see the children, 'because they like you and you can tell them about their old friends', and the IMS one 'to continue with us until we're used to being together again'.

The care of the children continued to be loving, at times over-indulgent, but Mr and Mrs Cabassi remained frightened of their potential violence to each other. On one occasion Mr Cabassi fell downstairs at a party, knocked himself unconscious and broke his arm. Mrs Cabassi said to the worker next day that she had been terrified that he had killed himself and added,

> 'But I expect you think I pushed him'.
> 'Did you?'
> 'No, but I'd have liked to'.

Knowing that their worker was leaving them in six months' time, as was the children's worker, they started trying to manoeuvre her, avoiding joint interviews, either keeping the children there and presenting a harmonious family picture, or one of them being out, leaving the other to make a string of the old-type complaints — that he was coming home late for meals, drinking too much and buying only cheap furniture for the sitting-room; that she, now working again, was not contributing anything from her wages and going out with unknown friends, leaving him to do all the baby-sitting. Concerned about leaving this family still in a fragile state, the workers offered them transfers. Mr and Mrs Cabassi refused, made an enormous effort to reassure the worker that 'all would be well', but added, 'We know where to find you if we need you'.

They did.

Six months later, already in serious trouble with rent arrears, Mr Cabassi was summoned for assaulting his wife in the street. He was given a suspended sentence and he asked the probation officer if he could be referred back to their previous worker. After two interviews this worker offered them a transfer to the IMS (a fee-paying service) where she would continue to work with them, but only on the basis that they guaranteed to pay off the rent arrears and subsequently maintain the basic necessities for the children. Mr Cabassi sold his car to meet the first requirement and Mrs Cabassi started making a contribution.

For six months they attended weekly. Similar explosions and rows occurred between them and the same old themes were worked over, but the children appeared to thrive at home and at school. Then Mr Cabassi withdrew from the interviews and wrote to say he did not feel able to do any more work 'on himself', but hoped his wife would continue to attend! She did so for another month and then decided they 'could manage', and again added, 'We know where to find you if we need you'.

A Christmas card from 'all the family' arrived a few months later and was the last news the worker had of them.

PART FIVE

The Clients, The Workers and The Organization

The problem is that of providing a professional service in a bureaucratic setting governed by political constraints.

A director of social services

15   Therapeutic Response and Institutional Temptation

Social services have accepted an impossible role and have passed it on smartly to the educators, saying 'Train us someone to do it.'

Another director of social services

Social services departments were set up to implement the recommendations of the Seebohm Committee that there should be a 'comprehensive approach to individuals, families and communities' - a 'community-based and family-orientated service, which will be available to all'.[1] (The committee asked itself the question 'What is a family?' and answered: 'We decided very early in our discussions that it would be impossible to restrict our work solely to the needs of two or even three-generation families. We could only make sense of our task by considering also childless couples and individuals without any close relatives: in other words, everybody.')

In practice, about half the money of these departments is spent on a small, often stigmatized, section of the community — those in residential care — while the remaining services are also very far from being genuinely open to everybody. The techniques for managing this gap between aspiration and reality form one theme of these next chapters. Our overriding concern, however, is how the organization influences the work with our core sample clients on whom the workers spend so much of their time.

The type of casework help which, we have suggested, benefits

---

[1]   Seebohm, F. (1968), *Report of the Committee on Local Authority and Allied Personal Social Services,* op. cit.

these clients can be summarized in terms of what they need the social worker to be: a specific figure

who will become familiar
with whom they can form a relationship within which emotional
    issues can be raised
who is reliable and trustworthy
who can survive and acknowledge anger and failure on his part and
    that of his client; good enough, not totally bad nor trying to be
    totally good
who can encourage the clients' own efforts
who can share and co-operate
who can leave in a way which is not too traumatic.

The question is, how far the organization helps its workers in their struggle to behave in this way. How far, for example, does it help its workers to form reliable relationships with their clients, to deal with splitting (the desire to see a person all good or all bad) and to manage their departure? In so far as it does not help them, why and how is that?

In pursuing these questions, we need to refer sometimes to the working culture and customary practices of the social workers; sometimes to resources; sometimes to the procedures and management style of the social work division; at yet other times to the wider context of the department as a whole in its political and legal context; and finally, to the expectations of the public and other professions.

In selecting factors from this institutional framework, we write not as sociologists, nor as organizational consultants, but as practitioners who have tried to make sense of the environment within which we worked from 1974 to 1977. Over this period we had discussions with staff at all levels within the department, but our view of it is most affected by the impact the working environment made on us when, alongside our local authority colleagues, we practised as basic-grade workers.

Influenced by this experience, we will be focusing on the feelings, particularly the anxiety, aroused by local authority social work and the cultural and organizational reactions to them. This focus is in keeping with our theory. The reader will remember from chapter 4 Menzies' statement: 'When the need of the member is to defend against what is felt to be intolerable anxiety, the organization will be used for this purpose.' Taking this theory as our starting-point, we hope to show how this institutional framework, in association with the clients, tends to produce anxiety, how the organization reacts and how this reaction influences the workers and encourages or diminishes the ability to do marital work.

Our focus on anxiety should not obscure the influence of other factors. Organizational procedures reflect practical constraints as well as defensive manoeuvres and sometimes both together. Moreover, an organization free of defensive procedures and the conflicts of which we write is an inherent impossibility.

We emphasize that we are not attempting to examine the social work division and its function as a blueprint for a new structure. To do so would be presumptuous. We do not believe that large-scale organizational change will eradicate some of the problems we discuss or that conflict in itself is something which has to be eliminated either between clients or between workers. The conflicts between the workers described in chapter 1 which related to the conflict between Mr and Mrs Jafferji will continue to occur and the important thing is that they should be contained and used more constructively. We believe an understanding of the organization helps in this respect. Although it is impossible to produce the perfect organization, it seems that it is wise to try to understand the organizations we have.

As a context to our enquiry, we begin with a straight account of the telephone calls and conversations held in the room of one of the teams in an area office, the only changes being for reasons of style and abbreviation.

THE DIARY

This 'extract' refers to the first morning one of us spent in a team room. The team consisted of John, the senior; Patrick, a basic-grade worker, who had been away on a course and was now ill; Rosemary and Eileen, also basic-grade workers; Betty, the group administrative assistant; and Tina, a social worker in training. On this morning, John and Betty were in all morning and Rosemary and Eileen for the second half of it; Tina was out all day.

> ... The morning was chiefly remarkable for the phone calls, of which there were ten incoming and two outgoing.

Call one was internal, from an administrative officer for Betty. A schoolgirl was living in a flat on her own and the department was subsidizing her. Something should have been marked red in her file. Betty could not understand what the officer was saying and, in the end, got the call transferred to Nicholas, the area administrative officer.

Call two was for Patrick and taken by Betty. The caller was told Patrick was not in.

Call three was from a fostermother for Patrick and was taken by John. The fostermother seemed anxious that Patrick had not visited. John told her that by regulation Patrick should have visited her by now, but that he was away ill.

Call four was internal, from a casework administrative officer for Rosemary and taken by John. The problem seemed to be that the department wanted parental rights over a child, after which they wanted to place him for adoption. The child's mother was ambivalent about this. The question was whether it was politically expedient to state the child had been introduced to would-be foster/ adoptive parents in a report to the committee. John thought this admission might make the committee think that the social workers had jumped the gun. The administrative officer apparently did not agree and also raised the question whether the maternal grandmother had been contacted. (When Rosemary came in, she said that the grandmother had been sent a letter by recorded delivery.) John said they had few cases of this sort, and every time they 'had to go back to the book'.

At this point, Mrs James, the home help organizer, came in. She was indignant about the fuss which a neighbour had made about an old person's budgerigar. John said that he had contacted the RSPCA and found that the budgie should not have been left covered up and that it was to be cared for by another neighbour. John later told me that the owner of the budgerigar (one of Patrick's clients) had committed suicide during the latter's course. This raised unfortunate memories for Mrs James, since two years previously she had found another suicide by hanging. On this last occasion, John had gone back with Mrs James and 'phoned the police, etc. John reassured Mrs James and told her that the neighbour was just trying to 'keep her oar in'.

Call five was from the fostermother again. John told her not to worry.

Call six was by John to Patrick, asking him when he would be coming back.

Call seven was by Betty to one of her friends, expressing her feelings about various administrative matters.

Call eight was from a Polish lady, asking for the address of an old person who had been moved to an old people's home. John gave it to her.

Call nine was from a medical social worker and taken by John. A Mr Yalden (one of Tina's clients) had walked out of a hospital ward, got drunk, borrowed a wig, and made passes at the male charge nurse. The hospital was now insisting that he be removed. John told the medical social worker that if the hospital discharged Mr Yalden, he should be told to come to the department.

Call ten was from an officer in central services for Tina and then John, and was taken by me as no one else was in the room. I said neither was available and the caller seemed surprisingly cross. ...

Call eleven was from a CAB worker for Rosemary and was taken by me. She said she would ring back.

Call twelve was from a neighbour of an elderly alcoholic lady on Rosemary's caseload and taken by Eileen. The neighbour was concerned. I heard more about this from Rosemary and the area officer. Rosemary said a lot of neighbours had rung up about this woman expressing their concern that she had, for example, left the gas on without lighting it. The area officer said that at one stage a rota of anonymous callers had rung at twenty-minute intervals to complain about the woman.

During the morning I grunted to Eileen, talked briefly to Rosemary and at greater length to John and the area officer. John said they were under pressure because of an unusually heavy period of referrals (47 in October), and also because Patrick had been away and a previous social worker had left suddenly with his cases not written up. It was also a bad time of the year as in winter there is a pervasive, vague anxiety that old people will die of cold. John said that he was not feeding all the new cases into the group. If social workers had too many cases, they became immobilized and tried to work with their most familiar ones. John himself seemed slightly tense and alluded to this ... John went on to talk of difficulties with the local general hospital. These mainly centred round sectioning people. The hospital had a 'phobia' that someone would jump out of an upstairs window as, indeed, one had. The housemen were insecure, psychiatric wards non-existent, and the relevant psychiatric hospital a long way away. Recently someone had hanged himself in the out-patient clinic. As a result, the hospital wanted social workers to section disturbed patients or get them out as quickly as possible. ... Many patients were discharged without seeing a psychiatrist. John was inclined to blame the suicide of the owner of the budgerigar on too early a discharge from this hospital, combined with the fact that her GP was away on holiday.

My conversation with Eileen was brief. She told me how terrified she had been when she was first left in the team room on her own with the telephones. I could understand this.

In the course of the morning, I also talked with the area officer, who discussed the pressure felt by social workers from external sources such as the press, councillors and the law. He himself had been told by an irate councillor that she would be gunning for him from now on.

THE NATURE OF THE PREVAILING ANXIETY

In describing this morning we have produced a snapshot without a context and this belies the long-drawn sagas of which many of these happenings were part. Four years later, two events described in this chapter gave important historical background to two managers who had been involved with the aftermath in the same week we presented the draft to them. We asked our local authority colleagues how typical they thought this morning was. Their replies varied. Some thought it was typical; others that, although typical of how things happened, the workers got used to it, so that an outsider reading this chapter would mistake the feelings of the participants; others that we had chosen an atypical day, but conveyed the feel of local authority work. Strangely, there is probably truth in all these comments. The morning was atypical in that there were more telephone calls than on some other mornings and in the mix of incidents to which these calls related. Nevertheless, it illustrates the variety of work with which a team can be involved and the possibility of simultaneous involvement in unpleasant crises of quite different kinds. For example, in one week a worker spent some time waiting for the birth of a baby on whom she knew she would need to apply for a place of safety order as soon as it was born. In the same week another client rang her from a tube station to announce that he was about to commit suicide. She reached the station just after he had done so. Another worker heard within a short time of the murder of one of her clients and of the death of another with whom she was closely involved in circumstances suggesting suicide. At one stage, one of us noted that this team was involved with suicide attempts (not all successful) in seven successive weeks.

The events involving one team quickly became known to other teams and provided a background of acknowledged and unacknowledged anxiety to the more humdrum day-to-day work. Since part of our task is to examine the way the institutional framework provokes some of the anxiety, we categorize the varied sources in so far as they can be seen in the morning we have described.

Firstly, there is the *quantity* of work. One crisis is easier to handle than a succession of them, and it was only after a number of calls that the senior worker alluded to his tension. In the course of the morning he also referred to the immobilizing effect on workers of having too much to do and the related pressure on himself of having a pending tray of unallocated cases.

Secondly, there is the *variety* of work, some of which obviously requires technical knowledge, not only of the law but also of such niceties as the need to send certain letters by recorded delivery. The senior's comment about 'going back to the book' suggests that the variety can prevent the workers from gaining confidence in dealing with a particular class of case.

Thirdly, there is the *insistence and seriousness of the events.* One person had died, and in the course of the morning there had been two mentions of deaths by hanging. A mother was being deprived of her rights over her child. A fostermother was anxious enough to ring up twice. A schoolgirl was living on her own in a flat. The bewigged client had indulged in a bizarre sexual gesture and another seemed in danger of causing a gas explosion.

Fourthly, there is the *sense of impossibility* in some of the demands and hence the feelings of anxiety and helplessness these demands are likely to arouse. Anxiety is less if there is something practical that can be done. What are social workers supposed to do about a man who is sick enough to be in hospital, but too reprehensible to remain there, or about a woman who is not mentally ill, does not wish to enter an old people's home, but is, nevertheless, a menace to her neighbours?

Fifthly, there is a *sense of a lack of context and unpredictability.* Crises are more worrying if they occur out of the blue, so that the worker has little basis for knowing whether they are genuinely serious or whether such events have happened many times before and always come to nothing. The sense of a lack of context obviously arises in part from the fact that this was the diarist's first day in the team. However, none of the incidents was being handled by the worker primarily responsible for the case who might have a more coherent idea of the background to what was happening. It is clear, for example, that no one knew why the fostermother was worried enough to ring up twice. Similarly, no one knows when or where an old person will die of cold. It is this unpredictability which raises the anxiety level. In fact, the actual incidence of death from cold among clients was low. We heard of none.

Finally, there is a *sense of a hostile environment.* There are battles, or potential battles, going on with the neighbours (over the alcoholic old lady) and with the hospitals (over the bewigged patient). Another neighbour is causing problems over a budgerigar. There was a suggestion that there should be a formal complaint to the hospital about the too early discharge of the budgerigar's owner. Councillors, who have demonstrated their interest in social services by serving on the committee, enter the morning's story as people who may attack social workers and with whom the political niceties have to be watched. Despite a professional disagreement, there was one friendly contact with the central administration over the rights and powers resolution; one much less friendly between the IMS worker and the officer who displayed considerable annoyance; and one which caused confusion, with a person who wanted something marked in red. Significantly perhaps, there are no direct contacts with clients, but the mother and grandmother of the child who may be placed for adoption may well not be friendly to the social workers. It is not surprising that the telephone, or rather the telephones, the omnipresent symbols of the team's connection with the outside world, are sometimes regarded with alarm.

It is worth noting that the difficulties between the team and the outside world are apparently centred around questions of responsibility and blame. Who is responsible for the alcoholic lady? And who will be to blame if she blows up herself or, worse still, someone else? Who is responsible for the difficult old man: the hospital because he is ill, or the social services because they got him into hospital? Who is to blame for the old lady's suicide: the GP and the social worker because they were on holiday or on a course, or the hospital who may have discharged her too early?

THE RESPONSE TO ANXIETY

These questions of responsibility and blame are entangled with issues of 'buck-passing' (as when the hospital demands the removal of its difficult patient), perhaps status (have the insecure housemen the right to make such demands?), and probably the feeling that awful things ought not to happen and that somebody must be to blame if they do. It is sad that the old lady has taken her life and also that one of the first human reactions to such an event is often that someone is to blame.

This reaction adds a source of stress to those whose day-to-day business involves such events, and faces them with the problem of how to respond. On this morning, the social workers were responding by considering a formal protest to the hospital and by handling the practical aftermath in the form of a budgerigar. The combined bureaucratic and practical response is within the idiom of the morning, which has shown the workers much concerned with procedure and, although to a lesser extent than we observed on other mornings, with managing the practical consequences of their clients' disasters.

The incident of the budgerigar and the continued and lengthy discussion about its fostering made a great impression on the IMS worker, who initially was amazed by the amount of concern the bird generated. This, however, became understandable during the course of the morning as his respect for the senior grew. He watched him turning his attention from one difficult situation to another, and back again. Either as light relief or as an object of displacement, the budgerigar served a purpose. Its problems were more easily solved than those of any other character mentioned in this book, and in this respect it afforded immediate satisfaction. And it was unlikely to complain.

The concern with the practical, the statutory and the procedural could conceivably divert attention from the underlying emotional issues with which the workers are also concerned. What is for the moment the issue is not the grandmother's or mother's feelings, but the rights and powers and boarding-out regulations; not the lonely position of the schoolgirl alone in a flat, but the form marked in red; not the suicide of an old lady, but the budgerigar. Offices are, of course, the place where administrative issues are handled, and this account cannot be used to judge the relationships between workers and clients. Nevertheless, it is clear that the organization and its culture offers the workers a chance to take on a bureaucratic role in self-protection and to blame others. It is also clear that it could allow or encourage practices whose primary purpose was to protect them against the demands and attacks of the outside world.

The defensive behaviour and counter-attack did not always occur. In the event, the area officer refused to agree to a formal protest against the hospital. Yet the temptation is there. In the next two chapters we shall try to understand these processes. In the first, we shall consider the temptation to react in such a way as to ignore the emotional needs of the clients; in the second, to become involved in a splitting and blaming process, and not to do marital work. These were the temptations to which our core sample clients were particularly subject and of which their social workers need to be correspondingly aware.

16 The Problem of Institutional Limits

And they said, Go to, let us build us a city,
and a tower whose top may reach unto heaven; ...

Genesis

THE SEEBOHM CONTEXT

By the mid-1960s, there were strong arguments for the reform of the segregated services designed in the 1940s and 1950s. The Children Act 1948 and the National Assistance Act 1948 had taken the work with children and the old out of the jurisdiction of the Poor Law and the work with the disabled from the voluntary societies. The 1959 Mental Health Act, both a radical and a consolidating Act, redefined the approach to the mentally ill and mentally handicapped and reorganized the services for them.

These arguments culminated in the 1968 Seebohm Report[1] and in the Local Authority Social Services Act 1970, which together provided the context for the events we described in our last chapter. In understanding the context we need to return briefly to the discussions which produced it.

Like most political events, the Seebohm Report had diverse origins, ranging from the wish to liberate some branches of social work from the hegemony of the medical officers of health to a desire to provide services for many groups of people who were then ineligible for them. One of the most influential of these origins was

[1] Seebohm, F. (1968), *Report of the Committee on Local Authority and Allied Personal Social Services,* op. cit.

253

the idea of a family service.[2] Under the terms of the 1963 Children and Young Persons Act, children's departments were allowed to offer 'advice, guidance and assistance' and they had responded with increased commitment to the prevention of neglect in the home. They had also used their new powers to provide financial assistance to families at risk, a trend which, it has been argued, led in the long term to quite widespread supplementation of social security benefits.[3]

In pursuit of this preventive role, the children's departments had also become increasingly dissatisfied with their lack of control over the resources they needed to perform it, and with their consequent dependence on other departments. They also noticed that the same families were often visited by a number of social workers concerned with diverse aspects of their welfare and not always able to agree as to the best way to help them. It seemed that resources were wasted. A unified family service seemed to some an attractive solution to these problems.

A further argument for such a service was provided by the wish to reverse the upward trend in juvenile delinquency. As the government reported in *The Child, the Family and the Young Offender:*[4]

The proposals in this paper for the reform of the law and practice relating to young offenders emphasize the need to improve the structure of the various services connected with the support of the family and the prevention of delinquency. The government believe that these services should be organized as a family service, but the form and scope of such a service will need detailed consideration.

The 1969 Children and Young Persons Act followed the preventive trend of the 1963 Act. It raised the age of criminal responsibility and brought more young delinquents into the fold of the children's

[2] Ingleby, M.R.P. (1960), *Report of the Committee on Children and Young Persons* (HMSO).
Labour Party (1964) *Crime a Challenge to us all.*
[3] Jordan, B. (1974), *Poor Parents* (Routledge & Kegan Paul).
Hill, M., and Laing, P. (1978), *Money Payments, Social Work and Supplementary Benefits* (School for Advanced Urban Studies, University of Bristol).
[4] Home Office (1965), *The Child, the Family and the Young Offender* (HMSO).

departments. It was hoped that a personal family service could be provided for juveniles who did break the law or who were deemed to be at risk of doing so. There was to be less distinction between the deprived and the delinquent.

These ideas were considered by the Seebohm Committee but viewed in conjunction with a contrasting strand of thought — 'the powerful voice of Professor Titmuss who had declared that much preventive thinking had been "too family and child oriented";[5] the new departments should emphasize provision of *services,* rather than support for the family or any other pattern of family relationships'.[6] This strand of thought was already exemplified in the welfare departments and was reinforced by a powerful lobby for the disabled. Significantly, the Chronically Sick and Disabled Persons Act 1971 laid the duty of providing aids and benefits not on the medical authorities, who were likely to be in touch with the disabled, but on the new social services departments, who were required to seek them out.

Clearly it is very difficult to try to stem the rising tide of juvenile delinquency with methods based on time-consuming personal relationships with social workers or on costly residential services. A department simultaneously faced with the need to provide services to the great number of disabled and elderly faces an acute problem of priorities and a question about the type of work it is supposed to perform. However, the Seebohm Committee itself saw no need to arbitrate between these potentially conflicting traditions. It was set on creating large departments whose political power would attract enough resources to provide for both personal and material needs. The committee sat amid a general climate of expansion and reorganization in which size was promoted as an aid to the better use of resources. There were arguments for big comprehensive schools, big district hospitals, big government departments and big local authorities. It was a period when bigger easily became equated with better and 'small is beautiful'[7] was a voice not recognized in this country.

[5] Titmuss, R.M. (1966), 'Social Work and Social Services. A Challenge for Local Government', *Royal Society of Health Journal,* Vol. 86, No. 1.

[6] Packman, J. (1975), *The Child's Generation* (Oxford, Basil Blackwell).

[7] Schumacher, E.F. (1973), *Small is Beautiful* (Blond & Briggs).

Despite the restraint of its prose, the Seebohm Report rivalled the yearnings of our core sample clients for a new Eden. The responsibilities the committee recommended for the new social services departments were to extend beyond those of the existing departments and integration was to be accompanied by reaching out 'far beyond the discovery and rescue of social casualties'[8] Services were to be extended to the great range of the needy and yet at the same time were to be based on assessments in depth.

Thus the legacies inherited by social services departments included the expectation placed on them by the Seebohm Committee and the huge potential demand for their services. Even if one refines the Seebohm categories of 'all' and 'everybody' to include only children at risk, delinquent, maladjusted or socially deprived adolescents, the mentally ill of all ages, the physically and mentally handicapped and the elderly, many groups of possible clients have been left out. The word 'family' has not been mentioned. 'The concept of a "family service" was thus swallowed up in something much larger and more ambitious before it was even born.'[9]

DEMAND, RESOURCE AND REACTION

The Local Authority Social Services Act 'followed the bare bones of the Report fairly faithfully, but it lacked most of its flesh'.[10] For flesh, the social work division of the new departments required an adequate supply of the resources which social services were expected to supply — for example, day nurseries, aids and adaptations — and, above all, enough experienced social workers to deal with the quantity and variety of the demand.

Unfortunately, over the three years we worked in the department the turnover of workers was high as, indeed, it was in all Inner London boroughs, and the number of experienced workers was correspondingly short. In one area only two of the basic-grade workers employed at the start of the project were still there three years later. Over the same period, the area officer had changed, as had three of the original four seniors, although two of their

---

[8] Seebohm, F. (1968), op. cit.
[9] Packman, J. (1975), op. cit.
[10] Packman, J., ibid.

replacements had come from within the area. In the other area the picture seems to have been comparable. At one stage in the project the social workers there surveyed the ninety-eight children on their caseloads who had been in care for at least six months. Nearly three out of four of the children had had two or more social workers in the previous two years and the percentage would no doubt have been higher if the children who had been in care for less than two years had not been included.

Social workers did not leave evenly throughout the year. There was a massive programme of secondment for training. The acute period of general post was in late summer when some workers were leaving to go on courses and the seconded were returning from them. A note of a meeting with the seniors in one area stated:

> Edward had only one worker remaining. He could not remember a supervision session which was not about closing cases. Hilary's group was still burdened with some heavy at risk cases and under such pressure that 'nothing is seen through'.

The word 'pressure' used in the above extract was often heard in the areas and was related to the experience that demand outstripped the resources available to meet it. Psychologically, pressure was associated with a feeling of being a dumping-ground for society's ills and waste and a feeling of no boundaries and no limits. There were complaints of being a 'dustbin department', of being unable to say 'no' and of being the place where 'the buck stopped', while the number of referrals was sometimes described as the 'bombardment rate'. It was said that clients could walk in and insist on service, and magistrates could get angry at the lack of treatment facilities and community home places, while in both diverse situations it was the social workers who bore the brunt. It was believed that those who controlled the resources which alone could satisfy the requirements were not in the firing line.

However, it was the variety of social work tasks more than the quantity of work to be done which was stressed. When we entered the department, we were frequently told that the social workers had too many different things to do and too many conflicting expectations placed upon them. It was explained that if there had ever been a consensus on what social workers did, there was one no longer. Departments were now too big to have an agreed ideology and courses had very different ideas on what they were training their students to do.

The variety of work created a difficulty in acquiring expertise in particular areas. As we previously mentioned, unpleasant tasks like removing children from home on an order were infrequent and even after nine months in the job a worker might not have accompanied a delinquent to court or received a child into care. Nevertheless, a large number of children were considered at risk, so that the anxiety related to the possibility of such events was much more prevalent than their incidence might suggest. Thus part of the anxieties surrounding these events related to uncertainty over the legal and administrative procedures.

There were similar difficulties in acquiring expertise in more mundane matters such as welfare rights. The great variety of benefits and the practice of reviewing the levels at regular intervals meant that it was extremely difficult for the social workers to know their clients' entitlements. Thus without looking through books, themselves sometimes out of date, it was impossible for them to help us with such details as the current family income supplement regulations or the allowances that could be claimed by an unmarried pregnant woman. Equally, because of the great variety of facilities of which they had to make use, they were often unaware of the characteristic of a particular one — for example, a luncheon club for the elderly.

These uncertainties were reflected in the half-jokes which were made to us by individuals at a variety of levels in the department. An administrative assistant in one team said that when she was acting as receptionist she received so many varied questions that she adopted a policy of sending callers to the CAB, on the grounds that if the referral was inappropriate there the caller would soon be back. A high-level administrator told us how difficult it was to allocate resources in a department without clear priorities, and when an IMS worker remarked that many clients did not appear to know what a social services department was for, another administrator replied, 'Well, if they know, I wish they'd tell us'.

The problems of too much and too varied work, conflicting expectations and staff turnover, demanded a solution if the department were to survive. Not everyone could be pleased, so, within the political and legal context, the social workers had to find ways of tailoring the potentially vast demand on expensive and, therefore, limited services. Implicitly or explicitly, the workers had to define a role for themselves in an organization experienced as having too few boundaries.

In this chapter we shall consider the tailoring solutions which helped to avoid institutional overload and provided the individual worker with a route to follow through the bewildering variety of things he might be expected to do. We shall follow the route and describe the definition of the role which emerged at the time we were working in the department. We then look at the compatibility of this role with the model of help we described in Part 4 and summarized in the last chapter. Finally we look at the institutional temptation to use this commonly defined role for defensive purposes to avoid anxieties which could be raised by clients, particularly those in our core sample.

THE ROUTE AND THE ROLE

Intake

Perhaps the most interesting point about the intake system is its name. The word 'intake' suggests receptivity and seems more applicable to residential institutions. It contrasts with words such as advice centre or surgery which are used by other professionals offering analogous services — a person is not 'intaken' by the CAB, his GP or his solicitor. The term expresses a desire to take care of some very deprived or unfortunate people, but it states only one side of the intake process and denies the inherent conflict when demand exceeds supply.

In practice an intake process has not one but several purposes:

to assist those in need of the services to obtain them;
to deal with those not in need by ensuring they do not apply, or handling them appropriately should they do so;
to tailor the demands to the resources available.

There are people who may be considered to need a service but who may not want it, and there are those who may want it and need it, and there are those who may want it and may be thought not to need it. Even given the coincidence of wants and assessed needs, there may not be the resources to satisfy them. Faced with potentially unlimited demand, any social services department is necessarily concerned with reducing it to manageable proportions and justifying the decisions to respond to one request and not to another.

The system in our areas was that the teams took duty days in rotation and workers within the teams took turns in acting as duty officer. Cases were kept by the intaking team unless it was exceptionally overloaded, but they were not necessarily kept by the worker who first encountered them. Most teams held a weekly allocation meeting at which bids were made by individual workers for cases which needed further attention.

The range of work which had to be processed on a duty day could be considerable and involve new clients and those already known to the team. On the first such day of which we took notes, the team was involved in considering whether to try to get power of attorney over the affairs of an old man; getting a schizophrenic out of bed into a day hospital; registering a request for a commode; seeing a known client whose wife had died the same day; interviewing a man whose wife had just left him and his children; registering a request to act as a volunteer; talking to another known client who was proposing to leave the putative father of her child; advising a woman in need of a maternity bed; and assessing two people for compulsory admission to the psychiatric hospital. The first of these admissions took nearly four hours and was distressing. The patient pleaded with her husband not to send her away; there was a long delay before the ambulance arrived and eventually a woman constable had to be involved.

Clearly there are parallels between this day and the morning described in chapter 15. There is the same background of death, madness, and separation and the foreground of tricky practical and procedural questions. However, it is also important to note that business was done and in such a way that the workers could pick up on their current work on the following day. The cases in psychiatric hospital could now, if necessary, be left for a while or even for good; the pregnant woman and the deserted father were going to try to manage on their own; the commode, the volunteer and the transport to the day hospital represented discrete manageable tasks. Obviously not all duty days were of this kind and some involved no more than one or two routine enquiries.

However, a day of the kind described gets near the limits of a team's capacity and, in keeping with the requirement to reduce demand, the social work division generally kept a low profile. The imposing flight of steps at the entrance to one area office seemed hardly calculated to attract mothers with young children or the disabled. The telephone system in one of the areas was such that only the most competent or motivated could negotiate it. The out-of-hours emergency number was not listed. (These comments apply to the time we were working in the division. Some changes have since been made.) Steps were taken to inform some referrers that certain types of referral (for example, requests to 'vet' applications for electricity meters) were inappropriate. Other types of referral (particularly those relating to delinquency and rent arrears) were almost automatically filed without further action, thus discouraging further referrals from the same source. Alternative routes had been provided for services, assessment for which was not thought to require social work skills — for example, bus passes and home helps. Some clients or referrers were told by the duty worker that she could not say whether the department could help until the matter had been discussed at an allocation meeting — a practice which enabled the referral to be considered in the context of other priorities. At times of acute overload, cases would enter the senior's pending box, which effectively constituted a waiting list.

Despite this mixture of conscious policy to exclude inappropriate clients and practical expedients to reduce the caseloads, the number of clients who could benefit from the department's help still outstripped the resources available, and decisions to accept or refuse work had to be made and justified. Justification involved several criteria, some reflecting good professional practice, and others organizational and political constraints.

The initial consideration was administrative boundaries, and sometimes disputes occurred between neighbouring authorities as to who should take responsibility for clients who had strayed temporarily over the border. Another consideration was the client's knowledge of and agreement to the demand. For example, a bailiff, arranging an eviction, found the tenant 'barricading the room against X-rays'. The tenant showed no desire for a social worker's intervention and the social workers, feeling they had been asked to do the dirty work of others, refused the case, much to the fury of the landlord's solicitors.

Other criteria included the authority of the referrer, the nature of the risk involved, statutory requirement, and the degree to which the problem could be seen as amenable to the services provided by the department. If a doctor had referred the lady afraid of X-rays, he would probably have obtained a different response from that received by the bailiff. A neighbour referring a frail old lady might be asked to make sure that the request was welcome, whereas a neighbour referring a child at risk might well get immediate action. A court order ensured that a case was taken on. A case where there was a possible need for a home help would be considered, whereas a case for which no possible concrete service seemed relevant might not.

The consequence of this very practical form of processing was that problems became defined in such a way that it was relatively clear what the department should do about them. Our survey of intake forms, described in appendix I, shows that the problems of referrals as described by social workers can be classified in terms of a small number of problem categories which, in effect, suggest a limited range of practical actions. A note in one of the diaries reads:

> Rita [a social worker] told me that after the formation of the social services department a number of old people had been referred because they were lonely. The department, unlike the old welfare departments, had refused to respond to this and would go and visit when there was a job to be done.

The concept of a 'job to be done' or a 'service to be provided' was equally important in other areas of intake such as homelessness. Not surprisingly, the actual homelessness usually dominated the consideration of the case. Appendix I contains two examples of cases in which women with extremely complex problems were considered as if the only aspect of these with which the department could concern itself was the lack of a house. Housing cases which did not fall within the council's policy for rehousing, such as an overcrowded family getting on each other's nerves, were quickly closed on the assumption that there was nothing to be done for them.

On one occasion an IMS worker challenged this approach:

> A couple had left the wife's mother's house in the neighbouring borough when the mother went to live with another daughter. The

wife, six months pregnant, was now staying with a relative within the borough in grossly overcrowded conditions. The husband was sleeping rough [in which borough was not clear]. The group discussed whether the wife could be accepted as homeless. I suggested there might be more in the interpersonal situation than met the eye. Diana was quite sharp with me: 'The thing we have to do is establish whether we can help them'.

This remark was made when the group was under pressure. By suggesting that it might consider or find out about the interpersonal situation of this homeless couple, the IMS worker not only held up the dispatch of business, but advocated a more expressive role which was not at that time acceptable. The question at issue was whether the couple was domiciled in the borough and hence eligible for rehousing.

The implied equation of help with practical assistance was a common one, not least because elaborate assessments could cause problems in terms of time:

Patricia told us that when she first became intake senior she insisted on what she considered, in the light of her previous experience, were adequate assessments. As a result, at 4.30 on the Friday afternoon of her first week, her team had three crises 'buzzing around their heads', whereas previously they would no doubt have managed to get them packed away much earlier.

A survey of one of the areas carried out by the department's research unit found that the intake team closed only 4 per cent of its cases with 'client's needs unmet'. This could be interpreted as a testimony to the efficiency of the workers, but it is more likely that it reflects how painful it is for the workers to consider need which they cannot meet.

Long-Term Work

Many of the concepts relevant to intake were also applicable to long-term work. Here, too, workers and organization struggled with the problems of too much to do, too many different ways in which time might be spent and too uncertain a definition of this task. As at intake, they justified their role and allocation of time through the concepts of crisis, need for practical services and basic statutory requirements.

As we showed in chapter 3, the bulk of the caseloads could not be managed by regular visiting unless the visits were spread very widely indeed. A variety of alternative methods of managing caseloads existed. They were used in differing ways by different workers and reflected the justification for their work.

One method could be called 'management by emergency'. Cases were visited as and when emergencies arose and time was allowed for possible future emergencies. This response to the problem provided a rationale for the worker's use of time and also, since emergencies were usually defined by the client or others, a justification of the worker's role. As one worker explained:

> In social services, if the clients are not presenting crises, they tend to get pushed into the background. You tend to deal with things just to keep them quiet.

Other justifications for contact with clients involved practical service and statutory obligations. Unfortunately, reasons for activity which might be regarded as valid by magistrates or the press could be regarded differently by clients. In statutory cases where there was anxiety about a child, workers sometimes solved the dilemma by emphasizing the practical tasks which they could undertake as an excuse for maintaining contact or fostering a relationship. In the words of one worker:

> ... and following that and within about a week she phoned up about an exceptional needs payment from the DHSS and asked if I would support this. I was a bit pleased that she had come to me for something and I immediately got on to the DHSS, explained the position and wrote them a letter.

Practical help provided a rationale for spacing visits which could then be timed according to the movements of the service with which the social worker was in contact on behalf of the client. Thus a worker might say she would make her next move after 'hearing from the housing department'.

These two methods did not always produce sufficient contact for the amount of anxiety the case generated. In some child care cases, part of what the worker did could be explained by the need to formulate, monitor and defend policy over where the child should be; this activity could require more frequent visits than could be justified by the need for practical services. Unwelcome visiting of this kind could be acutely uncomfortable for the workers (and presumably the clients), particularly if the workers felt they might be blamed if anything went wrong. In other cases the visiting could approximate to a friendly 'popping in'. When social workers felt that too long a period had elapsed since they saw a family, they might either write offering a date or visit without an appointment. The latter method was used particularly with clients about whom there was anxiety and who made a habit of being out even on agreed appointments. It was also the chosen method of some workers who said they never made appointments.

INSTITUTIONAL TEMPTATION

The social work division was inevitably much concerned with high-priority cases. In response to potential overload, the intake system weeded out clients who could be left without undue risk and those whose problems would be resolved by the provision of an immediate practical service. In its long-term work, the division had no choice but to respond to clients like those in our core sample who produced numerous crises, put their children at risk and complained of endless practical problems. The workers reacted to the crises, monitored those cases which were politically fraught and managed many of the practical issues.

The social workers' behaviour — for example, their concern with practical matters and their difficulty in keeping to reliable patterns of visiting — had some analogies with the behaviour of our core sample clients. These clients defended against their ambivalence about attachment, their underlying despair and lack of self-worth by denial of emotional need, an emphasis on material tokens and a hectic activity. They were faced with an organization which offered its social workers the temptation to behave in a similarly hectic way and to define their role primarily in terms of crisis relief and a practical 'job to be done'.

Obviously any organization is invited to respond in a way which fits the presenting behaviour of its predominant clients. However, in so far as our department responded in this way, it did not encourage the type of casework help which we believe our core sample clients needed in terms of a specific figure who would become familiar, with whom emotional issues could be raised and who would be reliable and trustworthy. We suggest that *the continuing response in the clients' own terms was a way of dealing not just with potential overload of numbers but also with the potential overload of feelings which could raise extreme discomfort.*

In practice it was difficult to respond creatively to many of these clients because of the feelings they aroused not only in the social workers but also in the referrers. Obviously individual workers have their own Achilles heels. Some workers are more vulnerable in some areas of feeling than their colleagues. There are, however, three sets of feelings or fears to which we wish to draw attention and which seemed to beset the division as a whole. These were, firstly, the general fear about impending catastrophe; secondly, the gloom concerning the general and chronic misery which provided a backcloth for so many of the encounters with these clients; and thirdly, a sense of helplessness in the face of expected crises and the intractability of some of the emotional problems.

These feelings, natural enough in the face of the events with which the workers were faced, nevertheless had a life beyond the immediate impact of the events themselves. Thus the fear of impending catastrophe could raise more anxiety than an actual crisis event. When we started working in the department, night duty was done by the day staff on a rota; it was admitted that the thought of what might happen was usually much worse than what actually did. The event, when it occurred, gave opportunity for action and thus relief from the tension of waiting, when imagination could run riot.

The depression engendered by the clients could become a prevailing mood. It was as if an adequate response to the clients' misery was for the workers to become equally miserable themselves. Surrounded by misery, pain and death, they appeared to find it intolerable to proclaim their own life and success. The IMS worker who carried out the survey of priority cases found evidence of much good work and some change in the clients. Although individually the workers had expressed enthusiasm and hope about some of their clients, collectively they were quite unable to accept such good news. During the feedback they sat with heads bowed and said that the optimistic insights of the survey were incorrect.

The sense of helplessness, again a natural response to impossible situations, was nevertheless increased, it seemed, by the badgering and expectation both from other professionals and from members of the community. One of us remembers the impact made on her during the first week she spent in a team room. Listening to the telephone conversations, she felt she had never previously heard a group of professional workers being told by so many people what to do. As one of our local authority colleagues commented:

> It makes me cross when people ring up and suggest there is a new situation which I ought to be changing. I don't write up much, but last time it happened I looked up the records and found that precisely the same thing happened last year.

The sense of helplessness and of not knowing accentuated the depression and the fear of catastrophe. Together they led to a reluctance on the part of some workers to become involved with clients whose demands could be so great and so impossible and to whom such terrible things might happen. The fear of becoming too important to clients was expressed in a variety of ways. Although many workers went far beyond the call of duty by working long hours and taking inordinate trouble over many things, client dependency caused discomfort and ambivalence. The workers in the project group grew uneasy when it became apparent that they were important to their clients. One client went to the trouble of discovering the whereabouts of her worker when he was in hospital. She sent him flowers. He explained this behaviour as being what this Englishwoman considered the appropriate behaviour towards social workers, rather than anything to do with her feelings for him.

The temptation to adopt such attitudes in individual instances is clear enough and was discussed in chapter 10. In this chapter we are concerned with the way in which the organization, through its culture, its rules and procedures, allows, excuses or encourages such a denial of relationships together with the related responses of helpless depression or frantic activity. We suggest, in Menzies' terms, that when workers are frequently faced with intolerable feelings, the organization is used to provide a structural defence. A role which is appropriate, or all but inevitable, with some clients can then be used inappropriately as a defence against the discomfort and anxiety raised by others.

There were, of course, many instances when defensive responses were avoided. For example, Patrick

> enabled an old lady to stay out of a psychiatric hospital. She was eccentric and Irish, had broken her leg and was immobilized in filth in her room. She was refusing to go into hospital and there was considerable anxiety among a number of people that she would somehow come to grief over the weekend. Efforts were being made to get her sectioned into a psychiatric hospital.

Patrick did not distance himself from this old lady by seeing her as mad, but instead saw her as pious and managed to get a nun to visit her on the Saturday and Sunday. He contained the anxieties of those pressing for compulsory admission and maintained his hope that, given more time, he would, more appropriately, be able to get her into an ordinary hospital.

Generally, however, a practical focus, crisis relief and busyness could all be used as socially acceptable defences against emotional pain, misery, catastrophe and dependence.

The role of intake as an antidote to helplessness and depression depended on its emphasis on practical tasks and crisis relief. After all, how many times can a worker be expected to bear the sadness, even though bearing with the sadness might be the most valuable response to a sad client?

> When I was on duty a Miss Yearsley, a seventy-year-old woman, came in. I discovered from the file that her mother, with whom she had been living previously and who had been known to the department, had died three years ago at a great age. Miss Yearsley wanted a telephone, but, as she was neither housebound nor obviously at risk she was not eligible. I told her so, adding that it must be hard picking up the threads of her life after having lived so long with her mother. She cried and I was distressed at having opened up an area that I had not the time to follow up.

In fact, Miss Yearsley may not have needed a follow-up. The sharing of the sadness would in itself, we believe, have offered some relief. It is difficult, however, to be able to do nothing for clients except bear with them in their uncertainty and sadness. A practical focus ensures that the worker is not exposed either to the client's pain or to the feeling that he has not helped.

Crises could also serve a similar function in defending the workers against much of the awfulness with which they were presented.

> At 4.30 on Friday my team was coping with three crises. Firstly, a Chinese man with an uncertain command of English was downstairs with a small baby, a bottle and some feeding instructions which he did not understand. He said his wife had left him and he wanted his child taken into care. At the same time, a single mother, believed to have once nearly smothered her child, was in a state at the day nursery, and was apparently expecting to have her sister's child at the weekend. And thirdly, the senior was waiting for a call from the police about two boys aged nine and fourteen apparently living on their own. The area officer, who came to help with all this, remarked 'If the *New Statesman* could see us now, they wouldn't say there was no need for social workers'.

Even before the reassurance that his social work role might be useful, the IMS worker was guiltily conscious of enjoying himself. Evading responsibility for the baby's feed, he went to the day nursery and got caught up in a feeling of hectic excitement and much joking shared by the young mother and the staff. Everyone responded to the drama and the mother spoke of her 'chances' of surviving the weekend as if this were a matter of luck and she had no control over what transpired.

Clearly, the division had to have some organization to deal with real emergencies. A senior was always available to the team on duty and the physical proximity of the senior's office to that of his team reflected the emphasis on ready access to an authoritative source of help. Some teams in one area arranged for one of their members to be available to cover crises during all working hours. However, the expectation and existence of crises dominated the atmosphere more than seemed strictly necessary.

Meetings were often disjointed affairs with social workers arriving late, leaving hurriedly or popping in and out. Before one project seminar, the Jafferjis' worker, knowing that the tipstaff wanted to speak to him, left a message with the covering worker to say that he was in a meeting and was not available till a certain time. Despite this, an 'urgent' request was brought to him in the seminar. A client wanted to speak to him. He again said that he would not be free till the end of the meeting and asked for a message to be taken. The message turned out to be a request for an alteration of an appointment.

When returning to the office we too were influenced by the expectation of disaster and adopted the habit of routinely enquiring whether things had been 'quiet' as if they might well have not been. People talked of so and so's caseload blowing up, and, when things were quiet, might well say with a sense of impending doom, 'It's been a funny week'.

The sense of excitement and general busyness were promoted by the rotating duty system which was said to prevent a worker from keeping regular appointments. We noticed a striking difference in one area (A) after it had moved offices and established an intake team. Previously the area had had a reputation for liveliness whose almost hysterical character contrasted sharply with the demeanour of the clients in the waiting-room and with that of the social workers in another area (B), with whom it shared an office. The workers in the other area seemed as depressed as their clients. In its new premises and with an intake team, the bustling fury of area A vanished. It became characterized by the depressed quietness of the new long-term teams whose need for relief and excitement was no longer being met by the old duty system.

To have something practical to do and to be surrounded by crises also helps the worker to avoid knowing how important she is to some clients. At an allocation meeting an IMS worker

> queried a phrase in an old lady's letter to her former worker about a radio. I asked 'Did she say "I miss it" or "I miss you"?' There was general laughter. 'I miss it, thank God'.

The question of the worker's importance to clients was also raised in relation to personal gifts. While the official position was clear, unofficially there seemed to be doubt over whether workers should accept such gifts from clients. Some clients who had been helped wanted to express their gratitude. The discomfort then experienced by many workers did not appear to relate solely to the official prohibition, but more to their own discomfort about being important to a client.

> A former client telephoned Terry wanting to give him money for his previous services. Terry asked his senior about this, was told not to

accept and to tell the client that he had just been doing his job. Later
the client called and gave Terry a bottle of sherry. Everyone laughed
when they heard about this. Terry offered us a glass and Janice said,
'To appease your guilt' and told him to keep it for himself. Beryl and
Janice then swopped stories about clients who had given them things.

The belief that the worker was not important to the client in that
what she did was only part of her job was sometimes buttressed by
beliefs about the importance of privacy and the danger of personal
revelations. The latter belief neglected the difference between
revelations made in the context of a reliable relationship and those
made without this security.

Mrs Izatt's worker, who had the reputation of being one of the best
caseworkers in the area, had a highly significant interview with Mrs
Izatt which she noted in full in the handover report. She also noted
that after this interview she had found it impossible to get hold of
Mrs Izatt again over a period of several months and she explained
this on the grounds that Mrs Izatt had told her too much. From
letters on the file, however, it was apparent that the worker had
missed two appointments following the interview and on neither
occasion had she been able to tell Mrs Izatt in advance. The first
interview was missed because the worker had to collect a teenager
from another part of the country. A letter contained her apology for
forgetting the second.

The forgetting of an interview is significant and may well have been
connected with the worker's own anxiety. As important is the fact
that this skilled and sensitive worker took no account of her own
failure to keep appointments and did not consider its implications
or the effects it could have had on the client. The whole of the
problem of maintaining contact was displaced on to the client. The
worker's own anxiety was left unexamined and its part in the
interaction was not considered. It can be guessed, however, that the
memory lapse might have had something to do with her own
uneasiness about her growing importance to the client, made
evident by the client starting to trust her with emotionally fraught
material. In reaction, the worker behaved as if she did not matter to
the client at all.

The high rate of staff turnover could also be used as a
justification for trying to minimize the value to a client of the social

worker as an individual. An expectation that workers would not remain long with a department was generated and experience confirmed its reality. Was it realistic then to encourage clients to value their workers? Lack of encouragement, however, could easily slip into a doctrine that social workers should operate in such a way that they were easily replaceable.

I started a conversation on a difficulty I had had in ending a case. Nigel said that it was often a mistake to discuss ending with a client as it burdened him with one's own doubts. Workers should not bring their personality into things and clients should not depend on particular workers although, unfortunately, they sometimes did. Priscilla said that she could not see how one could avoid bringing oneself into things but added that cases were often closed by not seeing a client for some time and then closing the case administratively.

Although the role implied in the above quotation was not one which either the workers or their managers consciously wanted, it was in fact reflected in two institutional practices: the period of notice and the 'six months' rule.

The period of notice required was one month. This was far too short a time to allow for satisfactory goodbyes and handovers and it is hard to imagine that social services departments would tolerate it if they were, as a whole, committed to relationship work. Many workers, of course, planned their departures well ahead, but others could and did avail themselves of the opportunity to leave at short notice and some were almost forced to do so by the fact that they could not obtain promotion unless they could take up the posts offered to them 'immediately'.

The 'six months' rule was a practice whereby cases which became active six months after they had officially been closed were picked up by the duty team of the day rather than by the team which had originally carried them. There was, of course, nothing to prevent the original team or worker from offering to take the case back and this sometimes happened. However, as the existence of this rule implies, this was an exception.

Mrs Dockeray, we believe, was not helped by the 'six months' rule. After her contact with the IMS worker, she married her 'desirable suitor' and later came in for advice concerning their adopting the two children of her previous marriage. Seen by a different social worker who did not consult the papers, she was referred to the CAB. It was not recorded whether she asked for her previous worker by name. Probably she did not, but in view of the distrust she had exhibited when he had cancelled an interview because he was ill, she would have been better served if she could have been referred back to him.

The existence and operation of the six months rule seem to encapsulate the themes of this chapter. It was an organizational rule perhaps devised to deal with overload on teams and to keep the work shared out as evenly as possible. Its operation, however, assisted the cultural defence against continuing involvement with clients' underlying emotional needs and devalued the importance of the client/worker relationship. By implication, it suggested that only short-term involvement was appropriate and that neither client nor worker should expect to meet again after the initial obligation had been discharged.

The importance of the familiarity of the worker may have been denied in an unconscious attempt to protect the worker from the splitting and blaming syndrome with which we are concerned in the next chapter. As one of the authors has argued elsewhere, however, we believe that lack of conscious involvement has the paradoxical effect of 'confirming the client's worst fears'.[11]

[11] Mattinson, J. (1975), *The Reflection Process in Casework Supervision* (Institute of Marital Studies).

17   The Problem of Institutional Splitting

While the disciplined love which alone could have employed these engines
Seemed far too difficult and dull, and when hatred promised
An immediate dividend, all of us hated.

W.H. Auden

In proposing an amalgamated service, the Seebohm Committee hoped to improve co-ordination between workers. It listed 'poor co-ordination' as one of the defects of the segregated services, and 'divided responsibility' as one of the 'underlying and closely associated explanations' for these defects, which were:

Inadequacies in the amount of provision
Inadequacies in the range of provision
Inadequacies in the quality of provision
Poor co-ordination
Difficult access
Insufficient adaptability

It added: 'The more fragmented the responsibility, the more pronounced the problem becomes.'

As the report explained, the divisions of responsibility demanded common and interlocking policies but, at the same time, made them extremely difficult to obtain. Staff in the separated departments were organized to achieve specific objectives rather than meet the full range of needs. This, the Committee believed, militated 'against the prospect of helping a family or individual with multiple needs'. And it noted that it was difficult to ascribe 'responsibility for failure to any particular service or to hold anyone responsible'.[1]

In ascribing the failure to co-operate to organizational structure, this analysis did not consider the part which may be played by clients, workers and referrers. Workers, whether in one department or several, will continue to be subjected to the clients' attempts to set them at odds and sometimes, but not always, they will succumb. We started this book with a description of the Jafferjis' marital war and their success in exporting it into their experienced workers, who began a fight amongst themselves. By contrast, in chapter 13, we described a more successful outcome with the Steggles family, who, at the point of referral, were splitting the caring agents into two categories — the 'amputators' and the 'non-colluders'. The co-operation that was achieved between all parties on that case appeared to be an important factor in helping Mr and Mrs Steggles resolve some of their ambivalence about their daughter's receiving treatment without being completely cut off from her family. Given the importance we attach to genuine co-operation, it is important to see how the organization and its culture encourage this or, by contrast, use the defences of splitting and blaming.

THE TEMPTATION TO BLAME

As we have seen, the clients frequently behaved as if they were trying to find an idealized figure who would banish all their pains and make everything right. Such behaviour is characteristic of the defence of splitting which we defined in chapter 4. The perceived world of a person using splitting as a predominant defence is typically inhabited by gods and devils or, in the language we used in chapter 9, by suckers and bastards. In part three we described the effect of such behaviour on the worker and the difficulty of resisting the response of trying to be all good before being turned into all bad.

It is not only the workers who are caught in this problem. The expectation of the Seebohm Report was that unmet needs were to be sought out and, by implication, fulfilled. The workers in the new departments had to contend not only with the clients' wishes for an idealized figure and their own unconscious wish to provide it, but

[1]   Seebohm, F. (1968), op. cit.

with the conscious or unconscious expectation that an idealized organization *should* exist. The practice of blaming individual social workers for their clients' disasters paradoxically preserves this expectation; deviations from the ideal can then be explained in terms of blameworthy individuals.

The situation is further complicated by the fact that social workers hold powers that are often associated with separation. For example, they can separate parents and children, inevitably, in our culture, stigmatizing the parents as bad. In work where one person is being separated from another, and in many other instances as well, pain is necessarily inflicted upon somebody. This in itself can give rise to guilt. It is not pleasant for the worker to feel, as in the case of Mrs Gibson (*née* Nanson), that what may be for the good of the child may result in the death of the mother, nor to be responsible for containing the anxiety of the foster-parents until a decision can be reached. Neither is it a joyful experience to have to face the wrath of clients who cannot be given what they envisage will make their lives less miserable.

In these situations the question inevitably arises as to who is to blame for events which no one desired. The rescued child may blame the 'bad' children's home in which he has been placed and idealize the lost parents; the parents may blame each other, the worker or the organization; and the worker may blame the parents, society or the organization which has compelled him to act in a controlling way. It is more comfortable to believe that controlling powers are not really exercised by 'good' workers and that blame should be attributed to someone else.

The Temptation to Blame within the Department
Not surprisingly, the department was characterized by an acute anxiety about being blamed, which was intensified by the various enquiries into the deaths of battered children which were preoccupying the national press over the period of the project. The concern was evident in the rules and procedure which were to be followed on notification of a potential battering of a child. What had been devised as an aid to good practice, offering the child maximum protection, was overtaken by the anxiety to ensure that nobody would be liable to blame in the case of disaster. The concern was also an element in many of our discussions with senior staff of the division, where the question 'who is to blame?' seemed

to hover uncomfortably much of the time. The same issue arose between the workers. In offering a regular seminar on their supervisory functions to senior social workers, the IMS workers found themselves caught up in unexpressed anxieties that these seminars might be seen by the basic-grade workers as the place where only their faults were exposed.

The insidious way in which blame crept up the hierarchy is well illustrated in the work with Mrs Yule discussed at two of these seminars. At the first of these, there was a strong note of blame in the senior's account of the worker's failure in getting on with the required work with Mrs Yule. Although the worker had, indeed, made several obvious mistakes, the anger of the senior was out of all proportion to the severity of them. It was then learnt that Mrs Yule had succeeded in making the previous worker also feel guilty and blamed. Both workers had had difficulty in keeping the relationship on a professional basis. The first worker had continued to be Mrs Yule's friend after leaving the department; the current one contrasted herself with her predecessor and felt quite incapacitated, particularly in relation to her inability to give Mrs Yule what the latter wanted. She felt blamed by Mrs Yule for not doing so and at the same time blamed Mrs Yule for not being a 'good' client. Both worker and supervisor, it seemed, were caught up in the feeling that somebody must be to blame.

At the second seminar, it was learned that Mrs Yule had by this time made complaints to the director and to the national press about the failure of the worker to provide what she demanded. The guilt of the worker was intensified and the blame was even more focused upon the mistakes she had actually made. In this, as in many other similar situations, it was difficult to hold on to the fact that neither the worker nor the agency was responsible for Mrs Yule's feeling of deprivation which led her into such blaming and guilt-provoking behaviour. Nor was it necessarily the worker's or the agency's fault that these deprivations could not easily be remedied. Only when the blaming behaviour of Mrs Yule, the worker and the supervisor were brought together could the connection be seen and the focus taken off the mistakes, some of which had been made in response to the worker's feeling of being blamed regardless of what she did.

It is interesting and indicative of the strength of the reflection that the blame expressed in these two seminars took over the seminar leaders to the extent that they recorded only the process of blaming and failed to record Mrs Yule's problem and what it was that she demanded. The problem and the demand cannot be recalled.

Obviously the question of blame was much more evident at some times than at others. For example, the suicide of a client who had 'escaped' while she was being considered for compulsory admission to a psychiatric hospital could lead to an issue about whether it was the social worker or the psychiatrist who was at fault, to a closing of ranks on the part of the social workers, and also to questions as to whose side the departmental hierarchy was on. At other times, questions of blame were less manifest, but there were some features of the organization which suggested that the fear of blame was latent.

One of these features was the difficulty of distinguishing clear lines of responsibility. It was, for example, difficult to determine the balance between the managerial and consultative roles of the seniors. How far were they managers with responsibility for the performance of their staff and how far were they consultants to professionals who carried responsibility for their own work? This question was further complicated by the fact that local authority social workers have statutory obligations. Inevitably, there is a potential conflict between the managerial demand to provide the expected services and a professional judgement on the part of both workers and managers about the quality of the service which is then offered.

A variety of factors contributed to this obscurity. At the intake stage when a practical problem was presented, and even at allocation, the severity of any underlying relationship problem was not necessarily apparent. At the best of times cases did not easily lend themselves to the kind of dissection which would enable less onerous duties to be handled by assistants while the more skilled work was undertaken by someone more senior. Even if such dissection were more possible with more cases, almost any element of a case could become politically fraught and, therefore, of concern to the director and even the committee. We suggest, however, that the fear of impending catastrophe for which blame could be apportioned tempted the workers into blurring the extent and limits of responsibility even further than was strictly necessary. At the same time, the fear of being blamed tempted workers into blaming someone above or below them in the hierarchy with whom they were not in regular or direct contact.

An example of these processes was found in the difficulty area officers experienced in taking responsibility for sanctioning neglect of work with some clients in order to provide a more reliable service for others. Although assurance had been given, there was no firm belief that top management would back such decisions if and when the worst happened.

During a period of excessive overload and shortage of staff, one area instituted an 'unallocated case cupboard'. Two problems arose in connection with this 'cupboard'. Firstly, although sophisticated efforts were made to determine what should be minimum intervention, no one felt sufficiently sanctioned to ensure that when such an intervention had been made the case was closed, allowing time to be spent on others. Many of these other cases went into the cupboard. Secondly, although management agreed to take responsibility for these unallocated cases, this in no way reduced the workers' sense of guilt or their belief that they would be blamed if a catastrophe occurred on one of these cases. Not surprisingly, this cupboard became the focus of anxiety of all levels of workers and continued to hang like the sword of Damocles over the whole area. It is an example of how failure to alleviate a primary anxiety and the social defence system set up against that anxiety can, in turn, arouse a secondary anxiety as crippling as the first.

A further feature affecting the nature of blame was the size of the department, which was considerably larger than its predecessors. Larger means much less contact between top management and basic-grade workers, much less identification with those who determine policy, much less understanding of some management decisions, and much less knowledge at the top of what it is really like at the coal-face. In our position as project workers, we crossed status lines and discussed various issues with the field workers and the members of the management team. Not surprisingly, their perceptions of each other's difficulties were discordant and sometimes we felt we had moved out of one world into another. In particular, field workers felt they had little power to influence management or effect change, and so were correspondingly free to blame management for the undesirable features of their own situation.

When the services were segregated, the blaming probably went predominantly between the departments; it could always be the welfare or the children's department which was seen to be at fault. In a unified and much larger social services department blame was still attributed but often between divisions and sub-divisions and up and down the hierarchy. Under the pressure of overload, anxiety and stress, and the expectation of being blamed, it was vital for workers to 'get on' with their immediate colleagues. This made it difficult to open up issues of disagreement or to allow for differences between workers to be publicly known in the team or even in the areas. The workers depended on each other to handle their cases when they were out. If professional survival in the face of ever-pending catastrophe requires mutual dependence, blame, when blame is around, is likely to be exported out of the team, out of the area and, if possible, out of the division.

The tendency for this to happen was accentuated by the separation in some instances between social workers who assessed for services, and the central administrators who determined whether the criteria for services had been fulfilled. The following example shows the type of transaction which could easily occur.

> Mrs Boothroyd arrived complete with Gary and suitcases and announced that she was homeless. In the approved fashion I telephoned Mr Boothroyd and asked if he were willing to have her back. He said that it was up to her. I informed Mrs Boothroyd that, as she was neither battered nor barred the house, she could not be said to be officially homeless, but, if she would like, I would check this. What was interesting about the telephone call I then made was that I and the person in the homeless families unit to whom I spoke managed to get into a fierce argument on the totally erroneous assumption that I was pressing for Mrs Boothroyd's reception into the accommodation.

In arguments of this kind the social worker generally falls into the role of portraying the client as ill-treated and helpless, the victim of old age, a brutal husband or other circumstances, while the distributor of scarce resources suggests the client is feigning helplessness, is no worse off than many others in a similar position, and indeed is more responsible for his plight than the department.

Some institutional practices reflected this type of argument. For example, social workers were not supposed to show clients over the homeless families' accommodation in advance of occupation for fear that the clients would refuse the accommodation and, presumably, that the social workers would support them in this. Generally the arguments oversimplified the truth. In the last example, Mrs Boothroyd was trying to coerce the worker, using threats which later events proved she had no intention of carrying out. She was also desperate and unhappy. The question of whether she was responsible and therefore to blame for her predicament, or the victim and therefore helpless, posed a false dichotomy. But it is easy to see how this dichotomy arises when the social worker wants to offer help, has a brief to do so, and is under pressure from his client.

As we have described in earlier chapters, many of the clients presented themselves as helpless and there was considerable emotional power in the appeal they made. For his part, the worker knew that resources were short and that he had to compete with the claims of other clients and their workers. Not knowing the details of the other claims or the limits of the resources and not having to take responsibility for the distribution and rationing, the pressure was on the worker to increase his eloquence about his client's helplessness, blamelessness and victimization. For their part, the distributors of the resources were apparently so used to being on the receiving end of this pressure that they could become inured and deaf to more moderate enquiry. The social worker, no doubt swayed by his own eloquence, became even more identified with his client. There was a strong temptation to take no responsibility for the refusal of resources and to portray the other officer as the villain.

The Temptation to Blame other Departments

Similar situations to that described above obviously existed between the workers and those who distributed resources to clients from outside the department, for example, the DHSS or the housing department. Moreover, relationships with other professionals, normally kept on a polite working basis, could quickly deteriorate under the stress of a crisis or pressure from such couples as Mr and Mrs Jafferji.

The differing positions of individual workers in these dramas were likely to arise from their professional bias. Schools, seeing the distress of some children or experiencing their disturbed behaviour, were more likely to want them received into care than the social workers, who knew the mother as well as, or better than, the children and would be the person who would actually have to take them from her. Education welfare officers were likely to give more weight to truancy and health visitors to cleanliness than were the social workers. Doctors were likely to feel that their training and status gave them paramount authority in situations concerning psychiatric illness, yet the law gave social workers powers of compulsory admission to hospital.

A striking example of the difficulty of co-operation was found in our survey of the priority cases. Although most of these cases involved children at risk on whose state of health the doctor might have crucial information, and although all of them involved women who were likely to turn to their doctor for anti-depressants, none of the social workers described close working relationships with the GPs of these families. A few of them described disputes with the doctors and one of them did not know whether her family had a GP.

Part of the explanation for this situation may have arisen from the pressure from the clients to keep the workers divided and separated, but differences in prestige were also important. When we first entered the area we were amazed at the peremptory and condescending way in which we were treated by some members of other professions, and we came to sympathize with the social workers' feelings that these professions looked down on them. One of the IMS workers was warned by a hospital social worker of the deference she must accord a registrar. On the ward the IMS worker was not impressed by the way he treated his patient (her client). Outraged and enjoying her 'immediate dividend' of hate, she left him stunned when she turned his 'joke' about the patient back against himself and his handling of the situation.

The difference between professions might have mattered less if it could have been held within ongoing working relationships; but the area was generally too large, time too short, the pattern formed by the boundaries of the various agencies too varied, and the role of the social worker too diffuse for this. The registrar, like many other different professionals, was never seen again. There were believed to be thirty GPs in one of the areas in which we worked and the chances of social workers who drew their cases from all over the area getting to know many of them well was slight, particularly as there was almost as good a case for getting to know health visitors, district nurses, education welfare officers and housing officers as well. Some of these services had also been extended or reorganized, and some had been affected by new legislation and additional tasks. Everyone seemed busy and hard to contact. In short, reorganization seemed to have multiplied the number of people with whom social workers might need to have contact without giving them in compensation a small enough base in the community in which to work and co-operate.

If social workers and other professionals each have no previous experience of how the other operates, it is much harder to understand and manage the conflicting relationships which disturbed clients can provoke. The disquiet roused by the bad or sad things which have happened between clients is easily relieved by an attack on other workers which, in its turn, invites a response.

BLAME AND THE TEMPTATION TO IGNORE
THE MARITAL RELATIONSHIP

The features we have been examining can easily exacerbate the type of triangular situation to which we have often referred in this book. In such triangles, somebody (for example, Mrs Jafferji) is defined as a helpless victim, somebody else (for example, the health visitor) as a rescuer, and yet another (for example, Mr Jafferji) as the cause of the trouble. Attempts to enter this triangle in order to help Mr Jafferji may result in battles with Mrs Jafferji's rescuer.

This situation — essentially one in which it is difficult to pause long enough to look at the marital interaction between the parties and their effect on the worker — is made more difficult by many of the statutes and local authority regulations under which the workers operate. In order to establish that Mrs Jafferji was entitled to homeless families accommodation, it was necessary to show that she was comparatively helpless (i.e. she had nowhere to go) and that Mr Jafferji was to blame (i.e. that he had hit her or debarred her the house). The law the social workers are administering is essentially concerned with need, as with the disabled, or blame, as with delinquency, or madness, which hovers uneasily between blame and need. It is also concerned with designated needy or blameworthy individuals rather than with interaction. In practice, the designation of an individual as needy or blameworthy often implicitly points the finger at a second individual. The youth's delinquency may be seen as his parents' fault and the old woman's need for an old people's home as the consequence of her daughter's failure to accept her responsibilities. This attribution of blame to a third party is particularly likely to occur when children are received into care. Most children need long-term care because of what most people would regard as a failure on their parents' part.

This triangular definition of a case was sometimes accentuated by the emphasis on statutory function. For example, the care of children, for which the department so often becomes directly responsible, overrides every other consideration. The problem is then seen as being only about the children, not about the interaction of the parents and, therefore, the interaction of the two parents with the children. An improved marital relationship might result in an improvement in the circumstances of the children.

For their part, the clients, as we have previously described, rarely asked for help with their marital problems. To judge from appendix I, they came describing a variety of problems and if they mentioned their marriage it was as a justification for their request rather than as a problem for which they wished to receive help.

In this respect the referrers were no different. Almost none of them had referred couples for marital help, and neither they nor the general public expected the department to do this type of work. When Mr and Mrs Levens had started regular weekly interviews, Mrs Levens made one of her frequent visits to her GP. By this time her definition of the problem had altered. Instead of saying that her husband's alcoholism was their only problem she told him of their marital one. The GP immediately referred them to the MGC.

A further example of the perceived irrelevance of social workers to marital problems was provided when one of the IMS workers and a local authority one decided to offer a group for couples with marital difficulties. The two hundred leaflets advertising this were beautifully illustrated and distributed to all doctors, clergy and ancillary and voluntary workers in the area. There was one response; it was not an application, but a letter from a GP to the director complaining that the two workers should know better how to be spending their time and should not be wasting the ratepayers' money.

In this situation, the workers, many of whom had been trained to see things in terms of individual pathology, had little incentive to attend to the marital aspect of their clients' lives. In the induction meetings which we had with the teams and with the areas as a whole before the project started, the workers told us they had few married clients and few marital problems on their caseloads. This was substantiated by the intake figures, although not by those relating to the current caseloads and high-priority cases. We could not help wondering how it was that a department set up in response to the recommendations of the Seebohm Committee could be unconscious of actually working with either married couples or couples with marital problems.

With our advent, marital work became more salient and it proved quite difficult not to be drawn into a conflict with those parts of the organization which were seen as standing for the concept of individual pathology. In one area we found ourselves being juxtaposed to the child care adviser, whose views were represented indirectly to us as emphasizing the interests of the child as opposed to that of his family.

When finding ourselves polarized from this adviser it was difficult to hold on to the knowledge that this externalization in the department of a real problem in the family had its potential for growth and change for both workers and clients. It was easier to remain polarized, taking one side or the other, and talking only of the protection of the child, or only of work with the parents. In their newly-aroused enthusiasm for the perspective we were promoting, some workers enacted the split in fervent and ideological terms, perceiving the adviser as standing only for the traditional emphasis, which actually he did not.

We ourselves were also far from immune from the temptation to ignore the marital relationship and concentrate instead on the concrete problem presented and the wickedness of those who refused to meet it. One of the IMS workers was on duty when

Mrs Yeomans came to the office asking for help as she was about to be evicted from the room she occupied with her eight-year-old son, Trevor. Her story was sad. A New Zealander, she had married a British citizen domiciled abroad, where they had continued to live. Two years previously he had died and Mrs Yeomans had returned to New Zealand, lived with her widowed father and worked to support herself and Trevor. After a year she came to London as she was concerned to establish Trevor's British nationality. Inevitably, life in this country turned out to be more difficult than she had anticipated.

She had always managed to find work, but accommodation had been a continuing problem. She was now desperate that she had nowhere to go when the current notice to quit expired.

Attention might have been given to her loneliness, the problems of widowhood or her feeling that she had to travel across the world to an unknown country to establish her son's right to be British like his father (Mrs Yeomans was one of our few clients who had been happily married). But the potential homelessness was pressing and the worker began exploring what could be done about this. Mrs Yeomans fell within the provisions of the policy for housing and homelessness which had been adopted by the borough, but this policy required that people should actually have been evicted before they were treated as homeless. The worker advised Mrs Yeomans that she should not leave her room until a court order had been made against her, and he also saw the landlord and advised him in similar terms.

Some of the workers in the team felt this was intolerable. Mrs Yeomans would have to be housed eventually, so why not sooner rather than later? They encouraged the IMS worker to take up the cudgels on her behalf by writing to the director to 'have the policy changed', if not completely, at least in respect of Mrs Yeomans. This he did and was duly rebuffed; there were good reasons for the general policy and Mrs Yeomans' circumstances did not merit her being made an exception. It was very tempting for the worker to continue a battle with the director and focus his attention on that problem. It was much more difficult to give that up and attempt to help Mrs Yeomans contain her anxiety while she waited to be evicted, not knowing where she would then be placed, particularly when his colleagues thought this latter course was painful and unnecessary and tried to encourage him back on to the former course. They were, however, able to acknowledge the distress they felt for Mrs Yeomans and Trevor, which the continued battle with the hierarchy was designed to relieve.

The IMS worker embarked on a programme of seeing Mrs Yeomans through the legal proceedings and of supporting her and the child in the very difficult circumstances from which they were to be evicted; he offered weekly interviews.

Difficult as were the practical problems of the accommodation and of making suitable arrangements for Trevor before and after school while Mrs Yeomans was working, the worker belatedly noticed that in the interviews Mrs Yeomans mentioned these less and less, but talked more and more of the issue of a Certificate of Patriality to be stamped in Trevor's passport. This involved lengthy proceedings with the Home Office in this country and the embassy in another, as proof was required of the nationality of her husband's parents, who had been born, lived and died abroad. Her current emotional preoccupation was keeping the memory of his father alive for Trevor and of retaining for him (and for her) something of his father which was represented by British nationality.

The eviction proceedings slowly got under way and occasioned anxiety, but the last the worker saw of Mrs Yeomans was the week before the court hearing was to take place. She had just received the Certificate of Patriality and the colourful and impressive stamp was inserted in the passport. She told the worker that her father, now aged eighty-two, really needed her to look after him and she had written and asked him to send her the fare back to New Zealand. Within a week they were gone.

Would the outcome have been different if the worker had succumbed to the temptation to engage in a gratifying administrative struggle instead of listening to Mrs Yeomans' feelings? Probably not, but the worker would have been less free to hear that the important emotional issue for Mrs Yeomans underlay the Certificate of Patriality and not the eviction. The latter, as it turned out, was important only in terms of adding to her anxiety and making it difficult for her to remain in London until she achieved her ends.

At times our particular training helped us to work in ways which other workers had found alien. The first worker with the Cabassis, described in chapter 13, had had the marital problem presented to her but in a way she found difficult to recognize. The reader will remember that the family was first evicted when Mr and Mrs Cabassi failed to keep up the mortgage payments. Money and its use were then clearly involved in the marital interaction. After the children were received into care a contribution order was made against both parents. Some time later an interview with Mrs Cabassi took place in which the following exchange occurred:

> Mrs Cabassi told me that she and Mr Cabassi were seeing each other
> at approximately two-daily intervals, but she felt she could not go

back to him until he had sorted out his financial position. I raised
with her the fact that she had not paid the department any money for
the children's upkeep during the past few weeks and I warned her
that she could be taken to court over this. She seemed rather
apathetic and said she had spent her money paying Mr Cabassi's
rent. I again stressed the importance of her paying this amount to us.

This worker could not hear that the parents of these children in care
were attempting to get together again and were expressing the
continued marital problem in their handling of the finances. She
did not take up the theme when in one interview it was presented to
her not once, but twice. She contented herself with issuing two
warnings about the consequences of non-payment of the
contribution order. Evidently, she was trying to foster Mrs
Cabassi's sense of responsibility for the children.

Once the children were in residential care the worker was acting
on behalf of that division of the department as well as the social
work one, and the concern for the children dominated the
transaction with the parents to the exclusion of the marital conflict
from which the need for the children to be received into care arose
and on which their return depended. In this case both the worker
and Mrs Cabassi seized the opportunity to avoid getting into the
work with Mr and Mrs Cabassi's marital problem which, as the
reader knows, was most severe.

The later work with the Cabassis was uncertain and exhausting
and in two ways at least atypical of much of the work of the
department. Firstly, it was explicitly focused on the marriage rather
than on the children in care. Secondly, it rested on the assumption
that both parents had a responsibility to help in resolving their
marital problems and that neither was exclusively the helpless
victim in the situation. These assumptions led to the practice of
holding regular joint interviews with the Cabassis for which they
had to attend at the office after Mr Cabassi's work. The unusual
nature of this practice was emphasized by the lack of facilities for
it. The IMS worker has vivid memories of difficult marital
interviews conducted in an open-plan office while cleaners, who
spoke no English, hoovered determinedly about her feet. Both the
contribution order and the hoover represented in their different
ways obstacles to working with marital problems in a social services
department. The contribution order deflected the worker from

hearing about an attempt at reconciliation. The presence of the cleaners suggested that such work, which often has to be done in the evenings when both husband and wife are available, was not expected.

It is certainly possible to do marital work in a social services department, but for the inexperienced worker, unsure of his own skill, it is certainly easier to avoid it.

18   In Conclusion

Celia   But even if I find my way out of the forest
             I shall be left with the inconsolable memory
             Of the treasure I went into the forest to find
             And never found, and which was not there
             And perhaps is not anywhere? But if not anywhere,
             Why do I feel guilty at not having found it?

Reilly   Disillusion can become itself an illusion
             If we rest in it.
                                                     T.S. Eliot

Our wish to work with marital problems in a social services
department had two main sources. We wanted to contribute from
our own specialized experience and also to learn by working
alongside colleagues tackling marital problems in a setting which
was unfamiliar to us. Out of our former experience and theories
and the new experience we acquired, we have written a book
focused on the interaction of client, worker and organization. In
this final chapter we summarize our argument and raise the issue of
the place of marital work in a local authority social services
department.

The assumption that we took with us to the department was that
social workers would be involved with a variety of clients who had
marital problems underlying the ones they presented. Our task
would be to assess the nature of these problems, if possible work
with them, and so develop a model that local authority social
workers could use. As we expected, the vast majority of clients
contacting the social services department were neither referred for
marital treatment nor did they ask for it. In most cases, however,
the type of work undertaken at the intake stage was such that there
was no possibility of determining whether a marital problem
existed, and even if such problems had been uncovered, only a

290

radical alteration of priorities would have given social workers the time to work with them.

In the long-term cases, marital problems were more common. Social workers in one area office had on average twelve cases in which somebody was married or cohabiting. The rationing system the workers adopted concentrated their attention on a group of priority cases of which approximately two-fifths involved a married or cohabiting couple. Almost all the priority couples had marital problems, which far from being hidden were of the most dramatic and obvious kind. These cases had a quite disproportionate effect on the agency in terms of the work and anxiety they generated. Compared with married clients who were not considered priority, they were more than twice as likely to remain on the caseloads for two years or more and roughly three times as likely to be seen in any given week. Because they seemed so central, and because they seemed the only cases likely to receive sustained marital work, we have built our analysis around couples of this kind.

In defining this core group of cases, we looked for the characteristics which were present in almost all of them. These were:

ambivalent marital bonds
lack of success in parental roles
lack of constructive support from families of origin
continual threats of separation from one or other member of the
    family.

During the course of the project we acquired a sample of sixty-eight couples drawn from our own caseloads or those of our local authority colleagues who chose to join us on the project. Within this sample we had a core sample of thirty-two couples definable by the four characteristics. In this book we have sometimes referred to clients in the larger sample who displayed some, if not all, of these characteristics, and to others who did not come into the sample but of whom we had knowledge. However, our core sample clients have provided the central themes.

In our analysis we interpreted the clients' behaviour in terms of Bowlby's theory of attachment and loss and our own theory of marital interaction, seeing both partners as two adults who both had difficulty in being attached. In our view, their ambivalence about their marital partner was based on the one hand on a lack of trust in attachment and on the other on a deep-seated longing for an ideal attachment and a fear that they would be unable to survive by themselves. Their previous experience seemed to have left them peculiarly helpless and lacking in confidence in their own ability, and yet unable to acknowledge their own emotional need for their partner. To do that was felt to invite only further rejection and, therefore, loss. Their defence against their own need and underlying feelings of inadequacy and misery was often the primitive one of splitting, whereby a spouse or the environment was seen as bad and the hope for something better and safer was maintained in the illusion of the distant ideal.

The couples were in a dilemma. Marriage was acutely uncomfortable for them and accompanied by constant separation or threats of separation in an attempt to avoid the discomfort; but being alone, or alone with children, was also uncomfortable and posed terrors akin, we felt, to a fear of death. The marriage seemed to serve a useful purpose not only in protecting them from their own helplessness and fears, but in providing a means whereby the simultaneous recognition of two contradictory feelings could be avoided. So long as one partner exhibited the yearning by anxious attachment, the other could exhibit the distrust by apparent detachment. Together they employed a variety of strategies whereby they could control and ensure the proximity of their partner while at the same time denying their need of each other except in material terms. Their difficulties in being attached to each other were also exhibited in their difficulty in being reliable attachment figures for their children. A third party in the form of a child, friend or relation was felt as a threat to the desired exclusive relationship between two people, or used by one partner as an alternative relationship which excluded the partner.

We then analysed some of the difficulties of the social workers when attempting to relate to these clients as couples. The clients came into contact in the crises with which their lives seemed to be ridden, and with many practical needs. The workers sought to maintain contact often by meeting material needs, when they were concerned about the care of the children. It was common for a worker to fall into the role of third party, often sought as an ally by one partner, and seen as a threat and someone to be avoided by the other, subjected to only one partner's definition of the problem and belief that 'it was all the fault of the other'. The worker could easily be drawn into the marital war and the conflict between the partners could become that of workers in different agencies and even of their senior officers, who were drawn in to support their staff.

The workers' ambivalence — on the one hand their wish to help these deprived people and meet their needs, and on the other their fear that they would be swamped by what seemed excessive need — played into the clients' ambivalence — their wish for an exclusive relationship with the worker, and their fear of their own vulnerability. The workers were fearful of hurting their clients and of being blamed, but were also in a position of power and able to influence events, particularly those concerned with separation. The clients knew of these powers but not always of the safeguards associated with them. Both clients and workers had cause for anxiety and cause to be wary, and each had strategies through which they attempted to control the other.

In keeping with this analysis, we came to believe that if we were to get into a potentially therapeutic relationship and get in touch with the underlying pain and misery of these clients, we had, as a starting-point, to offer them a *limited, reliable and defined contact* which persisted beyond the presenting crisis, and which challenged the clients' beliefs about potential attachment figures. We believed that it was vital that we should be there when we said we would be there, but we tried not to allow them constant and immediate access on all occasions. In this way we tried to help them to build up trust in us even when we were not there, and to encourage them to make more efforts for themselves. And from the beginning of the contact we tried to insist on our concern for their emotional as well as their practical problems. In this way we set out to deal with their feelings of helplessness and their tendency to deny attachment.

In the course of the work we endeavoured to avoid the trap of becoming idealized by one partner and set against the other, and we tried to survive with them their despair and depression and all the misery they inflicted on each other and on us. Inevitably we were drawn into their illusions, fights and predicaments, but we also tried to stand back and look at the part which we had played in the recent deadlock and to interpret our behaviour in relation to them. And throughout we had to insist that the attachment we offered was limited in duration, and that eventually we would leave them, in the belief that they could be more effective attachment figures to each other and to their children. As we saw it, our leaving, our faith in their continuing ability, our affection and, therefore, our loss as well as theirs when we said 'goodbye' were all part of the helping and strengthening process. We did not talk about cure, but we hoped that as a result of our work the couples could either remain more comfortably together or remain separated and manage better on their own.

When we could not make the marital work overt, we still used our understanding of the defensive interaction in determining our aims and level of work. In these terms we think it was possible to work with some of the emotional problems of these very deprived couples.

In the final part of our analysis, we looked at aspects of the institutional framework, not in search of a blueprint for a perfect organization, but in an attempt to understand how the organization constrained or advanced the model of help we thought the clients in our core sample required. In doing this, we tried to take account of those aspects of the legal, political and social context of the departments which impinged on the workers. We looked at how the organizational climate encouraged the workers to confront the anxiety inherent in the work with these clients, or alternatively tempted them into responding defensively in a way which echoed and reinforced the clients' defences. In Menzies' terms, how far could the organization be used as a defence against anxiety?

The sources of anxiety did not, of course, relate exclusively to our core sample clients. They could be found in much of the total volume of work. They seemed to lie in the quantity and variety of work expected in a social services department, in the seriousness of the events surrounding our core sample and other clients, in the feeling of impossibility and helplessness engendered by some of their demands, in the apparent unpredictability of events and, finally, in the sense of a hostile environment which placed high and idealized expectations on a department which had to deal with so many and varied unpleasant happenings.

To enable the workers to survive in such a climate, the demand had to be reduced to manageable proportions. In doing this, the department excluded at the intake stage those who could most easily be excluded. It was left with clients who for reasons of public concern, statutory requirements and common humanity were considered high priority, or were demanding. They were not, however, the most amenable to treatment.

The pattern of work with these long-term cases was similar in some ways to that carried out at intake. The social workers described their task in terms of responding to crises, assessing risks and managing practical problems. Such work had some analogy with the behaviour of our core sample. These clients defended against their ambivalence about attachment, and their underlying despair and lack of self-worth, by a denial of emotional need, an emphasis on material tokens, and hectic activity. They were faced with an organization whose social workers were liable to behave in a similarly hectic way and to define their role primarily in terms of crisis relief and a practical 'job to be done'. The maintenance of this pattern of work and its congruence to the clients' defensive behaviour suggested that the role served defensive purposes, but if so, it failed to alleviate the anxiety it was designed to dispel.

The workers were still left with a fear of pending catastrophe for which they could be blamed, a depression concerning the general and chronic misery of their long-term clients, a feeling of helplessness in the face of the intractability of many of the problems and a fear of becoming too important to their clients. It was difficult to develop skill in working with emotional problems, and there was a temptation to avoid the emotional issues which underlay problems, or to dabble with them in uncertain, undefined, and unreliable ways. The diverse functions and mixed caseloads in the two areas in which we worked gave numerous opportunities for avoiding regular and sustained contacts which, we considered, were the starting-point of work with the core sample. The need for an absconding adolescent to be removed from the other end of the country could, for example, override the routine visit to a core sample family. Indeed, it might provide a welcome relief. Similarly, the rotating duty day could provide a ready explanation for unreliability.

The core sample clients also raised the problem of co-operation in an acute form. The amalgamation of the previously separated departments was promoted, among other reasons, to ensure better co-ordination between social workers. However, the clients for whom the co-operation was most needed included many who were likely to evoke polarized responses and conflicts between workers. Genuine co-operation could falter just as easily between the divisions of one large department as it did between smaller segregated departments. Professional conflicts, like the fights of the clients, could always be used to protect the workers from the underlying pain and misery they could otherwise have to bear with these clients. The temptation to blame, and the fear of being blamed, influenced some organizational practices and blurred lines of responsibility further than may have been strictly necessary.

These two temptations — the avoidance of emotional issues and the process of blame — could be brought together in a third — the temptation not to do marital work. In this last temptation, the clients, workers and organization all had their part to play. The referrers did not expect the social workers and social services departments to do marital work. The clients themselves were ambivalent; they made it quite clear that they had marital problems, but used them as a justification for their predicaments rather than as something for which help might be sought. This approach enabled workers, diffident of their ability to work with marital problems, to avoid opening up what might prove to be painful areas of feeling to the clients and to the workers themselves. In addition, a legal framework conceived in terms of individual pathology, deviance or need, and many administrative preoccupations, could deflect the workers from hearing the clients' mixed messages about their marital dilemmas. Invited to accept only one definition of the problem, to be the all-good worker to one partner, the workers were often inveigled into participating in the fight, which was, in many cases, a continuing distraction from the underlying misery and ambivalence.

To summarize: resources of the social work division of the department in which we worked were heavily concentrated on a group of clients whose emotional problems related to disturbed attachment and actual and feared losses. An appropriate treatment for such clients requires, as a start, the offer of a limited attachment relationship. This presupposes time and reliability on the part of the social workers, which were difficult to offer within the existing context, structure and responsibilities of the area offices. Thus the social work division focused its major efforts on a group of clients it was ill-adapted to treat.

Stalemate? Not necessarily, but it leaves the question of whether no attempt should be made to offer treatment for the relationship problems of these married clients or whether the structure, or part of the structure, should be adapted to meet their treatment needs.

If, for whatever reasons, the decision is taken not to treat them, it must be remembered that statutory requirements and community pressures ensure that this group of clients cannot be left alone. Social workers still have a role: the task of handling practical problems, assessing levels of risk, withstanding community pressures for inappropriate action, and taking appropriate action in the least damaging way possible calls for a considerable level of skill. Such a definition of the social work role is, in fact, close to the one many of our local authority colleagues saw themselves carrying out. It involves relationship skills in so far as client and worker necessarily affect each other in the course of the work and in so far as judgements about relationships are crucial to the assessments of risk and proper disposal. We believe, however, that such work should not be termed treatment. It does not usually get these clients off the caseloads for any length of time and thus they remain a source of continuing anxiety which, in the long term, we believe, is more crippling to the workers than the anxiety which has to be faced in a treatment process.

If this alternative on its own is not considered satisfactory, it is still possible to try to provide clients with an attachment figure, who is not necessarily a trained social worker. It may be that the sustained contact and support we advocate could, in part, be provided by family aids, social work assistants or day nursery staff, and that the role of social worker could be that of case manager rather than that of front-line attachment figure. We cannot speak from experience about such approaches, and so would not want to discount them. However, we doubt whether such support would of itself improve the clients' marital relationships and, if these are not changed, we doubt if the clients would eventually be able to stand on their own. The NSPCC used a 'primary nurturing role' in their Denver House therapeutic project with parents of battered children.[1] The workers related primarily to the mothers and did not get much access to the fathers. They felt they had fulfilled their basic therapeutic intentions,

> but as the need for nurturing and support diminished, new needs did emerge ... For example, with several mothers, previously described

[1]   Baher, E. *et al.* (1976), *At Risk: An Account of the Work of the Battered Child Department. NSPCC* (Routledge & Kegan Paul).

as resistant, deep-seated marital problems began to emerge ... which required a different approach.

Another option within the alternative of not treating the core sample clients might be to refer more of them to voluntary organizations who are able to offer the time, reliability and skill that is required to help them in a more fundamental way. Unfortunately, there are not many such agencies. Even where they exist, it may be difficult to refer clients to them when the local authority retains statutory responsibility.

By making a greater use of referrals for marital problems, social workers would acknowledge the fact that the extent of these problems in the community far outstrips the capacity of their department. However, even if the department freed itself from treatment of the time-consuming core-sample clients, it would not be able to do more than a small fraction of the marital work that could be done. For example, the CAB in one of our areas produced figures for the number of clients who approached it seeking advice about marital problems and not simply asking for straightforward legal information. If these clients had approached the social services department instead, or had been referred to it, the intake system would have had to deal with an estimated 25 per cent increase of clients, any one of whom could have been time-consuming if marital work had been undertaken. Although social workers may hope to undertake all their work bearing in mind relationship factors, the hope that they themselves will have a sustained relationship with more than a small percentage of their potential clients is clearly vain.

The need to limit their direct marital work to a few clients means that social workers have to see their own efforts as part of a spectrum of response to marital problems which includes many others, such as GPs, marriage guidance counsellors, psychiatrists and priests.[2] The question is which kind of marital problem is most appropriate for social work help. In answering this question, the social workers may well choose to concentrate on the clients they

[2] Stotesbury, D. (1978), *Marriage Matters,* Consultative Document by the Working Party on Marriage Guidance set up by the Home Office in consultation with the Department of Health and Social Security (HMSO).

cannot avoid and whom other agencies are often unwilling to accept. In any case, it is difficult for them to recruit a different clientele. Sadly, perhaps, the average citizen does not see his local area office as an appropriate resource for his emotional difficulties.

If the second alternative is favoured and it is decided to provide treatment for the marital problems of our core sample clients, it does not necessarily mean that all clients in this category would receive a sustained approach or that other techniques and facilities could not be used with the same clients or with other priority clients. It does mean, however, that workers trying to stick with these clients would need the close support of a peer group doing the same type of work and smaller caseloads than they now have. They would need supervisory help from someone experienced and skilled in this type of work who could help them pick up the effect of the client on their behaviour as individuals and as a working group. The approach is expensive, but needs to be seen in the context of other provisions made for this group which are also expensive. Figures discussed in Appendix II suggest not only that certain clients are currently receiving a great deal of expensive attention from social workers, but also that the vision of smaller caseloads which would allow the kind of work we advocate, either for all social workers or for a few specialists, might not be wildly unrealistic. Even without additional resources, the workers in our two area offices have moved towards a more planned and reliable pattern of work with some of their clients.

We cannot resolve this issue of the place of marital work with core-sample clients in a local authority social services department. Its resolution involves managerial decisions which will be influenced by the prevailing political climate. In speculating what types of help might be offered to these clients — minimum provision of material aid and crisis relief or a sustained treatment process — we show not the path to be followed, let alone the details of the route, but only that all roads are not blocked. If, however, social workers are to undertake relationship work with their clients, they must first attain the preconditions of doing so.

Appendix 1 —
Survey of Referrals

All the information in this appendix came from one of the areas in which we were working. In this area all new referrals to the social work division were routed to a duty social worker who used a standard form to note, among other things, details of the composition of the potential client's family and the nature of the problem. It seems likely that some 'trivial' enquiries were not recorded and that recording practice varied between groups. Nevertheless, almost all enquiries and certainly all 'important' referrals were registered and provided a convenient way of sampling referrals.

At one stage in the project, we examined a year's batch of these forms, 1198 in all, and found to our surprise that only 265 (22 per cent) of them involved a client who was married — we use the term as in the main text — or said to belong to a family which included a married couple. Hoping for some inaccuracy, we examined every referral which immediately followed that of a married couple, and in a consecutive series of one hundred of these controls discovered four whom, given further information, we might have classified as married. Three of these were concerned with juveniles, who were referred by the police, and filed for no further action without the information on their families having been acquired. One was a common-law wife ringing to complain about her husband's treatment in the hostel where he was living. Here, perhaps, the cohabitation should have been considered as still in existence. Conceivably there were other doubtful cases. Ninety-six-year-old Mrs York, laconically described as 'needing a back-rest', was also referred without information about her family and may conceivably have been living with her spouse. Nevertheless, try as we might, it was clear that referrals involving married people amounted to little more than one in four of the total at most.

Before drawing conclusions from these figures one should remember that the number of clients concerned in a case were likely to be higher in cases involving married couples than in others. The intake forms on a series of 100 married couples mentioned an average of 2.98 family members as against an average of 1.36 family members in a hundred forms selected as controls. If this was an approximation to the true proportion, 38 per cent of the family members involved with referrals were associated with married couples. Nevertheless the contact of many of these family members with the department would be slight or non-existent and it remains true that the bulk of referrals did not involve a marriage.

In part, this situation arose from the nature of the area; according to the 1971 Census, 44 percent of the population was living in single persons' households. However, many of the services provided by the local authority were particularly adapted for the single-parent family, and the isolated and elderly. Cases involved with a married couple also reflected the services available: 88 per cent of the 265 clients of this sort were either in families with a child under school-leaving age or in families with an old-age pensioner. These, of course, are the main groups towards whom the social services department has responsibility. The remaining 12 per cent, adults of working age who had no children living with them or only children who had left school, were also involved with the social services largely for reasons sanctioned by statute. They included, for example, clients compulsorily admitted to psychiatric hospitals, clients seeking to adopt, and families in distress because of the behaviour of mentally subnormal or mentally ill children who could not live away from home.

We next examined a consecutive series of one hundred forms relating to married clients or their children. This series gave a vivid picture of the variety of problems presented and the extreme complexity of some of them. The following, for example, were six consecutive referrals.

Mrs Yeo suffers from rheumatoid arthritis and was discharged hurriedly from hospital without necessary bath aids.

Mrs Yewdall hurt her leg very badly some while ago; is due for another operation which will constrict her mobility severely. Mr Yewdall has to do shopping, housework, help her.

Mrs Yelland is getting a separation order and an injunction on her husband to stop him trying to murder her. She is epileptic and cause of his losing jobs and going to mental hospital. He has a solicitor building up evidence. One child died due to her neglect and he thinks the second child is not safe with her.

Mrs Yardley suffered a stroke some while ago which badly curtailed activities which took her out of the house. Situation with husband is not very stimulating and Mrs Yardley sought compensation in alcohol. She has just been discharged from mental hospital and needs support and bath aids.

Mr Yetts had a massive coronary ... family very bitter and in great poverty ... antagonistic to help but likely to accept what GP recommends.

Truancy of Arthur and possible family problems. See referral letter.

Obviously simple requests may cover a variety of problems. For example, Mr Yewdall may have been asking for more than a home help, felt aggrieved at what he has to do for his wife or even approached the local authority with the hidden end of seeking residential accommodation for her. Many of the applications arising from homelessness involved very young couples who were a long way from their parents' homes or had been ejected by their parents when, for example, the wife's pregnancy became known. It takes little imagination to see that these couples' marriages were likely to be under pressure. Nevertheless, the variety and urgency of the requests put pressure on the social workers to focus on the immediate practical issues. For example:

Miss Yare had been staying with her sister at the weekend and found living with cohabitee impossible since the cohabitee's family moved in. Five adults are said to be sleeping on the floor of one room. She has been living with cohabitee for over two years and is expecting a second child in two weeks. He does not give her money and she complains of derisory laughter from his family. Offered to visit to establish if homeless.

This case involved a medical social worker who may well have been attending to other aspects. From the local authority point of view, it was clearly a matter of 'homelessness'. Similarly, when Mrs Younger, a former client domiciled in another borough, came in, she told the social worker that her husband had tried to poison her, that she had absconded from a foreign psychiatric hospital a week previously and that she had now received a divorce petition and was uncertain what to do about it. She was referred to the CAB, as she was again a week later when she appeared homeless after quarrelling with her mother. This case was complicated by the fact that the client was not resident in the borough, but it was obviously dealt with as simply and practically as possible.

The social workers' need to focus their work meant that it was often easier to classify the problem which was apparently being negotiated than to formulate a more sophisticated explanation. Whether or not this classification denoted the 'real problem' is, to some extent, a matter of choice. Thus, a married woman approaching the department as 'homeless' may have been seen as having a housing problem or, for example, in addition, a financial one which made it difficult for her to obtain alternative accommodation on her own, or a marital one, or, lying behind that, a personality one. The choice of which to use out of a variety of possible descriptions tends to carry implications about blame (is society, the husband or the wife the source of the problem?), and about possible solutions. We have used the definition of the problem implied by the social worker's description on the form. In individual instances, this may have reflected the views of the client, the referrer or the social worker.

In our consecutive series of one hundred cases involving marriage, 19 per cent involved families who were squatting, or actually or potentially homeless. These were treated as requests for accommodation. A further 16 per cent were requests for the social worker to act as an advocate on housing matters since the family were suffering physically or mentally through poor housing. 14 per cent were direct, clearly stated requests for aids of various sorts. 7 per cent involved requests to adopt, to put children into short-term care or day care, or to get financial support for a handicapped child in long-term care. 3 per cent related to sections under the Mental Health Act. 5 per cent were requests for advice or advocacy relating to supplementary benefits, charities, or other social service departments. 4 per cent related to information passed on by other social service departments. The reason behind 3 per cent of the referrals was quite obscure; for example: 'Police called at six o'clock in the morning when a flower pot fell'.

This left 29 per cent of the referrals. 21 per cent involved family problems including delinquency and truancy (2 per cent), 3 per cent children at risk, and 3 per cent referrals arising out of anxiety that an old couple could not manage. Many of these cases also involved practical matters: for example, requests for bedrests as well as emotional support. However, the social workers were also expected to exercise professional judgement over, for example, whether a child or an old person could remain at home, and to prevent disasters, alter undesirable behaviour and relieve distress. Table 1 sets out these figures.

TABLE 1

Problems referred in a sample of 100 married couples

Old person cannot manage	3
Children at risk	3
Delinquency and truancy	2
Other family problems	21
Homelessness	19
Need for housing advocacy	16
Need for aids	14
Adoption/short-term care/day care	7
Compulsory admission to psychiatric hospital	3
Other advice/advocacy/finance	5
'For information only'	4
Obscure	3
	100

Note: Where a case could be coded in more than one category, the category mentioned higher in the table was used.

Many of the family difficulties involved marital problems which were explicitly mentioned. It became apparent, however, that if the intake of marital problems was to be studied it would be necessary to examine all the 1198 cases. Among these we found only thirty-seven (3 per cent) where marital problems were mentioned either explicitly or by direct implication. Detailed examination of what was, from our point of view, a depressingly small number of marital cases revealed that hardly any of them were presented initially as direct requests for marital help. Table 2 shows the reasons for these referrals.

TABLE 2

Problems associated with explicit marital difficulties

Housing	13
Child care	8
Deviant behaviour of one spouse	7
Wife's need for support	5
Other	4
	37

Of the thirteen (approximately one-third of the total) which involved housing, five were requests from women wanting reception into homeless families accommodation. Of these, three said that their husband had battered them, one that her husband was impossible to live with and one that their landlady was about to evict them as a result of their marital rows. Two further female clients sought accommodation following the break-up of their marriage but, as they had no children, they were not eligible for homeless families accommodation and were given lists of hostels or referred to the CAB. Three women wanted their husband's name removed from the housing list and theirs substituted or, alternatively, a separate offer of council accommodation for themselves. Three referrals, two from outside agencies, related to situations in which unsatisfactory housing or the necessity for husband and wife to live apart had exacerbated an already strained marital relationship.

Eight cases involved child care. In three cases (all apparently fended off), men came in seemingly to enlist the social worker's support in custody disputes with their wives. Two cases were referred because there was anxiety that the children of battered wives were at risk. Three further referrals arose from the fact that a wife had left without her children. Of these, one man sought advice and support; another day care for his children; and in the third, the mother-in-law applied for day care and financial assistance.

Three cases involved women (two of them former psychiatric patients) who were distressed or confused at their husband's departure and were thought to need support. In another case, the marriage was still in existence but the couple were referred directly for marital help since the psychiatrist believed that the marriage was a cause of the woman's depression. In another case, a volunteer referred 'a rapidly deteriorating marital situation' as in need of social work support.

In seven cases there was a request to control deviant behaviour. Excessive drinking was involved in four of these and the initial presentation in most of them was daunting.

> Letter from hospital doctor suggesting that this couple would benefit from social work help. Mrs Yuren has become depressed, aggressive and is drinking to excess. She says her problem is due to her unhappy marriage. Mr Yuren has a history of prison sentences and mental hospital admissions following drunken behaviour and stealing cars. Formerly Mrs Yuren was a quiet person with an even temper. Mrs Yuren has indicated that her husband will not accept social work help but doctor feels that some attempt should be made in this direction.

Four referrals completed the thirty-seven: a family in which the woman was seen as wishing to 'dump' her much older disabled husband in residential accommodation, two disabled people whose discussion of aids and recuperative holidays contained an allusion to marital problems, and a request to carry out a compulsory admission to a psychiatric hospital. In this latter case, 'admission was not appropriate' because the disturbance was caused by a 'prolonged, drunken, marital row'.

From the study of 1198 cases, two things are clear. Firstly, at the intake stage, the number of cases having an overt marital problem was very small. In only 3 per cent of the total did the social workers think it worth while mentioning a marital problem on the referral sheet.

Secondly, with negligible exceptions, those who had overt marital problems neither referred themselves, nor were referred with an overt request to deal with the marital problem for its own sake. Battered wives required accommodation and deserted husbands day care facilities on the grounds of their marital difficulties, but this was a far cry from requesting the social worker to intervene in their marital affairs. Two or three cases within the 1198 could be seen as requests to the social worker to carry out marital work as a means of reducing other problems (depression or alcoholism) and other cases left the social worker scope for deciding whether or not they would consider working with the marital problems. In these latter cases it seemed that the social workers often chose to concentrate on the immediate practical difficulties.

Appendix 2 — Survey of Long-term Cases

Three of the main themes of this book are that the resources of the social work division of the social services department were heavily devoted to a small number of married 'priority' cases (using both terms as in the main text); that such cases have a 'segmental structure' so that it is difficult for social workers to have contact with both husband and wife; and that it is hard for social workers to have regular and reliable contact with any case. This appendix gives some statistics from the survey of long-term cases which are relevant to these themes.

CONCENTRATION ON MARRIED CASES

Table 1 compares the proportion of married cases given priority with the proportion of unmarried cases.

TABLE 1

Priority cases and marital status

	Priority	Non-priority	Total
Married cases	40 (19%)	166 (81%)	206
Other cases	45 (10%)	416 (90%)	461
Total	85 (13%)	582 (87%)	667

Married cases were almost twice as likely as other cases to be given priority, a result unlikely to be due to chance. Table 2 compares priority and non-priority married cases in terms of the amount of time they take up and the likelihood that they will be assessed as having marital problems.

TABLE 2

Comparison of priority and other married cases

	Priority (40 cases)	Other (166 cases)	Total
Marital problems	88%	55%	61%
Open 0-12 months	32%	50%	47%
13-24 months	10%	23%	20%
25 + months	58%	27%	33%
Last seen 0-7 days	55%	19%	26%
8-28 days	38%	36%	36%
29 + days	7%	45%	38%

Priority married cases were almost certain to be seen as having marital problems, were over twice as likely to have been open for more than two years, and were nearly three times as likely to have been seen within the last seven days. Nearly all of them had been seen within the last twenty-eight days, a contrast to the non-priority cases, nearly half of whom had not.

DIFFICULTY OF HAVING CONTACT WITH ALL MEMBERS OF FAMILY

We asked for details of family members present when a social worker last saw the family. On our 'segmental' hypothesis we would expect that workers rarely saw husbands and wives together and that they would be particularly unlikely to do so in cases where there were marital problems. Table 3 sets out the relevant information.

TABLE 3

Family members present at last interview

	Marital Problems (126)	No Marital Problems (80)
Wife/husband/child	20%	10%
Wife/husband	21%	25%
Wife/child	7%	9%
Wife only	25%	33%
Husband/child	2%	1%
Husband only	8%	4%
Child only	12%	15%
Other/never seen	6%	3%

Table 3 does not suggest that it is more difficult to have contact with both husband and wife when there are marital problems, although to be more certain of this one would like information on the family members present at a number of interviews with each case. The table does illustrate the central position of the wife/mother in local authority work. In approximately three-quarters of the cases the wife was present at the last interview. In cases assessed as having marital problems she was three times as likely as her husband to have been seen on her own at the last interview, and in the other cases more than eight times as likely.

TIME AND CASELOAD SIZE

The seventeen social workers had seen an average of three married cases in the previous week. These married cases represented 30 per cent of their caseload, and as we have seen, they were more likely to receive priority. It is thus unlikely that social workers see more than ten cases from their caseloads in a face-to-face contact in any one week. Some of these cases may, of course, be seen more than once.

A much bigger exercise would be needed to establish that this figure was a reasonable norm for social workers, but assuming it is not too far from the mark, one can see that a worker could have, for example, ten 'weekly cases' or forty 'four-weekly cases'. A worker with a caseload of twenty-two might see four at weekly intervals, four two-weekly, six three-weekly and eight once every four weeks. Assuming that he saw them regularly, his interviews in any one week could include all his weekly clients, half his two-weekly ones, a third of his three-weekly ones, and a quarter of his four-weekly ones.

If one knew that a worker was operating this kind of regular schedule, one could work out how many clients he would have seen within the last week, how many he would not have seen for two weeks, and how many he would not have seen for three weeks. Conversely, from information on the number of clients not seen for three, two or one week, one could work out the number of clients he was seeing at weekly, two-weekly, three-weekly or four-weekly intervals. By applying this reasoning to the information on the time of last contact which we collected, we would deduce that the seventeen workers were seeing twenty-two married cases at weekly intervals, fourteen at two-weekly intervals, and fifteen at three-weekly intervals: or mathematically speaking:

$$W_1 = w_1 + \tfrac{1}{2}w_2 + \tfrac{1}{3}w_3 \dots\dots\dots\dots\dots\dots\dots\dots 1/n\ w_n$$
$$W_2 = \tfrac{1}{2}w_2 + \tfrac{1}{3}w_3 \dots\dots\dots\dots\dots\dots\dots\dots\dots 1/n\ w_n$$
$$W_3 = \tfrac{1}{3}w_3 \dots\dots\dots\dots\dots\dots\dots\dots\dots\dots\dots 1/n\ w_n$$

where W = number seen in last week, W_2 = number seen in previous week but not the first one and so on, and w_1 = number of weekly cases, w_2 = number of two-weekly cases and so on.

Thus, roughly a quarter of these clients could be seen at regular intervals of three weeks or less if the social workers were adopting a pattern of regular visiting.

In practice we do not believe that the social workers did adopt a practice of regular visiting, and a study of their actual visiting patterns would have been interesting. Our main point is that social workers did not see very many clients in a week. If they are to see clients regularly and frequently, their caseloads must be of a size which allows this.

Index of Clients

Ahmad, 103-4, 107-8

Arncrow, 88-90, 92, 96, 115, 198-9, 206, 215-6

Beattie, 113, 127, 129-30, 173-5

Boothroyd, 95, 104, 152-3, 280

Bootle, 203-8, 222

Briggs, 87-88, 92, 95, 111, 116, 128, 167, 197

Buzzard, 68-73, 79-85, 88, 92, 148-9, 175, 180, 187

Cabassi, 109, 172, 212, 223, 232-9, 287-9

Calder, 95, 98-9, 110-11, 124-5, 172, 220

Capstick, 114-5

Dockeray, 94, 97, 103-5, 151, 272-3

Doggart, 87, 109-10, 130

Eilbeck, 148

Entwhistle, 95, 109, 113, 115, 129

Fell, 148, 168-9

Flimsby, 68, 75-81, 83-5, 88, 92, 94, 102, 117, 143-4, 160-1

Frizington, 128, 218-20

Garlick, 171-2

Garstang, 89-90, 92, 148

Gibson (née Nanson), 163-5

Gilcrux, 109, 112-3, 145-6, 149-50, 186-7, 193-6, 207-9, 211

Greenhalgh, 162

Hardknott, 95-6, 111, 146-7

Ingledow, 106, 135, 148, 223-232

Izatt, 98, 105, 141, 271

Jafferji, 4-11, 46, 51-2, 55-7, 83-5, 88, 92-4, 193, 269, 275, 281, 283

Levens, 90-92, 96, 184-5, 187, 202, 205, 284

Mothersill, 93, 95-7, 109, 116-7, 129, 167, 182-3, 185, 197, 200-1, 210-11, 220-1

Nanson (Gibson), 163-5

Orton, 136, 147

Papcastle, 68, 73-5, 81, 84-5, 88

Parkin, 141, 147-8

Pennington, 169-70

Pooley, 166

Quinn, 168

Redhead, 114, 120-2, 144-5, 217-8

Ruddick, 161-2

312

Scattergood, 188-9
Skelton, 142-3
Sowerby, 128, 143-4
Steggles, 216-7, 275
Stockdale, 123-5

Thistlethwaite, 192-4, 213

Underwood, 150

Vasalli, 170-1

Waterhouse, 126, 130
Westgarth, 185-6
Whiteside, 86-7, 114, 116, 136, 149,
   189-91, 198-9, 202, 213-4

Yalden, 247
Yardley, 302
Yare, 302-3
Yarwood, 146
Yates, 137-40, 179
Yearsley, 268
Yelland, 302
Yellowly, 155
Yeo, 301
Yeomans, 285-7
Yetts, 302
Yewdall, 301-2
York, 300
Young, 40
Younger, 303
Yule, 277-8
Yuren, 306

General Index

(Note: roman type indicates a brief reference, bold type a lengthier discussion, and italic type an example from case or work records)

Ailing, 119, 120; *see also* Illness

Abortion, *98,* 106, 111, *147*

Alcoholism, *see* Drinking problems

Ambivalence, 51; of client **84,** 87, 107, 119, *127, 131, 139,* 291, 295, 296; of worker **141-56,** 160, 162, 265, 267, 293

Ambivalent behaviour, **83-5**

Ambivalent marital bonds, **32,** 44, 52, 291

Anger, 6, *10, 74-5,* 93, 121, 211, 215, *227*

Anxiety, in Nursing, Menzies Lyth study of **59-62;** of client *22,* 53, *86, 117,* 181, 184, *212, 221, 233, 286-7;* of worker **10,** *211, 237,* **244-52,** 266, *268, 271,* **279,** 280, 291, 294, 297

Area officer, 18, *138, 247-8,* 252, 256, *269,* 279

Attachment, **48-52,** 54, 63, *75,* 80, 87, 105, 108, 112, 141, 171, 292, 293; and loss (Bowlby's theory of) **48-52,** 92, 93; anxious *88,* 135, 170, 292; figure **49-50,** 53, 86, 88, 90, 93, 100, 101, 103, 105, 115, 116, 121, 132, *139,* 183, 191, 193, 196, 292, 293

Balint, E. and Balint, M., 63

"Battering", *6-7,* **122-5;** *see also* Violence

"Battered" wives, 26, 130-1, 167; children 41, *89,* 92, 276

Birth of child, 49, 50, 97-8, **106-8,** *124, 169*

Blame, clients' obsession with, 84-5, **92-4,** 130, 159, 198; among social workers 251, **275-89,** 296

Bowlby, J., **46-52,** 54, 62, 63, 64, 80, 89, 93, 96, 124, 183, 291

Burlingham, D. (and Freud, A.), 51

Caseloads, 25, **27-30,** 43, 261, 285, 295, 297, 299; high priority cases, 27, **28-44,** 62, 265, 282, 285, 291, **308-9;** management of, 264; proportion married or cohabiting, **27-8,** 291; proportion with marital problems, **28,** 43; overload, 280; size carried by IMS workers, 17; time cases open, 29, 31, 291; unallocated cases, 279

Casework, **12-15,** 16, 17, 19, 23, 43, 64, 199, 243, 265

Child abuse, *see* Children at risk

Child care adviser, 285
Child guidance, 31
Children Act 1948, 20, 33, 253
Children and Young Persons Act
    1933, 20
Children and Young Persons Act
    1963, 254; Section 1 money, 36,
    213
Children and Young Persons Act
    1969, 254
Children at risk, *10,* 14, 31, 33,
    36-7, 39, 41, 258, 262, 264, 282,
    304, 305
Children's homes, 36, *232, 236*
Children in care, *31,* 35, 37, *40, 72,
    73,* 80, 257, 284, *287-8;* reception
    into, 33, 41, 159, 163, *232,* 258,
    281-2; *see also* Place of safety
    order
Citizen's Advice Bureau, 26, *247,*
    258, 259, 298, 303, 305
Clients, changes in behaviour of
    197-9; characteristic local
    authority 25; childhoods of 206;
    complaints of neighbours about
    33, *247,* 250; married or
    cohabiting **25-30, 300-301;** need
    to control others 84, 90;
    overwhelming demands of **145-8;**
    time-consuming 21, **28-30;** view
    of themselves **102-5;** *see also*
    Social worker/client relationship
Coercing, 119, **120-6**
Compulsory admissions (Mental
    Health Act), 20, *75, 126,* 157,
    160-3, 167, *260,* 282, 303, 304
Containment, **183-191**
Core sample, **21-2, 31-2, 44,** 79-80,
    92, 106, 111, 132, 197, 243, 265,
    291, 295, 298, 299
Crises, 263-4, 265, **269-70,** 292, 295

Day care, 26, 303, 304, 305
Day centre, *216-7*

Day nursery, *22, 38, 143, 163, 220,
    269*
Debts, *see* Financial problems
Defences, **54-6,** 57, 58, **60-1,** 62, 63,
    131, 136-7; *see also*
    Organizational defence
Definition of problem, **167, 208-9,**
    292
Delinquency, 14, 53, 127, 254-6,
    261, 283, 304
Delinquent depending, 119, **128-9**
Department of Health and Social
    Security (DHSS), 20, 213, 281
Depression, *7,* 26, *30,* 107, *199, 206,*
    207, *217,* 266, 268, 270, 293, 295;
    link with violence **123-4**
Deprivation, 46, **54,** 64, 96, 105,
    209, *277*
Despair, 50, 93, 107, 175, **201-7,**
    226, 265, 293, 295
Disablement, *73, 188, 194,* 255,
    283, 306
Doctors, *4,* 158, 167, 282; *see also*
    GP, Psychiatrist
Drinking problems, 26, *78, 99, 106,*
    118, *218-9, 224-31,* 247, 306; and
    marital violence 122, *184;* and
    subversive caregiving **128-9**

Education Welfare Officers, 216,
    282, 283
Envy, 96, 108, 132

Fairbairn, W.R.D., 63
Families of origin, 92, **102-5;** lack
    of support from, 32, **34,** 44, 79,
    106, 131, 291; large size of, **96**
Family alliances, 85, 166, 169-70
Fear of being alone, **80-82**
Feedback, 63, 64
Financial problems, 42, *288;* debts
    33, *77, 98,* 116, *144, 195, 198,*
    222; rent arrears *22, 30, 214, 221,*
    239, 261

Food, as "token", **115-6**; in subversive caregiving, 128
Freud, S., 54, 62
Freud, A. (and Burlingham, D.), 51

General practitioners (GPs), 20, 26, *41, 75, 77,* 216, *221, 225, 248,* 251, 259, 282, *284,* 298
Guilt, 207, *208, 227,* 276, 277
Gynaecological complaints, **111**

Health visitors, *5-11,* 203, 282, 283
Helplessness, *77,* 84, **86-8,** 142, 159, 160, *210,* 212, 222, *226,* 266-7, 281, 292, 295
Home Help, *154, 246,* 262
Homeless families accommodation, 33, 36, *137, 150, 163-4,* 167, *184, 199,* 280, 283, 305
Homeless families unit, 20, 215, *280*
Homelessness, 14, 205, 262, *280, 286,* 302-3, 304
Hospital, 6, *247, 248,* 251; psychiatric *161, 217, 225, 248, 260,* 268
Housing, department, *212, 220,* 281; officers, 283; problems, *30, 31,* 33, *38,* 42, **205-6,** *212,* 228, *236,* 262-3, 303-4; as "token", **112-5**

Illness, *127,* **130**
Imprisoning, **121-2**
Institute of Marital Studies, 3, **13,** 36, 45, 47, **52-6,** 57, 58, 63, 180, 181
Institutional Defence, 47, **59-62** ("Organizational Defence"); Framework, **244-5,** 249
Intake, **25-6,** 44, **259-63,** 265, 268, 270, 278, 285, 290, 294
Interaction, 18; between clients 45, 64, 224, *234* (*see also* Marital Interaction); between clients and

workers 45, 64; influence of organization on 45-6

Jaques, E., 47
Jealousy, 39, 40, 85, **95-100,** 108,132
Jung, C.G., 53, 58, 63

Klein, M., 63

Local Authority Social Services Act 1970, **253-6**
Loneliness, *see* Fear of being alone
Loss, 54, 105, 218, 220, 292; Attachment and, **48-52,** 92, 93

Management team, 18, 19, 279
Marriage Guidance Council, 27, 125, 284, 298
Marriage, as vehicle for development **52-3**; as "emotional container" **53**
Marital, difficulties (associated with other problems), 14; interaction, 46, 47, **52-6,** 64, 283, *287,* 291; problems, **25-8,** 43, 47, 184, *233,* 284, 285, *288,* 290, 291, 296, 298, 299, **304-7**; work, 26, 27, **36-43,** 180, 245, 252, 285, *288,* 291, 294, 296, 298
Mattinson, J., 47, 57-9
Mental Health Act 1959, 20, 253
Mental illness, 14, *75-9;* madness, 53, 81
Menzies Lyth, I., 47, 59-61, 294

NSPCC, 297
Nursing, organizational defences in, **59-61**

Object relations, 63
Organization, 15, 47, 64, **243-5,** 275-6, 278, 294-5
Organizational defence, **59-62,** 267, 273, **294-5**

Parental roles, lack of success in, **33**, 44, *72, 78,* 80, 85, 106, 291; undermining of, **131**

Place of safety order, 20, 37, *41, 89,* 160, 161, 162, *164,* 249

Police, *9-10,* 125, *154, 163, 172, 201, 216*

Practical assistance, 38, **187-9, 262-5,** 268, 292, 295, 304; refusal to provide, 196, **212-5**

Pregnancy, *71,* **106-8,** *207, 210, 220, 227*

Probation officers, 125, *142*

Professional conflict, *5-11,* **12-15,** *163,* **281-3, 295-6**

Project cases, 21, 23, 43

Psychiatrists, 20, *41, 77, 126, 154, 162, 170, 248,* 278, 298

Referrals, 25, **26,** *224,* **261-2,** 284, 298, **300-307**

Reflection process, *8, 10, 18,* 47, **56-9,** 64, *144*

Rent arrears, *see* Financial problems

Research, clinical methods, **22-3;** clinical theories, **63-4;** control group studies, **22-3;** participant observation **19-20,** 23

Residential care, 31, *224,* 243

Resources, 256, 257, 281

Samaritans, *76-7*

Schools, 43, *87-8, 216,* 281; headmistress, *27*

Searles, H., 47, 57, 63

Seebohm Committee, 13, 243, **255-6,** 274, 285; Report, **253-6,** 274

Separation **50-52,** 62-3, 64, 84, 93, *124,* 125, 165, 199, 201, 206, **218-22,** 276; anxiety, 50, 53, 54; threat of, **34-6,** 44, 49, 85, 291, 292

Sex, *7,* 53, *77,* **108-11,** *234*

Social services departments, **255-9;** place of marital work in, 290-1, 296-7

Social services department of Inner London Borough, 3, **15-17**

Social workers, assistant, 297; basic grade, 18, 27, 245, 256; senior, 18, 19, 200, 245, 251, 256, 269, *277,* 278; trainee, 18, 27, *142;* complaints about, 167; compulsory powers of, **157-165;** role conflict of, 158-9; training, 257, 258; turnover of, **256-7,** 271-2; variety of tasks, **257-9**

Social worker/client relationship, **38-43,** 196, 197, 199, 203, 273, 293, 296; client's definition of, 167, 170, 174; clients' difficulty in sharing, **170-2,** 217; client's wish to control, **167-175;** forgotten interviews, 271; holidays of workers, 145, *210, 227;* importance to clients, **270-3;** initial negotiations, **181-196;** joint interviews, **193-6;** leaving clients, **155-6, 218-22,** *223, 231-2,* 272, 294; limited access, **192-3;** misperception of, 159-60, 166; regularity of contact, **183-4,** 191; diagnostic value of providing limits on, 192; rejection in, **148-52;** sexual attraction in, 171-2; short-term offer, **185-6;** surviving, 119, **200-209;** tokens of affection, 214-5

Splitting, **54-6,** 58, 62, 88, 93, 131, 160, 163, *169,* 199, **210-12,** 252, **275-89,** 292

Stress, 22, 59, 102, 122, 251, 280; young mothers under, 30-1, 41

Subversive caregiving, 119, **126-30,** 192, *219*

Suicide, *76, 246, 248, 249,* 278;

attempted, *89*, **120-1**, *144, 147, 217, 224, 230*, 249; threatened, *184, 230*
Sutherland, J.D., 45
Third parties, difficulty over, **85, 94-100**, 198, *230*, 292
Titmuss, R., 255
Transference (and countertransference), **57-9**

Unconscious, 54, 57, 62, 136

Venereal disease, *109*, 111, 207
Violence, 32, 54, *89, 92, 98, 103, 106*, **122-5**, *212, 224, 227-8, 238*; sex and, **109-110**; *see also* Battering
Voluntary agency, *7*, 298; workers, *228, 284*

Winnicott, D., 63, 211
Women's Aid, *7*